CUBA
*The Measure
of a
Revolution*

Published with assistance from
the Roger E. Joseph Memorial Fund
for greater understanding
of public affairs, a cause in which
Roger Joseph believed

CUBA
The Measure of a Revolution

Lowry Nelson

UNIVERSITY OF MINNESOTA PRESS
Minneapolis

© Copyright 1972
by the University of Minnesota.
All rights reserved.
Printed in the United States of America
at North Central Publishing Co.,
St. Paul, Minnesota.

Published in Great Britain, India, and
Pakistan by the Oxford University Press,
London and Delhi, and in Canada
by the Copp Clark Publishing Co.
Limited, Toronto

Library of Congress Catalog Card Number: 77-187163
ISBN 0-8166-0626-9

For BILL and CARMELITA

Foreword

The Cuban Revolution has had a far-reaching and profound impact on Cuba's domestic scene. The transformation of the economy, the attempts at changing the value system, the destruction of old institutions and their replacement with new ones, the traumatic restructuring of society, are all features which are giving rise to a radically new Cuba.

The unique attempt to develop a Communist system in a Latin American society at great geographic distance from the Communist bloc and the results of twelve years of Castroism are ably discussed in this volume by Professor Lowry Nelson, a long-time student of Cuban developments. His book throws light on the changes that have occurred in Cuba since Castro came to power and presents what the author considers to be the merits and failures of the revolution. He has also provided us with several important chapters on pre-revolutionary developments and problems which place the revolution in perspective.

This project was originally conceived as centering on a comparison of the data Professor Nelson collected in the late 1940s for his *Rural Cuba*, considered a pioneer book in the field, with data on the changed situation that has been brought about as a result of the revolution. Although Professor Nelson felt it highly desirable to supplement his "research at a distance" with a field trip to Cuba, he was unable to secure a visa from the Cuban government. However, he has made extensive use of the refugee interview program at the Center for Advanced International Studies, as well as of Cuban publications and documentary materials. In view of Professor Nelson's outstanding qualifications as a rural sociologist and the unusual opportunities he had in connection with the fieldwork for his original study, his book yields unusual insights into Cuban developments.

Professor Nelson is particularly sensitive to the sufferings of the Cuban people brought about by the revolution. Is the sacrificing of human values too high a price to pay for the sake of economic development? And must this economic development be achieved through revolution rather than through more peaceful, constructive means? Revolutions, especially Communist revolutions, Professor Nelson believes, are excessively destructive of human beings and of wealth; and up to now they have offered no model of change that could be called successful in terms of human welfare. The Cuban experiment is no exception. In their political fanaticism, in their conviction that they hold the only truth, the Cuban revolutionaries have resorted to any means to destroy the old "evil" order. Along with the shortcomings, the accomplishments of the past have been scrapped and replaced by a more authoritarian society devoted to the development of the elusive Communist "new man" and the building of communism.

This study is part of an ongoing research program at the Center for Advanced International Studies dealing with different aspects of the revolution and the subsequent shaping of the Castro regime. Part of the research effort concentrates on the gathering of the most significant Cuban, Soviet, Chinese, European, Latin American, and U.S. documents on the revolution and its continuing aftermath. Another part centers on a program to utilize interviews with newly arrived Cuban refugees as a basis for a memory bank of information on Cuba. We believe that this program is providing information and insights into Cuban developments otherwise unavailable. The written responses to the questionnaires as well as the documentary col-

viii

Foreword

lection are available to scholars for study and consultation at the center on the Coral Gables campus of the University of Miami.

The research for Professor Nelson's study has been supported in part by a generous grant from the Ford Foundation.

Mose L. Harvey
Director
Center for Advanced International Studies
University of Miami

Preface

Twenty-six years have elapsed since I made the field studies, the results of which were reported in *Rural Cuba*, published in 1950. The vast and traumatic changes of that quarter century inevitably called for a follow-up study. However, such a restudy presented serious difficulties. The Cuba of 1945–1946 was a free society in which scholars, whether foreign or local, could carry out research projects without arbitrary restrictions. More than that, in my case, I had the complete cooperation of the government, including the president of the republic. By contrast, the revolutionary government is wary of studies that may reflect unfavorably on it. That is to say, objective research is not possible under the Communist government.

Since my request for visas was rejected without explanation, I was under the necessity of working as best I could from source materials available outside the country. My hope had been to return to Cuba and conduct interviews in the same eleven areas covered in the earlier studies, but as that proved to be impossible, I turned to the sources available to me. Although no substitute for field studies, these materials proved to be far better than I expected. In fact, I came to realize that the data available were equal to any I might obtain in Cuba itself. The only official series of statistics which the government published in 1967 and 1968 soon became accessible, and all Cuban newspapers, journals, and magazines are readily obtainable. In addition there is the invaluable series of studies by devoted Cuban scholars in exile working on the Cuban Economic Research Project at the University of Miami. On the basis of these and other materials, I have been able to chart some of the widespread and radical changes that have occurred in Cuban society. So, while this book may be called a successor to the first one, it is not a sequel because I was not privileged to do the fieldwork that would have made it one.

The author hopes this volume will be of interest to the general reader, especially that large portion of Northamericans who know so little about Cuba in general and even less about the rebellion which began in 1952 and the work of the revolutionary government which took control on January 1, 1959. One is mindful of the fact that a generation of Americans has come to maturity who were too young to know of these events at the time they occurred. Yet Cuba is of such importance to the United States that citizens should be informed about it. This book is intended to provide such general information. It will provide little that is new for those relatively few specialists working on the Cuban "problem."

The contents of the volume fall into three general sections. The first three chapters recount the origin, progress, and final victory of the rebellion; the initial years of the revolution; and, for the sake of historical perspective, a brief review of the development of the country during the colonial and republican eras, including conditions at the time of the takeover. Then follow four chapters which concern changes in agriculture, the basic economic sector of the nation, reasons for the vanishing of the cane cutters, and the problem of worker productivity. The following three chapters describe the efforts of the regime to create the "new man" through the use of an expanded educational system, the neutralization of the culture-conserving institutions, and the drastic restructuring of society. In the final chapter the author presents what he considers the merits and failures of the revolution.

Anyone who writes a book of this kind incurs many debts to those who have in one way or another contributed aid and encouragement. My major debt is to Dr. Mose L. Harvey, director of the Center for

Preface

Advanced International Studies at the University of Miami. It was
he who suggested the work and provided the opportunity for me to
undertake it. My gratitude goes also to Dr. Clyde C. Wooten, associate director of the center, who read and made valuable suggestions
on parts of the manuscript and otherwise provided administrative
aid and encouragement. Professor Carmelo Mesa-Lago of the University of Pittsburgh provided major critical assistance on Chapters
6 and 7. Mr. Arch R. M. Ritter of the Department of Economics of
Carleton University, Ottawa, Canada, generously shared with me
some data he was able to obtain during several visits to Cuba in
pursuit of his own research. His help was crucial and claims my deep
gratitude. Georgina S. Palomares not only typed the original draft,
but called to my attention several important sources of information
which I would not otherwise have known. As always, however, despite all his debts to others, the author can share the limitations of
the work with nobody else.

L. N.

Coral Gables, Florida
January 1972

Contents

CUBA
*The Measure
of a
Revolution*

Chapter 1

The Cuban Rebellion

At about 2 A.M. on January 1, 1959, the president of the Republic of Cuba, Fulgencio Batista y Zaldívar, together with his family and closest associates, boarded a plane at Camp Columbia and departed from the island. It had become clear that he could no longer maintain either public order or his position as president. His dramatic departure marked the close of nearly 450 years of history under one economic system — that of private property and the utilization of material and human resources for profit — and the abrupt beginning of a new and vastly different one. The cliché "end of an era" was never more aptly applied, for on that fateful New Year's Day the way to Havana was open to the young leader who had been the immediate cause of Batista's departure, Fidel Castro Ruz. A new and extraordinary era began. We are to compare, or contrast, the old and new eras in this work.

As an introduction to the chapters which follow, it seems desirable, even necessary, to summarize the history of events beginning in 1953 that led to the condition in Cuba we refer to as the "new era." There are two phases. That which began in 1953 we will call the Rebellion, while that which began on January 1, 1959, we will consider as the Revolution. This distinction is based on the fact that all revolutions begin in rebellion, but not all rebellions eventuate

3

in revolution. Some rebellions have only limited goals: a resistance to some form of taxation, for example, or protests against other limited aspects of policy of the government in power. There are many uprisings against governments for the redress of grievances, real or fancied. If complaints are heard by those in control and corrective efforts are made, the matters at issue may be settled. Compromise and negotiation quiet most rebellions.

But a rebellion dedicated to the total elimination of the government in power and the transformation or reform of the society can only mean eventual revolution if it is successful. Such a rebellion becomes the precursor of revolution, aims at the overthrow of the existing government in its entirety. This, for example, was the aim of the American colonial rebellion of 1776. Such an uprising then becomes not a matter of mere replacement of those in authority by the rebels; no coup d'etat is enough; no benign settlement is possible.

Cuba has had a number of rebellions, but only two revolutions. The rebellion of 1868–1878 was suppressed, but that of 1896 was successful and broke the power of the mother country over her colony in 1898. There followed the revolutionary transformation of the government associated with its independence from Spain and the launching of the new nation as a republic. Another rebellion overthrew the dictatorship of President Gerardo Machado in 1933, only to have the revolution, for which so many had hoped and fought, frustrated by a series of developments.

It is well to take brief notice of those subsequent developments because they are part of the Castro story. The most important of them was the uprising of noncommissioned army officers at Camp Columbia on September 4, 1933, which overthrew the senior officers, who customarily did not live at the camps. The leader of this group was Fulgencio Batista. As the man in control of the army, he became the central power figure and arranged for a five-man commission to form a government headed by Ramón Grau San Martín.[1]

President Grau took immediate steps to implement some of the aspirations of the rebels. Laws were enacted to provide for an eight-hour day and a minimum wage. The government also demanded by decree that the electric and telephone companies owned by United

4

The Cuban Rebellion

States citizens reduce their rates and at the same time raise wages. When the companies refused to act, the government temporarily took them over. But there was near chaos throughout the country, Grau seemed unable to exercise control, and the United States refused to recognize his government. Batista forced his resignation on January 15, 1934. On January 24 the United States recognized Grau's successor, Carlos Mendieta, but Batista remained the power behind the government.

After a succession of several provisional presidents, plus one who was elected but later impeached, Batista himself became president in 1940 and was followed in 1944 by none other than Grau San Martín, who was elected in what was generally considered a free and honest election. His further reforms, together with those of his successor, Carlos Prío Socarrás, were not sufficient to quiet the unrest, while Batista's coup d'etat on March 10, 1952, served to inflame it. Most important, they had all failed to eliminate corruption in government.

It is well to note here that agrarian reforms were enacted in the late 1930's and in succeeding years. These will be discussed in a later chapter. It is also important to mention that the modern and progressive Constitution of 1940 was created during those years. Yet these actions and others were not enough.

The continuation of the political influence of the United States on Cuban affairs, along with the visible economic control of so much of the Cuban economy, was a constant source of annoyance. Even though in 1934 President Franklin D. Roosevelt had abrogated the controversial Platt Amendment to the Cuban Constitution of 1901, which had granted the United States the right to interfere in internal affairs, the memory of it still rankled. And while Roosevelt's Good Neighbor Policy forswore direct intervention in the internal affairs of Cuba, there was no denying the fact that the embassy of the United States was a powerful political factor in the country.[2]

It was against this background of Cuban history and, notably, Cuban-American relations that Fidel Castro was able to effect his rebellion. Since he is the central character of both the rebellion and the revolution, it is appropriate here to give a brief sketch of his early life and activities.

CUBA: THE MEASURE OF A REVOLUTION

Fidel Castro Ruz

This man who was destined to impoverish the wealthy and sustain the impoverished did not know any deprivation himself.[3] He was born April 13, 1926, to Angel Castro, a sugar planter whose farm consisted of some 23,300 acres. The father was an immigrant laborer from Galicia in northwest Spain. His plantation, reportedly acquired by his industry and frugality, was located near Biran in the municipality of Mayarí, near the north coast of Oriente province. After the death of his first wife, the mother of Lidia and Pedro Emilio, he and his second wife, Lina Ruz, had seven children: Angela, Agustina, Ramón, Fidel, Raúl, Emma, and Juana.

Revolutionaries usually have to forgo many ordinary personal associations. Fidel's relationship with his parents was not close. He told Lee Lockwood that his father exploited the peasants on his plantation and "paid no taxes on his land or income." [4] Angel Castro died in 1956 while Fidel was in Mexico preparing for his invasion of Cuba. During the struggle against Batista in 1957 and 1958, Fidel was to order the burning of sugarcane fields, including those of his own family, despite the pleas of his mother. He could hardly be expected to burn the crops of others and spare his own.[5] Over the years the member of the family to whom Fidel has remained closest is his brother Raúl, who is his designated political heir.

As the son of a well-to-do family, the future master of Cuba was sent to parochial schools in Santiago, the capital of Oriente province, for his elementary schooling. He took his high school work at Colegio Belén, a Jesuit school at Havana. In the fall of 1945 at the age of 19 he entered the law school of the University of Havana.

From this point on his course headed directly toward his ultimate career as a revolutionary. After the fall of the dictator Gerardo Machado in 1933, Cuban politics were in constant and bitter turmoil. For a time the country's preoccupation with World War II seemed to reduce slightly the bitter factionalism, but there followed a resurgence which was characterized by inter-gang fighting in the streets and finally on the campus of the university, which had been granted autonomy by the Constitution of 1940. As Jaime Suchlicki points out, "Student politics was only a microcosm of Cuba's political life. An entire system of nepotism, favoritism, and gangsterism predominated." [6] In 1948 the president of the FEU (*Federación Estudiantil Universitaria*) was assassinated. This led to the assassination of two other students who had allegedly been involved. An editorial in Havana's daily newspaper *El Mundo*, quoted by Suchlicki, described the situation as follows: "Violence holds sway at the University. Professors and students are nothing but the evident prisoners of a few groups of desperadoes who impose their will and pass their examinations at pistol points. The University Council itself has declared its inability to repress those gangs for lack of coercive powers." [7]

This was hardly an environment conducive to scholarly preparation for the ultimate practice of law — or for anything else except revolution. How much Castro was the creature and how much the creator of the atmosphere, and to what extent it suited his nature and ambition, only he can say. It is perfectly clear, however, that in the Cuba of that day any student who was able to become a recognized leader on the campus was well on the road to a political career in the nation. Although Castro did not achieve the presidency of the student body, he was elected a vice-president of the student organization of the law school. He was not averse to dropping his studies in order to participate in off-campus adventures such as the aborted invasion of the Dominican Republic designed to overthrow Dictator Trujillo. Or, with three other University of Havana students, to attend in 1948 a meeting at Bogotá, Colombia, to organize a Latin American Student Union against colonialism and imperialism, a project financed by Juan Perón of Argentina. Before the organization could be consummated, a bloody riot broke out in Bogotá triggered by the assassination of Liberal party leader Eliecer Gaitán. Castro and the other three students became actively involved.[8]

These episodes, together with the tensions prevalent at the university and in the community, reveal an activist and militant strain in the Castro personality. They also show that Castro was no stranger to violent confrontation, a condition that was to characterize his daily life in the years ahead, especially during the guerrilla warfare in the 1950's.

Castro's performance as a student at the University of Havana is as controversial as are most aspects of his career. He himself has deplored the lack of attention to studies, the skipping of classes, and the neglect of course work until the time of examinations. On the other side of the coin, Herbert L. Matthews reports that Raúl Castro showed him transcripts of Fidel's grades and that of the "thirteen or fourteen slips . . . eight or nine of the professors wrote *sobresaliente* (excellent), three gave him *notable*, and only two were *aprovechado* (approved, which is to say passing)." [9] There is no point in trying to prove either the dilatory or the scholarly attitude of Castro during his university days. There is testimony both ways. He is not stupid; that much is perfectly clear. Rather, he is undoubtedly very intelligent, but scholarly attainment was not a burning ambition or goal. He wanted to be a political leader, and that proved to be his destiny. His ability as a student did, at the least, enable him to obtain his diploma in law in 1950 and to begin private practice with two associates in Havana. But his heart was in politics.

Political Parties in Cuba

It is necessary at this point to describe briefly the political situation at the time. The party in power was known as the *Auténticos*, because its members claimed to be the "authentic" heirs of the *Partido revolucionario cubano*, organized in 1892 by the great hero of Cuban independence, José Martí. The Auténticos came to power when Ramón Grau San Martín was elected president in 1944 and continued after the election of his successor, Prío Socarrás. The party therefore shared the onus and odium for the graft, corruption, and violence which characterized the country. There was a strong running tide of opposition because of the failure of the administration to stamp out corruption and to maintain social order.

A leading critic of the administration was Senator Eduardo Chibás, a student leader in his day and one of the generation who had been frustrated by the failure of reforms in the 1930's. In 1947 he and some associates created a new party called *Partido del Pueblo Cubano* (Party of the Cuban People), popularly known as the Ortodoxo party. This group sought to bring to fruition the reforms for which the anti-Machado young people had fought. A systematically stated platform was not formulated. Chibás, a gifted orator, ceaselessly attacked the administration for corruption — "honor before money" was his slogan — on his Sunday night radio programs. He repeatedly dwelt on the familiar themes of economic independence, political liberty, and social justice. Says Suchlicki: "Chibás monopolized the rhetoric of the revolution, becoming the exponent of the frustrated old generation and the leader of a new generation bent on bringing morality and honesty to Cuban public life. It was he more than anyone else who, with his constant exhortation, calls for reform, and his attacks on Cuba's political leadership, paved the way for the revolution that followed." [10]

The Ortodoxos attracted large numbers of followers, especially among university students, and became a political phenomenon to be reckoned with. Chibás was expected to be its candidate for the presidency in the election of 1952, but at the end of one of his radio talks and for reasons which can be only speculative, he shot himself. His last words were "Cuban people awake!" [11]

The specific importance of the Ortodoxo party for our story is that its leader, Chibás, and its program, as far as there was one, had a strong appeal for Fidel Castro. He gave speeches in support of the party and became a candidate for Congress in the elections scheduled for 1952. The elections did not take place because of the reemergence in Cuban affairs of Fulgencio Batista.

We must go back a little in our story to bring him on the stage. Batista, who had gone into exile in Florida in 1944, had been allowed by President Prío to return from Miami in 1948 and be a candidate for election to the Senate. He was elected. With the approach of the general elections in 1952, he announced his candidacy for president. His two opponents for the office were Carlos Hevia of the Auténtico party, a respected public figure, and Roberto Agramonte, a professor of sociology at the University of Havana who became the substitute for Chibás on the Ortodoxo ticket. A public opinion poll conducted by the magazine *Bohemia* in December 1951 showed Agramonte far in the lead, with Hevia second, and Batista third. The results of this poll may have been a major factor in Batista's action. Under the pretext and charge that President Prío was planning some maneuver to remain in power, Batista executed a bloodless coup d'etat on March 10, 1952.

The Rebellion of Castro

This brief résumé of some of Cuba's political history serves to bring the two leading characters of this tragic drama to the point where they entered on a direct collision course. According to Jules Dubois, Castro's first response to Batista's coup d'etat was an angry letter written on March 15 in which he warned Batista that his action "was going to produce for Cuba graft and corruption, torture and death for many and a reaction of the people which would eventually overthrow him."[12] The charge proved to be prophetic. In the days immediately following, he filed a brief with the Court of Constitutional Guarantees asking that it declare Batista's assumption of power unconstitutional. Another and much longer brief was filed in the Urgency Court, which had jurisdiction over criminal cases, holding that Batista should be tried as a criminal. This second brief was ignored, but a reply to the first argued that the revolution engineered by Batista was the source of the law under which he took power.[13]

Castro immediately began to rally friends, mostly young followers of the late Eduardo Chibás, to discuss and plan future action. On July 26, 1953, about 160 Castro-led men attacked the Moncada military barracks in Santiago de Cuba. The attack failed and several of the men were killed or wounded. Along with some 120 others Castro was arrested and tried before the Urgency Court in Santiago. As a lawyer he conducted his own defense before the three judges. He was convicted of insurrection against the state and sentenced to fifteen years in the Isle of Pines prison.

In his final eloquent defense statement, however, he gave to the revolution a part of its "scripture." His speech later acquired its title from the emotional concluding line, "History will absolve me." In his address Castro described what would have been done if the revolt at Moncada had succeeded. The Constitution of 1940 was to be restored, he said, and elections held at an early date. There would be sweeping land reform, and workers in all big firms would be given the right to a 30 percent share of the profits. Property which had been acquired unjustly or fraudulently would be confiscated. Cooperatives would be encouraged; education was due for fundamental reform and teachers would be given better salaries. There was no serious threat to private property in general. This defense speech was to undergo considerable revision during Castro's prison term on the Isle of Pines before its final publication as a basic document of the revolution.

As it turned out, Castro was destined to serve only a short prison term rather than the fifteen years to which he was sentenced in 1953. Batista called a general election for 1955 in which he was elected president. Despite the boycott of the election by opposition parties, he interpreted the results as a legitimization of his government. In a magnanimous gesture in May 1955 he declared an amnesty for all political prisoners and Castro was freed to return to Havana. His stay there, however, was brief. He soon left for Mexico, where he proceeded at once to assemble clandestinely a group of trusted associates to be trained in guerrilla warfare for an invasion of Cuba. It was here that he met Ernesto (Che) Guevara, who joined the group and underwent the training course.

Castro was able to obtain financial support from a number of Batista exiles in the United States, among them former president Prío Socarrás. The latter is said to have provided the means for the purchase of the yacht *Granma* which carried the group of rebels across the Gulf of Mexico to Cuba late in 1956. The yacht was only 62 feet long and had a normal comfortable capacity of eight persons. The vessel was hardly adequate to carry the 82 men with their gear and weapons in addition to the crew, but after a risky voyage it landed on December 2, 1956, on the coast of Oriente province somewhere between Niquero and Cabo Cruz. The original plan had called for a simultaneous uprising on November 30 in Santiago de Cuba, to cover the landing, but a delay in the arrival of the *Granma* due to high winds upset the plan. Most of the group were seasick; the landing was discovered from the air and dispersed; several men were killed and many arrested.

Castro and eleven others, among them his brother Raúl and Guevara, escaped and were able to make their way to the Sierra Maestra. There was another trial before the Urgency Court of Santiago for those who fell into the hands of the government. One of the three judges who presided at this trial was Manuel Urrutia Lleó. Urrutia argued that the defendants were justified in their revolution against Batista. He was later rewarded by Castro, who chose him as provisional president of the revolutionary government.

Then began almost exactly two years of warfare between the rebels and the Batista army. The former had few weapons, few men, and few funds. What money they had in pocket was used to buy food from the farmers. Only twelve men, according to Dubois, survived to reach the mountains, and each had no more than a dozen cartridges.[14] The natives proved to be friendly and helpful. Fidel's brother Ramón on the family plantation was able to provide the rebel camp with supplies of all kinds, including weapons and ammunition. Ramón had considerable help from numerous clandestine supporters in the area of Oriente, mostly members of the so-called 26th of July Movement, a resistance group which Castro had created while he was still in Mexico and which took its name from the date of the 1953 attack on the Moncada Barracks. By slow but steady accretion of men and arms, and operating from a secure sanctuary, the rebels were soon able to undertake raids and sabotage which the government forces seemed powerless to prevent. Railway trains were dynamited, cane fields set afire, and the Central Highway made impassable at times. These harassments grew steadily in number and effectiveness.

Castro was, however, without effective means of communication with the Cuban people. Radio transmitters and receivers brought from Mexico on the *Granma* had to be abandoned with the ship. Meanwhile the government had complete control of the excellent Cuban radio and television networks and had invoked censorship of the press. The threat of Castro was constantly minimized by the government and the success of the government forces against him constantly exaggerated. It was reported for example that Castro had been killed after the landing and for some time no evidence to the contrary was forthcoming. However, a fortunate event for Castro occurred on February 17, 1957, a month and a half after his landing, when Herbert Matthews of the *New York Times* interviewed him at his camp in the mountains.[15] The publication of this interview broke the communication barrier and it can probably be considered a turning point for the better in Castro's fortunes. There followed increased support in arms, money, and men not only from within Cuba but from Cubans and others in the United States. It also brought about a temporary relaxation of press control by the Batista government. *Bohemia*, the weekly magazine published in Havana and one of the most prestigious in the hemisphere, reprinted the Matthews interview in May 1957. The interview not only let the world, and especially Cuba, know that Castro was alive and well but gave a very favorable account of the progress of the rebellion and the plans for reforms in Cuban life.

From that time on fighting accelerated. The rebels, who had previously avoided direct confrontation with the government forces, finally felt sufficiently strong to engage them in battle. On May 28, 1957, the rebels attacked and overwhelmed the military garrison at Uvero on the south coast of Oriente province, acquiring much-needed arms and ammunition. It was the first victory and one which gave confidence to the guerrillas. It also stirred hopes, as well as fears, throughout Cuba that the rebellion might after all succeed.

Meantime, with every foray, every act of sabotage, every raid by the rebels, the government forces reacted with greater terror and brutality. This in turn only increased the bitterness of many Cuban citizens and intensified their opposition to the regime. It was a vicious circle; every action of the rebels brought more severe reaction from the police, which fired still more the passions of the opposition. Many highly respected persons, deeply distressed by what was happening to the country, sought to stay the bloodshed by urging negotiation, but to no avail. Things had gone too far. Finally the regime itself was no longer able to maintain order. Growing numbers of the regular army were defecting to Castro; there was virtually nationwide revulsion against the brutality of the police and the regular army in attempting to counter the rebellion. At last it became clear to Batista that he could not prevail. He left the country and unwillingly, if not unwittingly, bequeathed the control of Cuba to Fidel Castro.

For the winners the difficulties and hardships of the campaign had provided no inkling of the far more difficult problems of governing a nation and managing its economy. We turn now to a brief description of what transpired in the early years of the revolution.

Chapter 2

The Revolution
Takes Over

The story of the rebellion and its success is a truly remarkable one. Starting out with only a dozen poorly armed men, the rebels never managed to accumulate more than a few hundred recruits, except at the very end of the campaign when success was already assured. Yet with their limited numbers and weapons these amateur soldiers and officers "defeated" a professionally trained and led army of some 30,000 men well equipped with all types of weapons and supported by an air force.[1] Because of the dramatic climax to the campaign and the people's weariness of the terror of the last months of the Batista regime, the *barbudos* ("bearded ones") were welcomed as conquering heros. Although they got the credit for success and inherited the spoils, they had benefited from struggles waged by the Second Front of Escambray, a University of Havana group known as the Student Revolutionary Directorate (*Directorio Revolucionario Estudiantil*) that was independent of Castro. Also, there were many underground fighters who identified themselves with the 26th of July Movement.

Yet there were some final moments of anxiety for Fidel Castro. On January 1 he learned that before flying out of Cuba Batista had written a resignation which proposed the transfer of his "powers as President of the Republic . . . to the constitutional substitute." [2] This "constitutional substitute" was the senior justice of the Supreme Court, Carlos M. Piedra, though as we shall see he was not permitted

14

finally to take office. When the news of Batista's departure reached him, Castro was commanding a column headed for Santiago de Cuba. On learning of Batista's effort to set up a successor, Castro ordered his column to hasten to Santiago. Addressing the citizens of that city on January 2, he announced that Manuel Urrutia Lleó would be the provisional president of the republic and declared Santiago to be the provisional capital. In order to further frustrate the goings-on in Havana — especially any plan to name a successor to Batista, which he termed a "betrayal of the Revolution" — he called for a general strike. This strike was effective, unlike the one he had attempted from the Sierra Maestra in April 1958.[3]

An Unsteady Beginning

In naming Urrutia as provisional president, Castro took the first step toward forming a government. It was intended that the president would serve until elections were held. Castro himself had earlier called upon all anti-Batista elements, including those in exile, to unite on a candidate for this office. However, he disapproved of Felipe Pazos, the candidate suggested by the exiles in Miami, and as we have seen named Urrutia instead.[4]

Castro left Santiago on January 2 for his triumphal journey to Havana. Stopping at the principal centers along the way, he addressed the adoring crowds, savored their fervid applause, and basked in the glow of their hero worship. He was everybody's idol, every man's hope.

While Havana awaited the arrival of the man of the hour, which was to occur on January 8, conditions bordered on a kind of anarchy. Little was being done to set up the new regime, and the provisional president soon discovered that he could not function in Santiago, the declared provisional capital. On January 5 he flew to Santa Clara for a conference with Castro, and it was agreed that he should proceed to Havana and occupy the presidential palace. Although conditions in Havana were in a sense anarchical, one should not overlook the fact that order was being maintained. There was none of the rioting, looting, and murdering that had taken place after the overthrow of Machado twenty-five years earlier, or at least not on the same scale.

15

The reason was that the anti-Batista underground in Havana, composed mainly of 26th of July members, had surfaced and under the command of Manuel Ray had taken over the policing of the city. Moreover, in the general euphoria of the great victory and relief from the terrorist past, nobody wanted to see disorder perpetuated.

When Urrutia arrived in Havana, the presidential palace was already occupied by representatives of the *Directorio Revolucionario Estudiantil*, mentioned earlier, which had fought without coordination with Castro. Under the leadership of Fauré Chomón and Rolando Cubela, the *Directorio* had occupied not only the palace but the university as well, and both places were well stocked with arms. Negotiations soon settled matters, however, and Urrutia was permitted to take over the palace. Both Chomón and Cubela accepted positions in the Castro government. Urrutia immediately designated a cabinet led by José Miró Cardona as prime minister and composed of other distinguished and respected individuals. Roberto Agramonte, the Ortodoxo party candidate for president, was made minister of foreign affairs. On January 7 the United States recognized the government of President Urrutia and on January 21 named Philip Bonsal, a career foreign service officer, to replace Ambassador Earl E. T. Smith. Bonsal presented his credentials on March 3.

Meanwhile it soon became clear to the members of the new government that the real center of power was not in themselves but in Fidel Castro. Castro, however, was not sitting at a desk working out the organization of his government and developing its future plans. He was giving long speeches on the radio and television networks, mingling with the people, and enjoying with them the euphoria of the great victory. Rarely in one place for long, he went up and down the country making promises of a vast and glorious future for the nation. The cabinet, lacking guidelines, floundered about like a rudderless ship. During the first week in February it finally passed the Fundamental Law to replace the Constitution of 1940, much of the latter being incorporated in it. However, the law also contained some important new provisions. It broadened the powers of the premier, reduced to thirty the age of eligibility for the presidency (making Castro eligible), and ratified measures to facilitate the confiscation of property. It

16

made the executive supreme over the legislature and judiciary and authorized the death penalty retroactively.

On February 13, only little more than a month after taking office, Miró Cardona resigned as prime minister, saying "The Fundamental Law . . . grants to the post the powers of a true chief of government which, in my judgment, corresponds to those assumed by Dr. Fidel Castro, who, because of his historic hierarchy, is the chief of the Revolution." [5]

The Consolidation of Power

Castro was appointed prime minister to succeed Miró and was sworn in on February 16. Two days earlier, he had had a long cabinet meeting in which he presented a twenty-point program. But Castro was apparently not able to get things done, even though he held supreme power. Legally, President Urrutia also had some authority to veto proposals or delay their implementation. There were in addition continuing uncertainties in regard to the attitude of the government toward communism. For one thing, the Cuban Telephone Company, largely American owned, was "intervened" in March, and although this action was in line with commitments to Cubanize foreign companies it could not fail to stir apprehension of things to come. (To "intervene" an enterprise meant to appoint a government agent as manager.) President Urrutia was an anti-Communist and had so declared himself in a television interview. Since Castro himself had repeatedly denied that he was a Communist, Urrutia had a right to expect that his utterance on this point was within the limits of policy.

It proved to be otherwise. On July 17 Castro shocked the nation by announcing his resignation as prime minister. There followed a great demonstration at the presidential palace, with the crowd, as Jay Mallin, an eyewitness, phrased it, "chanting support for Castro and carrying pre-readied signs with such slogans as 'Fidel, Cuba needs you.'" [6] President Urrutia assured the crowd that Castro was indispensable and the resignation would not be accepted. It was not long before the hapless president watched television with incredulity as Castro lashed out at him, accusing him of "near treason," of trying to blackmail him with the "problem of Communism," and of slowing down the revolution. Urrutia wrote his resignation and left the palace by a back door in order to escape harm from an aroused mob. He was placed under house arrest and early in 1961 sought political asylum in the Venezuelan embassy.

In thus ridding his regime of his former defender, Castro cleared the way for his complete and absolute control of the government. The new president was a former minister of revolutionary laws, Osvaldo Dorticós Torrado. In the 1940's he had been a candidate of the (Communist) People's Socialist party in elections for the municipal council of Cienfuegos. Curiously, he had also held office under Batista as "legal assessor of the Cienfuegos waterworks," which, says Goldenberg, was in fact a sinecure.[7]

In addition to making his position secure by the replacement of high government officials not in agreement with his plans, Castro eliminated any possible threat from the remnants of the old power structure. Three groups were marked for removal by one means or another. The first group included members of the police and military forces who had committed crimes against the people. The second group comprised the wealthy. "When we speak of the people," Castro had said in his "History Will Absolve Me" speech, "we do not mean the comfortable ones, the conservative elements of the nation who welcome any regime of oppression." The third group, to quote again from the same address, included "those who had committed fraud during previous regimes." Their "ill-gotten holdings and [the] ill-gotten gains of their legatees and heirs" were to be confiscated.

The trials of accused persons began on January 22, 1959, when three Batista officers faced charges of murdering and torturing civilians. This was a show trial before a revolutionary court of three judges. It was held in the Sports City Stadium and attended by a crowd of 18,000, including many news correspondents and even United States Congressmen invited by the government. The defendants were condemned to death by firing squad.[8] This trial and subsequent similar ones brought widespread criticism from the world press, notably in the United States. It was plain to observers that with the crowd calling *paredón* whenever an accused person was brought up before the court, there was scarcely any chance for a fair trial.

Castro reacted angrily to the adverse criticism of the American press to "Operation Truth," as it was called. Why, he asked, with some reason, hadn't the press protested against the murder of innocent people by Batista's henchmen, persons shot down in cold blood without charges or trials? Granted that Castro had a point, still two things need to be said here: In the first place, no government today can execute hundreds of its citizens within a few weeks after taking power without inviting scrutiny and probable condemnation not only by the United States but by most other nations as well. This is especially the case because such wholesale and vengeful killing as occurred in Cuba was without parallel in the history of Latin America. Secondly, the "trials" can hardly be regarded as having been conducted by standards acceptable to the Western world. "Most of the members [of the revolutionary courts]," concluded the International Commission of Jurists, "are not lawyers, and in many cases are illiterate." 9

Since the very wealthy had been forewarned, most of them went into hiding or exile or sought asylum in one of the foreign embassies. All "collaborators" with Batista were subject to the vengeance of the new government. The word "collaboration" was never defined and could be applied to practically anyone who had served the previous government in any post. The properties of these men were confiscated and, if the truth were known, many were executed. There was inevitably overlap among the three categories, of persons designated by Castro for removal, and the same person might be adjudged guilty under more than one.

One other action needs to be noted, namely, the dismantling of the Batista-era army. This policy was made clear by Castro in his reply to a message from the Civilian Revolutionary Front in Miami proposing that the "revolutionary forces will be incorporated into the regular armed forces of the Republic with their arms." Castro angrily disagreed with this suggestion, saying that "the 26th of July Movement claims the function of keeping public order." 10

Thus after roguing the government of those who were not in full agreement with him, by executing, imprisoning, or forcing into exile formerly influential individuals and confiscating their possessions, and by dismantling the army, Castro was in full charge of the situation. He would still have dissenters to deal with, but his power was now well consolidated.

CUBA: THE MEASURE OF A REVOLUTION

The Problem of Communism

Much of Castro's trouble, domestic and foreign, after May 1959 arose out of the uncertainty as to the kind of movement he was leading. Was it to be a revolution along democratic lines as he had so often promised, or was it to be something quite different, perhaps even communism? During the rebellion and after Castro arrived in Havana in January 1959, he was repeatedly asked about communism. This was particularly true of reporters from the United States, but it was also a major concern of Cuban journalists as well. Would Cuba become a socialist state, a satellite of the USSR? While Castro had frequently denied being a Communist, the subject of his ideological orientation could not be put aside. Even now, many years after the event, the controversy and speculation continue. Had Castro been a Communist all the while during the rebellion, or had he gradually drifted to the far left? The question remains unanswered, but the evolution of the Cuban government into socialism or communism is a matter of history.

In order to fully appreciate the extraordinary and prevalent anxiety about Castro's attitude toward communism, it is necessary to recall the world political climate of the postwar years. The Soviet Union and the United States had been allies during World War II, but soon thereafter the USSR began its imperialist expansion into Eastern Europe and became a threat to Greece, Iran, and Western Europe itself. Thus began the cold war, with all its heated emotions and hostility.

There was near hysteria in the United States as the demagoguery of Senator Joseph McCarthy stirred suspicions and internal controversy to a point seldom if ever experienced before. This was the period of loyalty oaths, the blacklisting of organizations reputed to be Communist fronts, "guilt by association" charges, and the screening of the political background of people applying for jobs. While the intensity of this mood abated somewhat after the death of Stalin in 1953, it by no means disappeared.

At the same time, the Cuban people were equally concerned. The Communist party on the island had been organized in 1925 and had at times acquired considerable influence in the labor movement and even in the government. During Batista's rule from 1938 to 1944, the Communist party functioned openly and two members served as ministers without portfolio from 1940 to 1944. During the early 1940's, when the USSR was a wartime ally, Communists dominated the Cuban labor movement. Nevertheless, the Grau and Prío administrations ousted Communists from the labor leadership and in 1953, during the later Batista regime, the Communist *Partido Socialista Popular* (People's Socialist party) was declared illegal. The party was therefore not considered a particular threat, especially since it had not openly supported Castro until it appeared that the rebels were going to win. However, the Cuban as well as the American people were much concerned over what line Castro would follow.

Developments after May 1959 increased the feelings of anxiety. As the months passed, Castro seemed to become more determined to prohibit the expression of opposition to communism. Individuals and organized groups and institutions had not yet learned that freedom of speech and press would be strictly limited, despite Castro's earlier assurances to the contrary. One of the best-known and most disillusioning acts in this regard was his harsh treatment of his comrade-in-arms, Major Hubert Matos. Matos, disturbed by growing evidence of Communist infiltration into the revolution, decided to resign his position as military commander of the province of Camagüey. His letter of resignation of October 13 provoked a public outburst of vituperation and charges against him by Castro. Castro himself headed an armed contingent that went to Camagüey to arrest Matos and several of his staff. Tried and convicted of conspiracy, Matos was sentenced to twenty years in prison. This event was extremely upsetting to the members of the 26th of July Movement, who had assumed that it would be the governing instrument. On October 21 Díaz Lanz, chief of the revolutionary air force, defected to the United States and numerous others began the dismal flight into exile. The extremely popular rebel leader Camilo Cienfuegos mysteriously disappeared during this period and was never heard from again. These three popular leaders of the fight against Batista, along with Urrutia and others, had clearly not understood Fidel Castro, his ambitions, and what he hoped to accomplish in the revolution.

As the government came into possession of the enormous resources

21

confiscated from the groups discussed above, apprehension about the future grew. This fear was heightened after the passage of the Agrarian Reform Law in May 1959 and the subsequent further acquisitions of property by the agency administering the law, the *Instituto Nacional de Reforma Agraria*, known as INRA. In the United States there was concern about legal compensation for American citizens whose properties were expropriated.

Toward Cuban-American Confrontation

In addition to the cold-war atmosphere in which Cuban-American discussions took place, there was the undeniable attitude of hostility of Fidel Castro toward the United States. Both factors made rational diplomatic exchanges virtually impossible. Castro's attitude was not uncommon among Cuban reformists.

Cuban-American relations over the years had left many wounds that were easily inflamed. The story has been told and retold and there is a vast literature on the subject. While it can be shown that both countries have benefited by their relationships, there are Cuban and American scholars who will argue that Cuba benefited least. Most students of the subject would agree with Robert F. Smith that "in the long-range perspective of United States policy the emphasis has been placed on order, stability, and the protection of American interests. From the 1890's to the present the United States has supported the conservative upper classes and their American allies." [11] Yet it is not at all clear what alternative policy was practicable. Nations have to deal with each other on the basis of the governments in power. Nevertheless this was the philosophy that inspired the imposition of the Platt Amendment and that produced resentment among the rebel Cubans of the 1930's and those who followed them, in particular Fidel Castro.

The early months of 1959 were characterized by what might be called a wariness on the part of both Castro and the United States. On the one hand, Castro could not be certain on the basis of past history that the United States would not again intervene militarily to overthrow him; on the other hand, he was clearly determined to realize the deferred hope of the Machado rebels for economic and political independence from the United States. The situation was a delicate one, for achievement of the latter goal might provoke the unwanted reaction from the United States. The United States government for its part was perplexed by the confused pronouncements coming from Cuba regarding the plans of the revolution, and it was under pressure from both right and left as it tried to reach a definite policy.

Whether or not Castro was trying deliberately to confuse Washington he succeeded rather well in doing so. The Cuban Telephone Company was taken over in March, but the next month, during a visit to Washington, Castro assured the American Society of Newspaper Editors that foreign investment would be welcome. He professed devotion to the principle of a free press in April 1959, but the erosion of such freedom began soon after and was completed within a year and a half.

Castro's visit to Washington was a private one and, according to Teresa Casuso, who was in charge of arrangements for the trip, that is the way Fidel wanted it. She reports that the Cuban ambassador in Washington asked whether Castro wished an official invitation and that Castro said no; thus no initiative was taken in Washington by the United States government. Casuso believes that if Castro "had been invited, he would have accepted in spite of what he had said; but he could not go looking for an invitation." She implies that if some gesture had been made by the United States government to reach a relationship of understanding, the future might have been different.[12] However, it is a fact that Castro met with Secretary of State Christian A. Herter, with the undersecretary for Latin American affairs, Roy R. Rubottom, Jr., and with Vice-President Richard M. Nixon. (President Dwight D. Eisenhower was in Georgia.)

Nixon's comments on this encounter with Castro in his book *Six Crises* confirm the suspicion in which Castro was held by many Americans at the time. "After the conference," Nixon said, "I wrote a confidential memorandum for distribution to the CIA, the State Department, and the White House. In it I stated flatly that I was convinced Castro was 'either incredibly naive about Communism or under Communist discipline' and that we should treat him and deal with him accordingly."[13]

Nine months later Nixon's recommendation became policy and the Central Intelligence Agency was given authority to secretly arm and train exiled Cubans for an invasion of the island. By then Nixon was the Republican candidate for president and, as he pointed out in his book, since the operation was a secret one, he was not at liberty to answer the criticism of his opponent, John F. Kennedy, on the administration's Cuban policy. Nevertheless, speaking in September at Miami, Nixon came out publicly for a "policy of all-out 'quarantine' — economically, politically, and diplomatically — of the Castro regime . . ."[14]

Nixon admitted in his book that his position was a "minority one within the Administration and particularly so within the Latin American branch of the State Department," since the state department's line was, "trying to get along with" and "understand" Castro.[15] Without doubt, however, there were many others, both public officials and private individuals, who shared Nixon's suspicion of Fidel Castro.

As for Castro himself, whether or not he resented the failure of the American government to take more official notice of his visit, it could hardly be considered a decisive factor in determining his attitude. The experience could only have reinforced the attitudes which, as Ruiz and others have pointed out, were generated during a half century of experience.

Knowledgeable students of the revolution no longer take seriously the theory that the action or lack of it by officials in Washington forced Castro into the arms of the Soviet Union. This thesis was put forward by American pro-Castro apologists with the idea of blaming Castro's behavior on the errors of American diplomacy. Others have argued against this thesis.[16] Nevertheless, in retrospect, it seems to have been a mistake for the United States government to fail to give Castro greater official attention. He was the man of the hour in Cuba and as the head of the government deserved special official consideration. There was nothing to lose, it would seem, and some benefit might have followed.

Before returning to Cuba, Castro flew from the United States to Buenos Aires, where he addressed the Economic Conference of the American States and put forth proposals for a Marshall Plan for Latin

America. In this speech, as well as in the addresses, interviews, and press conferences he gave in the United States, nothing was said to foreshadow the attacks on the United States that were to come. Indeed, Goldenberg reports that at this time there was considerable anxiety among Cuban Communists about Castro's apparent "pro-*Yanqui* deviations."[17] His brother Raúl even flew to Texas to see him on his way to Buenos Aires and inquired "angrily if he had sold out to the Yanquis." Perhaps Fidel was going through a period of some uncertainty, or perhaps he was merely beguiling his "enemies" until his own position was more secure. It is of interest to note also that shortly after his return from Buenos Aires, he denounced communism and the People's Socialist party (*Prensa Libre,* May 23, 1959). It was only a few days later that, as we have previously noted, he arrested Hubert Matos. Truly, Fidel was a difficult man to follow — and in more ways than one. In reviewing the events of 1959 one is inclined to accept the judgment of Goldenberg that Castro was "certainly more anti-capitalist and anti-American than he publicly declared." Yet, as Goldenberg points out, "much of what Castro said could not have been proclaimed by a 'Marxist-Leninist': the glorification of representative democracy, of human individual liberties, and the condemnation of all kinds of dictatorship. However, the radical turn of the revolution could hardly have been avoided even with a different American policy." Nevertheless, Javier Pazos has added his tentative support to the notion that Castro was experiencing some indecision at this point.[18]

The verbal exchanges between the United States and Cuba that would eventually end diplomatic relations began mildly enough. During the first weeks after the passage of the Agrarian Reform Law in May, concern in regard to compensation arose in the minds of Americans who owned property in Cuba. On June 11 the Department of State sent a note to Cuba which supported the goals of land reform but expressed the wish that expropriation would be accompanied by reasonable compensation and that the rights of American citizens would generally be respected. The Cubans answered on June 15 that the economic condition of the country would not permit immediate compensation but that a bond issue would be arranged to compensate owners.[19]

The attempted invasions of Panama on April 18 and of the Dominican Republic on June 14, in which Cubans participated, naturally aroused concern over Castro's plans regarding other Latin American countries. President Eisenhower voiced his own uneasiness on July 1 and suggested that conditions in the Caribbean should be considered by the Organization of American States.

On July 14 Major Díaz Lanz testified before the Senate Subcommittee to Investigate the Administration of the Internal Security Act that Communists were taking over the revolution. He gave the names of several Communists who were in charge of important sectors of the government, mentioning also the establishment of indoctrination schools and attempts at invasion of other Latin countries. In a press conference on July 15 President Eisenhower took note of this testimony but said there was no concrete proof that Castro was a Communist; the United States, he added, was watching developments in the Caribbean and would cooperate with the OAS in its forthcoming conference.

The OAS foreign ministers met at Santiago, Chile, on August 17–18 and agreed to a full study of the Caribbean situation. Meantime, on August 14, a group composed mainly of Cubans attempted to invade Haiti and was repulsed.

On October 21 Díaz Lanz, flying a plane from American soil, swooped low over Havana and dropped leaflets. In the ensuing firing of antiaircraft batteries and guns mounted on the roofs of police stations, two persons were killed and about fifty wounded. Government publications referred to the incident as Havana's Pearl Harbor, charging that the city had been bombed and accusing the United States of being involved. On October 26 Castro, speaking at a rally, denounced the United States for permitting planes to fly from its soil to "bomb defenseless" people in Havana. The "bombs" proved to be propaganda leaflets.

The Department of State protested this charge the next day and expressed concern at the "distrust and hostility" fostered by some Cubans; at the same time it denied any backing of Castro's enemies. President Eisenhower on October 28 said that the United States was doing all it could to prevent illegal flights to Cuba. Again on November 9 the state department in more heated language denounced the "inaccurate, malicious, and misleading reports" on the alleged bombing of Havana. On November 11 Moscow radio issued a statement supporting Cuba's interpretation of the affair. On November 13 Cuba rejected the United States protest and reiterated old charges of economic and political offenses. On December 10 Secretary of State Herter stated at a press conference that "relations with Cuba have deteriorated."

On December 22 the Cuban cabinet decreed the confiscation of property of counterrevolutionaries. (As we have noted, the regime had previously dealt with everyone who could by any means be associated with the Batista government.) In a cabinet reorganization, Manuel Ray, Faustino Pérez, and Manuel Fernández, all important members of the 26th of July Movement, were replaced by pro-Communists. On December 18 Castro called Vice-President Nixon "insolent" and charged the United States with seeking to dominate Cuba. On December 26 President Eisenhower reaffirmed the policy of no reprisals against the Cuban people and no intervention in their internal affairs, but he also protested the violation of United States rights and expressed the hope that the Cuban people would defeat Communist influence. On January 27, 1960, President Dorticós rejected Eisenhower's insinuation that Communist intrigue was poisoning American-Cuban relations and demanded that the United States respect Cuban sovereignty.

Still another factor in what Smith calls the "cross fertilization of antagonisms"[20] occurred when the deputy prime minister of the USSR, Anastas Mikoyan, arrived in Havana and opened a Soviet trade fair on February 5. This event could hardly cool the anxiety of people in the United States. At the same time it had become evident that one freedom after another was being suppressed in Cuba. According to the official newspaper *Revolución,* anyone who expressed criticism of the Communists was considered to be an opponent of the revolution and therefore a counterrevolutionary, subject to possible penalties including the confiscation of his property. Castro and Mikoyan concluded a trade agreement under which the Soviets were to buy five million tons of sugar during a five-year period and extend a credit of $100 million to Cuba.

On February 18 Castro claimed to have documentary evidence that a plane which had recently "bombed" Cuba came from the United States. (He was not referring to the flight of Díaz Lanz on January 2.) The following day, the United States acknowledged that a plane which had crashed in Cuba came from the United States and offered regrets.

On February 22 Cuba stated it would discuss differences with the United States but specified that the latter must agree not to adopt any measures harmful to Cuba. This precondition was rejected by the United States on February 29 in a statement which said in part: "The government of the United States must remain free, in the exercise of its own sovereignty, to take what steps it deems necessary, fully consistent with its international obligations, in the defense of the legitimate rights and interests of its people. The Government of the United States believes that these rights and interests have been adversely affected by the unilateral acts of the Government of Cuba." [21] Thus another opportunity for conciliation was lost.

In early March the French munitions ship *Le Coubre* exploded in the harbor of Havana while being unloaded. Fifty persons were killed and some two hundred wounded. Cuba implied that the United States was involved, and the latter protested the charge. Although Castro denied having accused the United States of sabotage, he insisted on his "right to wonder." [22] As relations steadily worsened, the Central Intelligence Agency was authorized on March 17 to equip a force of Cuban exiles who were preparing to attempt an invasion of the island.

Another matter that rankled on the United States side was the treatment of its ambassador. Since March 3, 1959, the United States had been represented in Cuba by Ambassador Philip Bonsal, but he was kept waiting for an appointment with Castro until September 4. No Cuban official met him on March 20, 1960, when he returned to Havana after a trip to Washington.

In April hostility mounted further between the two countries. The United States charged that Cuba had increased tensions in the Caribbean and the result was an excessive demand for arms throughout the area. A few days later Castro charged the United States with plotting aggression against Cuba through the OAS and urged instead an alliance of Cuba and other Latin American countries against the

United States. Guatemala broke diplomatic relations with Cuba after Castro charged that an invasion was being planned on Guatemalan soil by the United Fruit Company. (Castro's intelligence was correct except for the sponsor!)

In a May Day address Castro complained that "war criminals," the "assassins of yesterday," had appeared before the Senate of the United States to testify about the affairs of Cuba. He was referring to an appearance by Díaz Lanz. Again he mentioned the danger of armed invasion. Turning to the diplomatic break with Guatemala, he repeated his claim that soldiers were being trained there.

Hot Words: Acts and Counter Acts

On May 6, 1960, the United States submarine *Sea Poacher* was fired on by the Cuban coast guard. There followed conflicting claims between the two countries as to whether or not the submarine was in Cuban territorial waters. On May 23 President Dorticós began a tour of Latin American countries, allegedly to win their support against the United States. On May 27 the United States announced the termination of technical assistance projects in Cuba and on June 4 it accused Castro and Dorticós, both of whom were traveling in Latin America, of conducting a campaign of slander against it. On June 21 a memorandum by the United States was submitted to the Inter-American Peace Committee charging that the "government of Cuba has for many months conducted an intense campaign of distortion, half-truths, and outright falsehoods against the United States Government, its officials, and the people of the United States. The United States has responded to these hostile attitudes and actions of the Cuban government with patience and forbearance, in the hope of avoiding to the extent possible, impairment of the friendliness and mutual confidence which traditionally have existed between the two countries and their peoples."[23] The document reviewed a number of charges and allegations made by Cuba against the United States and the refutations made in answer. There was special reference to Cuban charges resulting from the explosion of *Le Coubre*, the "bombing" incident in Havana, and the attack on the *Sea Poacher* by the Cuban coast guard.

29

From this point onward exchanges became increasingly heated. Meantime the expropriation of American-owned property continued. When refineries owned mainly by the United States and Britain refused to process Soviet oil which arrived in April, they were taken over by the government of Cuba. On June 11 American-owned hotels in Havana were seized.

The month of July opened on a somber chord as Congress passed a bill authorizing the president to alter sugar quotas, an act clearly aimed at giving him economic leverage in dealing with Cuba. On July 6 Eisenhower announced a cut in the Cuban quota for the balance of the year. This meant a reduction of 700,000 short tons. The original 1960 quota for Cuba was 3,119,655 tons, equal to nearly a third of the total needs of the United States. "I believe," said the president, "we would fail in our obligation to our people if we did not take a step to reduce our reliance for a major food product upon a nation which has embarked on a deliberate policy of hostility toward the United States." The estimated loss to Cuba was $92,500,000. The Cuban government immediately retaliated by passing a law authorizing the nationalization of all American-owned enterprises. The following day Castro attacked the reduction in the sugar quota as imperialism and an attempt to destroy the Revolution, although earlier the regime had called the quota a form of colonialism.[24] Again he assailed opponents of the revolution as traitors.

Premier Nikita Khrushchev of the Soviet Union, as he had done on previous recent occasions, once more seized the opportunity to express his support for Cuba. President Eisenhower responded that the United States would not permit a regime dominated by international communism in the Western Hemisphere. (These brave words proved to have no influence on events.) The Soviet Union promptly agreed to buy the 700,000 tons cut from the Cuban quota and Castro went on television to accept the Soviet offer. When the United States announced a plan for aid to Latin America on July 11, Cuba was told it would have to change its ways before it could participate.

Cuba registered a complaint with the United Nations Security Council on July 11 against actions of the United States. The next day Khrushchev, by way of offering further support to Cuba, issued a statement claiming the Monroe Doctrine to be a dead issue and again promising to back Cuba in any effort to get rid of the naval base at Guantánamo. In answer to Khrushchev's statement on the Monroe Doctrine, the state department accused him of seeking to establish a Bolshevik Doctrine that would provide for the use of Soviet military power in support of communism anywhere in the world. So the battle of words took on triangular dimensions.

When Cuba repeated its charges of economic aggression in the Security Council on July 18, the United States declared that its policy would continue to be the one expressed in the Monroe Doctrine and in treaties with other American republics to oppose alien domination of any part of the Western Hemisphere. On the same day the OAS agreed unanimously to hold a foreign ministers' conference on Cuban-United States differences.

The OAS conference was held at San José, Costa Rica, in late August. A major concern was Cuba's action in conducting training camps to prepare agents for guerrilla warfare in other Latin American countries. Cuba already had been charged with attempted invasions of the Dominican Republic, Panama, Guatemala, and Haiti, and on July 26 Castro had openly called for guerrilla wars in Latin America. On August 28 the conference issued what is known as the Declaration of San José. It condemned intervention by extracontinental powers in the affairs of the American states and reaffirmed the principle of the nonintervention of any American state in the internal affairs of another. The document also declared that the inter-American system was incompatible with any form of totalitarianism.

This declaration left a number of vulnerable openings and Cuba promptly responded with the Declaration of Havana on September 2. It condemned the San José statement, charging American imperialism, and noted the many United States interventions of the past. It also rejected the Monroe Doctrine and insisted that in any case the Soviet promise of economic aid to Cuba did not constitute intervention. It announced Cuba's intention to resume diplomatic relations with Communist countries including mainland China, along with breaking relations with Taiwan. The document went on to lecture the authors of the San José declaration by challenging the implication of

31

totalitarianism in Cuba, maintaining that "democracy is not compatible with financial oligarchies, racial discrimination, the Ku Klux Klan, persecution of intellectuals . . . and the execution of the Rosenbergs." [25] After specifying the abuses that existed in Latin America, it promised to make those countries "free."

During September the Cuban government made further expropriations, including all United States banks, all cigar and cigarette factories, and CMQ, the leading radio and television network. All newspapers and magazines had already been suppressed, except for two operated by the regime. Castro attended the General Assembly of the United Nations and spoke for five hours on September 26, reviewing all the familiar charges against the United States. Upon his return to Cuba on September 28, he announced the organization of the Committees for the Defense of the Revolution (CDR), which were to become one of the most important mass organizations in the political and social control of the regime. For its part the United States took another step toward ending relations when it advised its citizens in Cuba to send out dependents and suggested that travelers avoid the island.

On October 14 all Cuban-owned sugar mills and nearly four hundred other commercial and industrial enterprises were nationalized. On this day too the government announced the Urban Reform Law, which granted a limited title to renters of houses and apartments, who were thereafter to pay their rent to the state. Owners were indemnified by a grant of monthly payments based upon the value of their properties.[26]

On October 19 a further step toward an open break with Cuba was taken by the United States when it announced an embargo on all trade with the island except for food and medicine. There were many reasons for this action, but the main one was Cuban discrimination against imports of United States goods by means of taxes and import duties. In addition American exporters were finding it impossible to collect payments for goods they sent to Cuba. It was estimated that by the end of 1960, $150 million was owed to American exporters.[27] On December 16 President Eisenhower cancelled the Cuban sugar quota for the first quarter of 1961 and on January 3, 1961, provoked by Castro's demand that the personnel of the large United States embassy be reduced to eleven, he broke off diplomatic relations, turning over American affairs in Cuba to the Swiss embassy.

Conclusion

In reviewing the events involving the relations between the United States and Cuba after mid-1959, one finds it difficult to avoid the conviction that from that time on Fidel Castro was determined to obtain complete isolation from the United States. In the face of his repeated provocations, the United States had manifested an unusual measure of "patience and forbearance" (in the words of the June 21, 1960, memorandum) despite the demands of many high officials that strong action be taken because they feared that Cuba was becoming a Communist country, allied to if not dominated by the USSR. The unfortunate consequences of the American diplomatic failure could be seen in the condition of Cuba in 1971.

The responsibility for this lamentable result will long remain a matter of controversy. Critics of the performance of the United States fall into two main categories: "hard-liners" and "soft-liners." The hard-liners, such as Paul Bethel and R. Hart Phillips think the United States should have reacted strongly against what they consider the intolerable provocations of the Castro regime. The other group, including such men as Matthews, Zeitlin, Scheer, and others, are critical of the government for not embracing Castro and supporting his program. For his part the prime minister could hardly have expected a friendly reaction to the flow of philippics against the United States, tirades surely designed to bring forth the kind of unfriendly answers which finally came out of Washington. The blame for the unhappy consequences for the Cuban people must be shared by both governments.[28]

As for the United States and its diplomacy throughout the affair, one can detect in the foregoing recital of events a sort of bewilderment among the diplomatic personnel. The state department obviously was at a loss to know how to deal with Castro's unorthodox diplomatic behavior. His relentless hostility, his repeated charges of "imperialism" and "economic aggression," and his distortion of events in such a way as to point an accusing finger of blame at what had always been a friendly country — all this was outside the rules of diplomatic intercourse. The situation was unprecedented.

But Castro's rebellion against the United States was possible only because of the cold war and the existence of the Sino-Soviet bloc. Ready to take advantage of uprisings against capitalist nations anywhere, Moscow kept a careful eye on Cuba. The Soviets let it be known very early that Castro had their support. Although diplomatic relations with the USSR had been ended during the Batista regime, the official newspaper *Revolución* announced on December 16, 1959, the arrival of Alexander Alexiev, a correspondent of Tass, the Soviet news agency. After the restoration of diplomatic relations on May 7, 1960, Alexiev became the Soviet ambassador to Cuba. On January 21, 1960, the Cuban government announced the establishment of its own press agency, *Prensa Latina*, and declared that it was obligatory for all Cuban papers to subscribe to the agency. An important part of the announcement was that agreements had been made for the cooperation of *Prensa Latina* with Tass and other East European news agencies. The propaganda mechanism was now entirely under the control of the regime.

It was shortly after this that Mikoyan visited Havana and signed a trade agreement. The eager grasp of any opportunity for ingratiating itself in Cuban affairs was manifested by the USSR and China in supporting Cuba's interpretation of the explosion of *Le Coubre*. The arrival of the first Soviet oil tanker in April 1960; the reestablishment of diplomatic relations in May, followed shortly by announcements of the establishment of diplomatic relations with Poland, Rumania, Bulgaria, Hungary, North Vietnam, Albania, Czechoslovakia, and Communist China; and finally the physical embracing of Castro and Khrushchev at the Harlem Hotel during the meeting of United Nations General Assembly rather solidified the identification of Cuba with the Communist world.

The die was cast. Cuba was "free" of the apron strings of the United States and had adopted political, social, and economic ties with the Communist camp. On April 16, 1961, Castro formally declared that the revolution was socialist; on May 1 he termed Cuba a socialist country; and on December 1 he declared himself to be a "Marxist-

Leninist." He had always been one, Castro said, and he always would be.[29]

Meantime the revolution was consolidated by several measures for political and social control. The power of the Roman Catholic Church was broken and it was told to keep out of politics. Labor organizations were firmly under control of the regime. The revolutionary defense committees had been created as a vigilance mechanism. The press had been brought under government ownership and control, as had the excellent radio and television networks.[30] The educational system, from the universities down to the kindergartens, was under complete government control and special schools for indoctrination at all levels had been set up. In the assault on private property, the revolution had come into ownership of virtually the entire island. In the process, the former leaders, the skilled managerial and professional classes had fled into exile — those who were not already executed or imprisoned — leaving the tasks of reorganizing and managing the society in the hands of untrained and inexperienced youths.

Thus the revolution became the sole property of Fidel Castro, as had the rebellion before it. He had instigated the rebellion and by unwavering persistence against all odds had brought the revolutionary government into power. He had come into control of the destinies of 6,800,000 people; their lives, their freedoms, were in his hands. It is impossible to conceive of the revolution without Fidel Castro. He made it, he owns it, and he runs it.

The development of Cuba before the revolution came to power will be briefly reviewed in Chapter 3.

Chapter **3**

The Development
of Prerevolutionary Cuba

It required only two years to undo and overturn the gradual economic development of four and a half centuries under the ethos of European-American capitalism. Social structures rooted in age-old values were swept away, as a fire destroys in a few minutes physical structures that may have required years to construct. Cuba constitutes a unique example of a country launched on a classical linear path of capitalist development, a course that is suddenly truncated by revolution and re-routed on another course in many ways contradictory to the first. This drastic replacement of a free enterprise system and its concomitant social structures by a system of state capitalism under a totalitarian political regime had traumatic consequences not only for the economy but for the entire social system as well.

To understand the magnitude of the social change in its varied aspects, it is necessary to have in mind something of the history of the country, its natural resources, and the growth and characteristics of the Cuban people.

The Setting

That Cuba is an island is an important geographic fact which has conditioned its social, economic, and political development. The further fact that it lies so close to the continental United States has had a complementary developmental influence. The United States — rich in natural resources of soil, coal, iron, and numerous other kinds of metallic and nonmetallic wealth, highly industrialized with a population drawn originally from the countries of Western Europe and motivated by the ethos of capitalism — could not be otherwise than the dominant factor in the development of Cuba as well as of other nearby small countries. For its own part, Cuba has large areas of level and good soil and one of the most salubrious climates in the world. It has large deposits of nickel, with less significant amounts of copper, cobalt, chromium, manganese, and tungsten. There are large deposits of iron, but the ore is not high grade on the whole and there are serious problems in extracting it. The most grave lack in Cuba's resource inventory is fuel. There is no coal and only small quantities of oil have as yet been discovered.

To these natural resources must be added a number of excellent harbors, which because of the strategic location of the island have played a very important role in its historic development. On the other hand, the rivers of the island have not been as important to its history. They do not provide a major source for hydroelectric power. Because of the shape and topography of the island, the rivers are generally not large. On the contrary, they are often a menace in periods of heavy rainfall, due to the flooding of the lowlands. Only in recent decades has there been a significant development in the control of these water channels through dam construction.

Cuba then is almost entirely dependent on outside sources for the fuel needed in modern industrial development. This is all-important, though the country is also dependent on imports for many other items which the island cannot supply. The dim outlook for industrial growth, recognized after the fiasco of the industrialization plans of the first four years of the revolution, was reaffirmed by Prime Minister Castro on December 22, 1969, in an address to the graduates of the Institute of Economics at the University of Havana. "Our country," he said, "does not have the basic industries which will allow it to work out a program based only on its own internal resources, and therefore to a considerable degree it will depend on outside factors for its development program."

CUBA: THE MEASURE OF A REVOLUTION

Historical Development

For present purposes the history of Cuba may be considered under three chronological periods: (1) the moribund years, 1511–1763; (2) the growth of an agrarian society, 1763–1850; and (3) the capitalist sugar society, 1850–1958. These chronological periods are inevitably somewhat arbitrary as to dates, since precision is not possible. Nevertheless, they will be discussed in turn, though only in a most superficial manner because of limitations of space.

The Moribund Years

Although the conquest of Cuba under Diego de Velázquez was undertaken in 1511, the settlement of the island was extremely slow during the succeeding two centuries and a half. There were several reasons for this. As already mentioned, Cuba's major resource lay in its soil and climate, that is, in its agricultural potential; but the early immigrants from Spain were more concerned with precious metals, as were the monarchs themselves. Thus primary attention was focused on the wealth of the Aztecs and Incas; Cuba was essentially a camping ground for travelers to Mexico and Peru. After almost a century the population of Cuba in 1602 was reported to be only 20,000, of whom 13,000 were in Havana. The latter was a way station for ships traveling between Spain and the gulf ports of entry to Mexico and Peru. The population was a shifting one, the main activities being the provision of food and lodging, and supplying ships with food in limited quantities and such exportable items as cassava, dried meat, tobacco, hides, and tallow. (Often the boats were too fully loaded to take on additional cargo at Havana.) The excellent harbor, in addition to providing a place of rest and refreshment for travelers, was also equipped to make repairs of ships.

Despite the emphasis on the continent, the first settlers in Cuba set out to find such gold as might be there. To this end they were made the beneficiaries of *encomiendas,* or rights to the labor of the natives of a certain locality, in return for which the grantee fed and cared for the Indians and converted them to Christianity. The natives were put to trenching soil that might contain gold deposits and working the streams, and they were so maltreated that by 1550 there were few survivors.[1] This led to a demand for African slaves. A license was granted a British company to import slaves and even before the end of the encomiendas Negroes were said to be numerous in the island. However, as interest in mining for gold decreased so did the requirement for workers.

Although the energies of the settlers had to shift somewhat toward agriculture, what developed was a largely pastoral economy that required relatively few workers. Primary emphasis was upon cattle raising although the production of food was an ever-present need. A system of land grants to individuals was inaugurated in 1536, when the city council (*cabildo*) of Sancti Spíritus granted to one Fernando Gómez a circular hacienda three leagues in radius from a center. The circular form grew from two facts: the abundance of land and the scarcity of surveyors. It was a comparatively simple procedure to have the applicant describe his general location and to grant him an area with a given radius.

Eventually, practically the whole island was granted to private individuals by the municipal councils, notably those of Sancti Spíritus and Havana.[2]

These circular land grants were originally made to individuals, but as a result of sales and inheritance they soon became communal properties — that is, they were held without subdivision by many persons. Some of them endured for a century, by which time there well might be scores of people with rights in them. But to divide them was not considered practical. The alternative to subdivision was at first the use of marks and brands on the livestock to identify ownership. Later the property was divided into shares based upon the total valuation of the land and stock. These were called *pesos de posesión*, an interesting and useful invention for the time. As long as there was no pressure to expand sugar production, the *haciendas comuneras* were in no serious danger of dissolution. Labor requirements were minimal and could easily be supplied by the comuneras themselves. However, as a growth industry, the raising of livestock at the time was extremely limited. In the first place, the only market open to Cuba was Spain itself. Secondly, the lack of processing and cold storage facilities meant that only hides, tallow (for making candles), and dried meat could be regarded as exportable.[3]

Sugarcane was brought to Hispaniola (now Haiti and the Dominican Republic) by Columbus on his second voyage in 1493, and Velázquez, the conquerer of Cuba, is himself reported to have brought it to that island. However, it was a century before any significant growth began. The most serious impediment was the fact that the greedy merchants of Seville, who had a monopoly on Cuban trade, charged such heavy commissions, not only on incoming products but on outgoing ones as well, that it was impossible for Cuban sugar growers to meet the competition of other sources. Machinery for the sugar mills was bought in Portugal but had to pass through the port of Seville, where commissions were added before it could be shipped. Moreover, the market for Cuban sugar was limited to Spain itself, which supplied part of its needs from production in its own province of Granada. In addition, there was no capital available from outside Cuba until Philip II authorized loans to entrepreneurs willing to go into the sugar business. He also granted certain exemptions from levies on machinery.

This early period was therefore one of torpor and extremely slow development as a result of the focus of metropolitan attention on the continent, the unreasonable strictures on trade and commerce, the isolation of the island from Spain, and the lack of a labor supply necessary for intensive kinds of agriculture. Socially, there was gradually forming a society based on cattle ranching with wide and essentially equal distribution of land to those who worked on it. There was little social stratification. Social organization was essentially familistic. Left so largely to their own devices, the settlers had little relation to the central government. The municipal council was the government. The church, of course, was in evidence, but it probably functioned only in the centers of population. These two and a half centuries were a gestation period, economically and socially.

Toward an Agrarian Society

A number of events of tremendous importance to Cuba took place in the world during the latter part of the eighteenth century. These included the industrial revolution in England, the revolt of the American colonies, the French Revolution of 1789 and the resulting uprising in Haiti, and the occupation of Havana by the British in

The Development of Prerevolutionary Cuba

1762–1763. We have space for only a few lines regarding each. The application of steam as industrial power was destined to become one of the basic technological factors in the evolution of the sugar industry, with all that it has meant to the social structure of Cuba. Not only was it to become the power for operating the mills themselves, thus replacing animal power, but in the latter half of the nineteenth century, when it was practicable to build railroads, it made possible the extension of the area that could be served by a single mill.

The success of the American Revolution opened the United States as a market for Cuban sugar and other commodities. But the climactic event was the Haitian revolt. Under the French Haiti had been the most productive and profitable colony in the Caribbean. It supplied the European market not only with sugar but with coffee as well. The revolt of the slaves resulted in the expulsion of the French plantation owners and managers — or their assassination — and the vast devastation of the plantations. Some of the owners and managers escaped to Cuba where they were the first to introduce coffee growing. They also brought with them a level of culture which Cuba had had little opportunity to develop due to its enforced isolation from the mother country. With the Haitian production largely destroyed, Cuba was able to become a substitute source for both sugar and coffee.

Yet it would have been impossible to capitalize on this opportunity if Britain had not broken Cuba's isolation by capturing Havana in August 1762. For the first time in its 250 years the port of Havana was open to all commerce. Instead of the one to six ships a year that had previously entered the port, a reported one thousand vessels arrived during the approximately ten months of British occupation. The English surrendered the port in April 1763 when Spain agreed to transfer Florida to them. Havana and Cuba could never be the same after that event. The island was now joined to the world, although by no means all its problems of commerce were solved.

The accession to the Spanish throne of Carlos III (1759–1788) was another favorable event of this period. This liberal monarch relaxed the restrictive regulations to a considerable extent. Other Cuban ports than Havana were opened to commerce and the monopoly of the port of Seville was broken. In 1774 Carlos decreed free entry into Spain of Cuban products, and the number of ships in the Cuban-Spanish trade increased from one, before the British capture of Havana, to two hundred in 1778. Carlos also encouraged trade between Cuba and the United States, although by 1784 the fear grew in Spain that Cuba would become too dependent on the United States and the old monopolistic restrictions were restored.

Thus the course of worldwide events in the latter part of the eighteenth century brought a great awakening to Cuba. It was really the period of birth and infancy for the society of the island. The first census of Cuba was taken in 1774 and it revealed a marked development, much of which undoubtedly had occurred in the most recent decades. The population consisted of 96,440 whites, 31,847 free colored, and 44,333 slaves. Some 10,000 of the latter had been brought in by the British during their occupation of Havana. There were 399 large cattle ranches, 477 sugar mills, and 7,814 small holdings.

Despite this rapid growth, Cuban society remained largely agrarian with wide distribution of land among the settlers. The demand for sugar for export to the new markets brought pressure for more sugarcane land, which meant the gradual dissolution of many of the large cattle ranches. The sugar mills were small and served areas limited by the use of ox-power, not only for transporting cane to the mill but also for hauling wood to fuel the boilers, since the use of bagasse as fuel was not yet known to be possible. The use of oxen necessitated the growing of feed for them. In addition the island had to be largely self-sufficient in the food supply for its human population. Thus general farming could not be neglected.

The sugar mills increased rapidly in numbers, but each served a limited area, perhaps no more than one or two thousand acres. It was estimated by Pezuela that there were two thousand small mills (*trapiches*) in 1860.[4] This was the peak; from that time forward the influence of technological improvements in the mills and, above all, the introduction of the railroad made possible a vast expansion of the area which one mill could serve.

During this time of economic awakening, Cuban society became much more complex. In contrast with the earlier period marked by a largely homogeneous Spanish settlement and equality in possessions, the influx of Africans was so large that the slave population almost equaled the white population. A growing feeling of nationhood was evident, however. Under the colonial regime of Don Luís de las Casas (1790–1796) there was founded the famous *Sociedad Económica de Amigos del País*, which by royal order was charged with the sponsorship of education. An inventory made by it in 1793 showed thirty-nine schools in Havana, thirty-two of them for girls. Those that were functioning taught only reading. In 1816 the society established the first free public school. Its activities were, however, opposed by the bishop of Havana, who also opposed the educational efforts of the Jesuits, whom he had banished from the country earlier. The bishop feared that education would affect adversely the faith of the young.

Capitalist Sugar Society

During its long colonial period Cuba developed a feeling of nationhood unlike that in most other colonies. This was due to its isolation from and neglect by the mother country, as well as by the growth of a predominantly Creole population (those native-born of Spanish parents). In all Spanish American countries, the Creole population was the spearhead of the wars for independence. They came to demand control of their own affairs and to resent the intrusion of the officialdom from Spain which held authority over them. Cuba was the last, along with Puerto Rico, to begin the fight for independence. The last half of the nineteenth century was a period of unrest and of open war, culminating in the defeat of Spain in 1898. Because of the wars, progress in agriculture was slowed though by no means stopped. And up to the beginning of the republic, Cuba remained an agrarian society.

Without attempting to describe in detail the developments of this period, we offer a few general comments. The establishment of the republic in 1902, along with the famous Platt Amendment to the new constitution, signaled the beginning of a vast transformation from many small farm units to the large sugar plantations. Under the benign protection of the Platt Amendment ("benign" only in the sense of reducing the risk to capital resulting from political upheavals), capital from the United States and other more developed countries flowed into Cuba in enormous amounts. Land was bought in extensive tracts from small and large farmers and joined to the enlarged and enlarging areas around the mills. Railroad trackage grew by

43

kilometers daily. The outcome was the virtual destruction of the agrarian society based on the widespread ownership of land by those who worked on it. The two thousand small mills of 1860 had been gradually declining in number, but after independence they completely disappeared and only 165 *centrales* or large mills processed all the cane that was needed to supply the sugar market. During and after World War I that market became a bonanza as the price of sugar soared to unprecedented levels. The 1920's became known in Cuba as the "dance of the millions"; at this time vast fortunes were made and the luxurious suburbs of Havana were constructed. The story is well known.

Then came the "hangover." The overproduction of sugar demanded world agreements on the control of production. Cuba became a signatory of these agreements. Meantime, the erstwhile independent farmers and their children became workers on the plantations or tenants on cane, tobacco, and coffee farms. Instead of a relatively unstratified society, rural Cuba now became a highly stratified one, with the large plantation owners at the top, followed by the few independent farmers who still remained, the tenants of various types, the squatters, and finally the great mass of often impoverished laborers.

Cuba in the 1950's

In spite of the well-known corruption of some of the governments of the republican period, the economy became increasingly diversified. By 1953, when the latest census was taken, about 60 percent of the labor force was engaged in nonagricultural occupations. The percentage would have been greater had not the labor unions opposed further mechanization of agriculture. Although by 1959 Cuba was still far from achieving its potential in economic growth, by Latin American standards it was reasonably well provided with food and the daily average consumption was exceeded only by Argentina and Uruguay. It had more motor vehicles in relation to population than any of its Caribbean neighbors except Venezuela and exceeded all of the Caribbean in telephones and newspapers per thousand population. It ranked near the top of all Latin America in the number of radios and had well-established television networks. (See Table 1.)

The Development of Prerevolutionary Cuba

Cuban citizens, meanwhile, had been able to purchase many of the foreign-owned sugar mills, which declined from 66 in 1939 to only 36 by 1958. The number of Cuban-owned sugar mills increased from 56 to 121 in the same period and their percentage of the sugar production from 22 to 62. This is evidence that the capital accumulation within the country was accelerating. The per capita annual income, while still low in 1958, was among the highest in Latin America. Cuban workers enjoyed a number of benefits gained through their organizations, including the eight-hour day with time and a half for excess hours, along with many fringe benefits such as vacations with pay. Worst off were the agricultural workers, who suffered long periods of unemployment and underemployment.

Table 1. Transportation and Communication Facilities in Cuba Compared with Other Latin American Countries in 1958

Item	Number	Per Thousand Inhabi- tants[a]	Rank in Latin America
Communication			
Radio stations	160		...
Radio receivers	900,000	184	2
Television stations	23		...
Television receivers	365,000	56	1
Telephones	151,458	26	3
Transportation			
Air: Passenger-kilometers (in thousands) ..	272,827		7
Rail trackage in kilometers	4,784		...
Rail trackage per square kilometer	42		1
Passenger motor vehicles	159,000	25	1

SOURCE: *América en Cifras*, 1960 (Washington, D.C.: Pan American Union).
[a] Figures are given only for relevant categories.

Educational facilities were slowly improving, although they were still inadequate. The illiteracy rate of more than 20 percent in 1953 for the country as a whole was by no means the worst in Latin America; only about three other countries had a more favorable percentage. Nevertheless, it was the rural people who suffered the greatest deprivation in education. Illiteracy for all rural Cuba was more than 40 percent and in Oriente province rose to 50 percent.

By 1953 the population had risen to nearly 6,000,000. Almost three-fifths lived in the cities. The social structure was marked by a steady growth of what we may term the middle class: the professional, semi-professional, managerial, and proprietary groups. In relation to population, Cuba's middle class was probably the strongest in Latin America. Yet the disparity in well-being between the very wealthy and the very poor was great indeed.

Although leaders of the Cuban Revolution like to paint a dismal picture of the country before they came to power and particularly of the retarded state of industrialization, a condition they attribute to United States policy, the facts available indicate that rather impressive progress had been made in the nonagricultural sector. For example, estimates for 1957 of the number of nonagricultural units give the impressive total of 20,731. The estimated total capital investment in these units was $3,222,712,823 and the total number of employees 890,675. The largest single industry, not surprisingly, was that related to cane sugar and cane derivatives. The 276 centers employed 485,231 persons and represented an investment of $1,158,850,000. This did not include the agricultural sector of the sugar industry. The second ranking nonagricultural activity was transportation and communication with a combined capital investment of $645,414,000, and employment of 47,770 people. In third place, in terms of capitalization, was metal ore mining and the metallurgical industries. This was followed by electric, gas, and water installations, fuels and lubricants, foods and beverages, textiles, garments, etc., tobacco and derivatives, coffee, cocoa, and derivatives, and so on through a list grouped under twenty-six general types.[5]

A country so well equipped with communication devices — telephones, television sets (even color ones), and radios all but universal — can hardly be called totally undeveloped. Moreover, the transportation system, both air and ground, was excellent. Railroads ran the length of the island but had suffered from competition with motor transportation until 1952, when the government purchased the system. In addition to the railway trackage given in Table 1, there were almost as many more kilometers of rail on the sugar plantations, some of which were used in a small way during the off season for the transportation of persons and cargo. As the *Report on Cuba* by the International Bank for Reconstruction and Development noted in 1950: "In comparison with many other countries of similar economic and social development, Cuba possessed a great asset in her highways and roads. Few — if any — countries of the same general economic status have anything comparable to the Central Highway [1,144 kms.] either in quality or extent to which it traverses the entire country" (p. 264) .

By 1959 Cuba had a total of 7,224 kilometers of paved road. Additional all-weather roads were needed to link more of the rural territory to the paved highways. In response to surveys made in 1946 and reported in *Rural Cuba*, farm people placed good roads first among their needs.

Undeveloped countries usually lack electricity or have very little. A considerable expansion in capacity to meet the rising demands after World War II placed Cuba among the top countries in Latin America in this regard. Cuba's first large hydroelectric plant was under construction on the Hanabanilla River when the revolutionary government came to power. It represented an investment of $16 million.

This brief résumé of developments in the nonagricultural sector should be adequate to dispel any claim that in a material sense the revolution inherited very little from the past. There remains the additional fact that among its legacies the revolution fell heir to the largest cane-sugar-producing complex in the world. It was composed of 161 mills under expert management and supplied with first-class technical and skilled personnel. It had an enormous capacity, much of it unused under the world quota system to which Cuba subscribed. The agricultural situation at the time of the takeover will be discussed in a subsequent chapter, as will also conditions in the areas of education, health, and welfare.

Despite the data we have just presented, Cuba in 1958 needed much more than it possessed in the way of material man-made resources. This fact was fully recognized by the responsible leaders of the nation. A national bank had been created, along with a bank for agricultural and industrial development. The country could begin to envision the time when it could finance its own industrial growth with less and less dependency on capital from the outside. Indeed there was much wealth in the country; but, as has so often been said, it was poorly distributed. By contrast, as we shall see in the pages to follow, after

47

thirteen years of the revolution there is a general scarcity of material goods, but a scarcity that is shared by all.

At what point on a scale of economic development, or in what stage thereof, was Cuba in 1958? There have been attempts to answer this question both by the winners and the losers of the revolutionary campaign that ended January 1, 1959. Not unexpectedly, their assessments are poles apart. It is common political practice for the opposition to castigate the regime in power for its sins and errors of commission or omission and flay it for its failures. Prime Minister Castro plays the game according to form and tradition. His assessment of the Cuba of 1958 would place the country near the bottom of any scale, and he has even said at "zero."

On the other side, the losers — and they represent most of the half million or more who have left the island, and more specifically the economists in exile — would score the country at a pretty high point on the scale. In a massive review of Cuba's socioeconomic history since settlement, these economists have presented evidence which convinces them that Cuba had satisfied the preconditions for a "take-off" into self-sustained growth as described by W. W. Rostow.[6]

A vast literature on economic development has accumulated since World War II as scholars have attempted to describe and measure the characteristics of developed and undeveloped countries. Throughout all the elaborate analyses, there appears to be no better single index for placing a country on a scale than its per capita income. The rationale behind this index is that it provides at least a rough measure of the extent to which a country, in utilizing its natural and human resources, is able to supply the needs of its population for goods and services. A related index is the percentage of the labor force employed in nonagricultural production, since per capita income is closely correlated with it. It is an observable fact that with a few notable exceptions (Denmark is one) high per capita income is found in the more industrialized countries. In 1953 Cuba reported nearly 60 percent of the labor force outside of agriculture. In one compilation of the per capita incomes of 127 countries in 1957, Cuba ranked thirty-second. It was outranked in Latin America by Venezuela (20), Puerto Rico (24), Argentina (27.5), and Uruguay (29). Chile was number 36. Comparable rankings of countries of Europe and Soviet bloc nations were as follows: Italy, 26, Hungary, 27.5, Poland, 30, Bulgaria, 38, and Rumania, 40.[7]

Far from being among the least developed countries of the world, Cuba ranked in the upper quarter in this calculation. Its position was due largely to the consistent economic growth following World War II. It is speculative, of course, but one cannot help wondering what Cuba would have been like in 1970 if the elections of 1952 had been allowed to take place and, as seemed probable, the Ortodoxo party had won. Its program of reform was very much in line with the dreams of the generation of the 1930's, and it had in the race a slate of highly respected candidates headed by Roberto Agramonte. Speculation, however, is interesting but futile.

There is one more point to be made on the subject of economic development. Castro has claimed that a country can achieve economic development only under socialism. This statement conveniently ignores the fact that none of the world's more highly developed countries gained their status under socialism. Western Europe, North America, and Japan are not, nor have they ever been, socialist.

We now turn to a discussion of Cuba's agriculture.

Chapter 4

Cuban Agriculture
Before the Revolution

As we have noted in Chapter 3, agriculture developed in Cuba at fluctuating rates throughout the four and a half centuries up to 1959. But despite the merciless exploitation by the Seville commission merchants and the suppressions of the colonial governments; despite the wars of independence which brought so much material destruction and loss of human life; despite the corruption of governments in the period of the republic and any mistakes of United States policy — despite all these impediments, agriculture continued to grow. This is a tribute to the conscientious, hard-working population who were willing to perform the daily tasks necessary to the survival of the society, even in the face of deprivations not of their making. Above all, the development must be credited to the masses of the peasantry and the agricultural laborers.[1]

Although the eyes of the world have been focused for thirteen years on developments under the new regime, a better understanding of the prerevolutionary condition is indispensable to an appraisal of the achievements of postrevolutionary Cuba. Such a presentation necessarily involves a great many statistics, and we begin with the census of agriculture made in 1946 (the only agricultural census ever taken in Cuba). The information was for the most part applicable to the year 1945 and must constitute the benchmark for the measurement of change since that year. For developments since 1946, we have to depend on the estimates of knowledgeable students of the Cuban economy. The establishment of the Cuban National Bank in 1948 and the Bank for Agricultural and Industrial Development (BANFAIC) in 1950, along with the creation of the National Economic Council and other government agencies, provided opportunities for economic studies. Most of the distinguished economists involved in these studies later went into exile. In Miami they organized themselves for continued studies of Cuba and were subsidized by grants from sources in the United States. They were thus able to bring together a vast amount of data regarding developments before 1959.[2]

Land Utilization in the Benchmark Year

Table 2 presents some of the facts revealed by the 1946 census. It should be borne in mind that the manner in which the land is held is a matter of great social as well as economic importance because the tenure groups represent a stratification of the rural population.

Table 2. Number of Farms and Total Area by Type of Tenure in 1946

| Type of Tenure | Farms | | Total Area | |
	Number	Percentage of Total	Hectares	Percentage of Total
Proprietor ...	48,792	30.5	2,958,694.5	32.4
Administrator .	9,342	5.8	2,320,444.7	25.6
Renter	46,048	28.8	2,713,929.7	30.0
Subrenter	6,987	4.4	215,215.5	2.4
Sharecropper .	33,064	20.7	552,078.9	6.1
Squatter	13,718	8.6	244,558.8	2.7
Other	2,007	1.2	72,134.2	0.8
Total	159,958	100.0	9,077,056.3	100.0

SOURCE: Ministry of Agriculture, National Agricultural Census, 1946.

The farms designated as "administrator" were mainly the larger enterprises, including sugar plantations, livestock ranches, and others. Squatters (*precaristas*) are farmers who occupy and use land without authorization of the owner. Less than a third of the farms were owned by the men who worked them, but it is interesting that they covered approximately a third of the land. The extremes in

51

terms of number of farms and the areas covered are shown in the administrator category, where 5.8 percent of the farms encompassed
over 25 percent of the area, and in the sharecropper farms, which
represented 20.7 percent of the total number but included only 6.1
percent of the area. The sharecroppers, it should be pointed out, included the tobacco farmers who practiced very intensive farming on
a very small area.

The vast majority of Cuban farms were small, as Table 3 shows.
Of the total number, 78.5 percent were less than 26.8 hectares. At
the same time, this large percentage of small operators controlled but
15 percent of the total area in farms. At the other end of the scale was
a small proportion (2.8 percent) of the total number of farms which
included nearly three-fifths of the area.

Table 3. Distribution of Farms according to Size in 1946

Size of Farms in Hectares[a]	Farms		Percentage of Total Area in Farms
	Number	Percent	
Less than 26.8	125,619	78.5	15.0
26.8–67.0	16,766	10.5	9.1
67.0–402.0	13,150	8.2	19.0
402.0 or more	4,423	2.8	56.9
Total	159,958	100.0	100.0

SOURCE: Ministry of Agriculture, National Agricultural Census, 1946.
[a] A hectare equals 2.47 acres.

It is important to keep in mind that the land included in farms
as defined by the census was only partially cultivated. There were
significant differences in the utilization of land by the tenure classes.
(See Table 4.) The groups with the smallest percentages under cultivation were the proprietors and administrators. The managed farms
devoted to surgarcane and livestock often had large areas idle or in
pasture or other extensive uses. The sharecroppers, who as we have
noted included tobacco farmers among others, had the highest proportion of cultivated land. We must keep in mind that these data
were twelve or thirteen years old when the revolutionary government
came to power and that some changes probably took place in the
interim. While no further census has been taken, an estimate is avail-

able for the year 1957 on the amount of cultivated land devoted to various crops. Table 5 compares these estimated figures with the census figures of 1946.

If we grant the approximate accuracy of the estimates for 1957, it will be seen that the cultivated acreage increased by 369,654 hectares or 18.5 percent. In the same twelve-year period, the population grew at an estimated rate of 2.2 percent per year or 26.4 percent for the period. Thus despite the increase in the area under cultivation, the amount of crop land per capita was less in 1957 than in 1946.

Table 4. Utilization of Land in Farms by Type of Tenure in 1946

Type of Tenure	Area (in Hectares)	Uses (in Percentage)		
		Under Cultivation	Pasture	Other Uses[a]
Proprietor	2,958,700	16.2	50.1	11.3
Administrator	2,320,400	14.9	43.7	41.4
Renter	2,713,900	28.3	39.1	32.6
Subrenter	215,200	36.8	42.9	20.3
Sharecropper	552,100	40.7	31.2	28.1
Squatter	244,600	21.1	24.4	54.5
Other	72,100	29.0	21.9	49.1
All land in farms ...	9,077,000	21.7	42.9	35.4

SOURCE: Ministry of Agriculture, National Agricultural Census, 1946.

[a] Forested areas including *marabú* (a shrub of little value), farmsteads, riverbeds, field roads, etc. Marabú occupied 3 percent of the land in farms in 1946. According to the Cuban Economic Research Project, in 1957–58 the cultivated area had increased to 25.8 percent of the land in farms largely due to the reduction in marabú infestation. *Cuba: Agriculture and Planning*, p. 59.

A notable fact in this camparison is that of the 369,654-hectare increase, 319,897 hectares are accounted for in two crops, sugarcane and rice. Only in rice growing was there a real expansion of the food-production capacity. As we shall note presently, Cuba has for a long time been a large importer of food despite its favorable soil and climate for such production.

As Table 5 shows, not much attention was paid to the expansion of areas devoted to other food crops that would make the island more nearly self-sustaining. There are several explanations, both economic and cultural. The *Report on Cuba* of the International Bank for

Reconstruction and Development (IBRD) pointed to a number of factors: (1) the dominance of sugarcane and the wealth from it that enabled the purchase of other food; (2) the lack of capital for other than cane production; (3) the farmers' lack of knowledge of how to produce other crops; (4) the ease of growing cane; (5) the availability of credit only for cane production; (6) the lack of farm-to-market roads; (7) the chaotic market conditions and the power of greedy, unregulated middlemen.[3]

Table 5. Land Devoted to Principal Crops in 1946 Compared with Estimates for 1957 (in Hectares)

Crop	1946	1957	Change
Sugarcane	1,103,143	1,326,600	223,457
Corn	179,762	198,320	18,558
Coffee	88,864	126,804	8,375
Plantains	80,601	88,976	8,375
Tobacco	66,211	58,960	−7,251
Beans	59,365	66,209	6,844
Edible yucca	57,524	...	...
Rice	57,472	153,912	96,440
Sweet potatoes	53,291	59,898	6,607
Malanga	32,794	39,449	6,655
Pumpkins	22,679	25,486	2,807
Citrus fruits	15,683	17,647	1,964
Millet	14,737	16,656	1,919
Pineapples	14,362	15,761	1,399
Peanuts	13,172	14,740	1,568
Garden vegetables	12,591	15,544	2,952
Henequen	11,208	13,065	1,857
Potatoes	8,475	8,897	422
Cocoa	7,169	9,246	2,077
Other crops	71,302	78,889	7,587
Total	1,970,405	2,335,059	369,654

SOURCE: Adapted from CERP, *Cuba: Agriculture and Planning*, p. 184. Original sources are the 1946 agricultural census and José Arteaga, *Estimados technicos*, National Economic Council, 1958.

These are explanations for the failure of Cuban farmers to engage in specialized commercial production of other crops, but they do not account for their failure to produce food for the family table. A Northamerican, visiting Cuba during World War II, could not fail to be impressed by the apparent impossibility of getting farm families to grow vegetable gardens even when seeds were distributed free. The family garden, at one time an adjunct to practically every farm home in the United States, was not characteristic of Cuban rural culture. True, there were farms with a plantain (banana tree) or two, and perhaps a small plot of yucca or some other edible tuber such as malanga or sweet potato, but never a garden of green or yellow vegetables.

There were some areas of diversified farming in 1946. One of these, in northwest Camagüey province, supported some canning factories, and a few growers specialized in packing and shipping fresh tomatoes to United States markets. Another area was at Güines, where rice was an important alternative to sugarcane.[4] Since World War II rice growing has been greatly expanded in Güines and other parts of the island.

Nevertheless, Cuba has had to continue heavy importations of food. In 1958 the value of agricultural imports from the United States alone amounted to $145 million.[5] The largest single imported commodity was rice ($40 million), followed by lard ($21 million), and other pork and pork products ($11 million). Imports of wheat and wheat flour together amounted to over $14 million, and imports of beans to nearly $8 million. The resources existed for a much larger production of most of these crops, with the exception of wheat, but the use of land was not patterned to realize self-sufficiency.

Advances during the 1950's

The preceding discussion has focused on the conditions of agriculture as reflected in the census of 1946, except for the change in land utilization given in Table 5. The gathering of current statistics after 1946 was greatly improved over earlier periods, and there is reason to use the estimates of competent authorities with confidence. Let us take a closer look at the rice problem, since rice is the cereal of universal consumption in Cuba.

Despite its wide popularity as a food, very little rice was grown before World War II. Up to that time the main supplies came from Burma, Thailand, Indochina, and India. When the war eliminated these sources, it was necessary to turn to the United States. A tariff agreement in the Geneva negotiations of 1947 provided a quota of imports from the United States and at the same time offered protection to Cuban growers. This encouraged the expansion of local production, which in 1940 had amounted to only 18 million pounds of hulled rice out of a total consumption of over 411 million pounds. After the war expansion was rapid and by 1956 Cuba was producing 55.5 percent of its rice needs. By 1957–1958, although production was slightly less than half of the 741.8 million pounds consumed, it was holding up well.[6]

The increased production was due not only to the expansion of the planted area, but also to increased yield per unit of area. This is revealed when we divide the reported production for 1946 and 1957 by the number of hectares as given in Table 5. The yield per hectare of hulled rice was approximately 1,409 pounds in 1946 and 2,374 pounds in 1957.[7] One reason, perhaps the main one, for the increase in yield was the increased use of fertilizers. The consumption of chemical fertilizers for all crops grew from 41,787 metric tons in 1945, covering 7.4 percent of the cropped land, to 244,760 metric tons in 1958, when it was used on 20 percent of the cultivated area. The manufacture of fertilizers did not become important in Cuba until after 1951 when the newly established Bank for Development of Agriculture and Industry (BANFAIC) provided financing for several fertilizer plants. In 1957, 20,361 tons of fertilizer were used in the production of rice.[8] Also important in increasing rice yields was the development of irrigation. While only 59,809 hectares of farm land were irrigated in 1946, it was estimated that by 1958 the area had increased to 350,000 hectares.[9]

The development in rice production was the most spectacular, but there was also expansion in the production of the other crops listed in Table 5, with the exception of tobacco. Although, as we have pointed out, the total increase in cultivated area did not equal the estimated percentage growth of the population, it is possible that the increase in food production was equal to the population increase, and for reasons mentioned in the case of rice. The increased use of fertilizer was important in the production of other crops as well. Figures on the application of fertilizer to other crops are available for the years 1955–1958. The figures (in tons) for 1955 and 1958 respectively are as follows: vegetables, 15,207 and 30,707; potatoes, 25,380 and 26,642; fruits, 3,365 and 3,518; garden produce, 824 and 1,473.[10]

One estimate has placed the "annual accumulated growth rate" of agricultural production during the 1950's at 3.7 percent, compared with an average population growth rate of 2.3 percent. The same source concludes that "agricultural production had increased to the point where it met 75 percent of the domestic demand."[11] This estimate may be somewhat optimistic in view of the amount of food imported during the 1950's, but if it even approximates the truth, it means that considerable progress was made in the decade of the 1950's. Further evidence of the expanded production of food crops in spite of a limited increase in the area devoted to them is given in Table 6.

In addition to the increased use of fertilizers, mention should also be made of advances in other aspects of agricultural technology. Mechanization of farm operations made some progress during the

Table 6. Comparative Production of Principal Food Crops for 1946 and 1957–58

Item	Unit of Measure	1946	1957–58
Beans	kilogram	35,014,852	36,935,545
Salad tomatoes	kilogram	39,861,593	105,000,000
Sweet potatoes	kilogram	159,685,916	161,289,131
Malanga	kilogram	85,051,298	191,206,000
Yucca	kilogram	178,748,943	186,350,000
Potatoes	kilogram	56,892,187	120,000,000
Plantain	Thousand of bunches	390,102	430,500
Onions	kilogram	1,159,388	1,290,000
Rice	kilogram	63,613,062	172,500,000
Beef	pound	385,000,000	459,250,000
Pork	pound	90,000,000	237,000,000
Poultry	pound	10,153,355	79,000,000
Fish	pound	20,000,000	70,000,000
Eggs	dozen	6,541,507	26,978,000
Milk	liter	408,159,413	959,946,000

SOURCE: Adapted from CERP, *Cuba: Agriculture and Planning*, p. 260, Table 120, and p. 313, Table 129. The original sources are the agricultural census of 1946 and estimates of the National Economic Council and Ministry of Agriculture, 1957–58.

period. The increase in the number of tractors is one of the best indicators of this. The agricultural census of 1946 reported only 1,888 tractors on the farms of Cuba. These, it could safely be assumed, were on the large farms and especially the cane farms. There are indications that important numbers of tractors were imported after that enumeration. Between 1947 and 1958 the United States exported 14,771 tractors to Cuba.[12] The Cuban Ministry of Hacienda, in its report on foreign commerce for the years 1957 and 1958, listed imports of 2,031 tractors in 1957 and 2,287 in 1958. While obviously these tractors were used on only a small fraction of the total number of farms, they represent a remarkable increase from the 1946 base. As a counterpoint to the increase in tractors, there was a notable decrease in the number of oxen between the 1946 census and the census of livestock in 1952. The former reported 576,542 head and the latter 384,259, a decrease of one-third.[13]

Tractor power was especially important in the sugarcane fields, not only in plowing and preparing the fields for planting but especially in the harvest operations. The high-wheeled oxcart was rapidly being replaced by trucks and rubber-tired carts drawn by tractors. These carts, incidentally, were manufactured in Cuba, as were many of the smaller farm implements.

Finally, there was an increasing use of insecticides and herbicides in crop production and a reported eighty planes used in dusting and fertilization operations. Agricultural technology was being applied gradually by 1959, though admittedly much remained to be done.[14]

Systems of Farming

In describing the various forms of agricultural organization in my earlier work on Cuba, I listed five principal types of farm units: the sugar plantation; the tobacco *vega* or farm; the *cafetal* or coffee farm; the family farm; and the livestock ranch. The basic structure of these systems changed little between 1946 and 1958.

The Sugar Plantation

The sugarcane plant is of such enormous importance to Cuba — and to the world in general — that a few words of description are appropriate here. To begin with, this plant is the major though not the only source of the world's sugar supply. The sugar beet is, of course, the other important source. According to the *United Nations Statistical Yearbook*, the total world production of sugar in 1968 was 66,891,000 metric tons, a little over half of which came from cane. The two plants, beet and cane, differ in several ways. The beet grows from seed and the cane from slips or joints. The beet stores the sugar in the root, the cane in the stalk above ground. Yet the chemical composition of the sugar from the two sources is identical. While cane grows only in tropical or subtropical climates, the beet thrives only in temperate zones, most importantly in Europe, in the USSR including Siberia, and in North America. The leading beet grower is the USSR, which produces between 9 and 10 million metric tons. The world's leading producer of cane is Cuba, followed by Brazil, other countries of the Caribbean and South America, Australia, Indonesia, India, and China. The beet, it might be added, has been exploited for sugar only since the beginning of the nineteenth century, while cane has been used as a source since prehistoric times.

Sugarcane is a member of the botanical family of grasses. It grows best in clay or loam soils with high water-holding capacity. The stalks grow in clumps from cuttings planted in furrows and lightly covered with soil. It grows to heights of ten to twenty feet, but the usual height in Cuba is about twelve to fifteen feet. The stalk consists of several joints quite regularly spaced several inches apart; each joint contains several buds from which new plants can sprout when it is planted. The leaves resemble those of corn, a plant also belonging to the family of grasses. At the top there is a tassel, also similar to corn. This tassel yields small seeds and only in recent decades was it discovered that the seeds were fertile and could be used for cross-breeding and inbreeding to produce new varieties. In commercial planting, however, seeds are never used, only the joints or slips. These slips are about twelve inches in length.

Although cane is a perennial and with care will yield two or more crops, it has been found desirable to replant at least after every second crop, depending on the fertility of the soil and the moisture supply. The cane requires about twelve months to mature, depending on the variety. The cutting of the first crop requires a certain skill to prevent injury to the buds on the stubble that is left and to make sure that all the high-sugar part of the stalk is harvested.

The combined potential production of sugar from beet and cane is so great that international agreements have been necessary to keep supply somewhere near the needs of the population. Under these agreements producing countries are given certain quotas in the world market. Interestingly, the consumption reported by the United Nations for 1968 was 67,481,000 metric tons, exceeding by only about half a million tons the amount produced. In that year the USSR had a deficit of 1,407,000 metric tons, which were supplied from abroad, undoubtedly from Cuba. The United States, the other great consumer, produced less than half the 10,218,000 tons it used and had to import the balance.

The United States — where both beet and cane are produced — has imposed a two-cent tariff on sugar to protect its own growers. The result of the tariff is that the United States pays about two cents a pound more to suppliers than is available to them in the world market. Naturally, then, the quotas awarded to producing countries that supply the five-million-ton American deficit are in great demand. Until the recent break in diplomatic relations, Cuba had the largest quota.

The production of sugar from cane has involved a combination of agriculture and industry, or farming and manufacturing, usually under a common ownership and management or control. As was pointed out in Chapter 3, the original trapiches were relatively small mills for the extraction of the juice, and consequently the cane area used by each was relatively small. With the growth in the technology of manufacturing, and especially the building of railroads, many trapiches in an area were combined into a single *central* or large mill. The larger mills required larger plantations. Before slavery was abolished, the centrals grew their own cane, but after that wage labor was employed. There also developed a new tenure class known as the *colono*. The term referred to a grower who was permitted to lease company land and assume responsibility for raising cane and delivering it to the mill. He therefore stood in a middle position between the central and the wage laborers whom he employed. Although the centrals continued to grow cane on their own account for many years, "administration cane," as it was called, became progressively less important. There were also some mills that depended almost entirely on cane supplied by independent farmers. One such was Central Araujo, near Manguito in Matanzas province, which was supplied by 353 small farmers who grew cane as a cash crop.

Administration cane steadily declined as a proportion of the total production after the passage of the Law of Sugar Coordination of September 1937, which favored the colono over the company in the awarding of quotas. (The system of quotas derived from the International Sugar Agreement signed in Brussels on May 9, 1931, as a measure for reviving the stagnant sugar market through self-imposed restrictions on output by the producing countries.) The sugar coordination law of 1937 was extremely important in several ways. It established a formula by which the product was allotted among the factors producing it: the mills, the colonos, and the wageworkers. But the law went beyond that important step when it guaranteed the right of permanent occupancy of the land which the colono was operating. It was, in fact, a law of agrarian reform. In practice it established the colono in a land tenure class nearly equivalent to ownership. The small colono was favored over other growers — the mill and the large colono — in the awarding of quotas. These quotas were inalienable; they could not be mortgaged or sold but could be inherited by specified heirs. Naturally, there were certain attendant obligations imposed upon the colonos. They were required to produce the quota of cane, to pay certain rent, and so forth. But as long as they complied with the law, they could not be evicted. They were now entrepreneurs in their own right and not essentially foremen for the mill.[15]

A notable fact concerning the sugar industry is that ownership had shifted markedly into the hands of Cubans in both the manufacturing and agricultural sectors. In 1939, as noted earlier, 66 of the 174 mills were under United States ownership and produced 55.07 percent of the crop. The Cuban-owned mills numbered 56 and produced 22.42 percent of the crop. The remainder were owned by Spain (33), Canada (10), England (4), Holland (3), and France (2). By 1959 the total number of mills had declined to 161. Of these, American citizens owned 36 mills producing 36.74 percent of the sugar. The 121 Cuban-owned mills produced 62 percent. Spain still had 3 mills and France 1. All other foreign ownership had disappeared. Actually, Cubanization had proceeded even further than these figures indicate, because many Cubans owned stock in the American sugar companies.[16]

The Tobacco Vega

The tobacco plant is indigenous to the western hemisphere. On his first voyage, Columbus found the natives of Cuba smoking tobacco in much the same way that it is smoked today. It was used by the Northamerican Indians before white settlement, as well as in the Caribbean and South America. It is a plant of remarkable adaptability to different environments, able to grow even as far north as the Arctic Circle.

Soon after the discoveries, the use of tobacco was introduced in Europe. At first forbidden in Spain by Queen Isabella I, it found acceptance in France (1556) and Portugal (1558). Spanish opposition to tobacco relaxed in 1559, and Sir Walter Raleigh introduced it to England in 1563.

The plant is an annual with large leaves and grows to a height of four or five feet. The leaves, of course, constitute the crop. They contain the alkaloid nicotine, which has a narcotic effect that accounts for its popularity and habit-forming quality. The varieties of the plant are numerous, since different kinds of leaves are desired for different purposes. The quality is also determined by the type of soil and climate.

Tobacco has been an important export crop for Cuba since the early eighteenth century, but as in the case of sugar the product is subject to severe competition in the world market. Moreover the labor unions in Cuba resisted mechanized manufacture, fearing a loss of jobs, especially in rolling cigars. This resulted in the transfer of manufacturing by machine to the United States. Although the United States was the chief importer of Cuban tobacco, the Depression of the early 1930's resulted in the assignment of quotas not only on imports but also on domestic tobacco production which also was suffering from surplus supplies. Yet some forms of Cuban tobacco, notably that used in cigars, enjoyed a worldwide reputation and could always find a market, albeit a somewhat fluctuating one. Nevertheless, as a consequence of the worldwide depression, Cuban exports fell from $43 million in 1929 to only $13.8 million in 1933.[17] The Reciprocal Trade Agreement with the United States in 1934 granted tariff reductions on Cuban tobacco imports but established an import quota. Nevertheless, it stimulated exports of Cuban tobacco.

According to the census of agriculture of 1946, about 160,000 acres were devoted to tobacco, grown by 22,750 farmers. The average size of farms for this crop was, therefore, about eight acres. Production is concentrated in five areas: Vuelta Abajo and Semi-Vuelta in Pinar del Río province; Partido in Havana province; Remedios in Las Villas province, and Oriente in Oriente province. The most highly prized tobacco leaf comes from Pinar del Río, which in 1956 produced over half the national total. The next most important area is Remedios, which grew about 40 percent of the total crop in 1956.[18]

In the common parlance of producers there are two kinds of tobacco, "sun" and "shade." Sun tobacco is grown in the open field, while shade tobacco is grown under an artificial cover consisting of cheesecloth spread over a supporting framework of poles. The effect of shading is to produce a leaf lighter in color than that grown without cover. There are also two methods of curing or drying the leaves — one by heating, known as flue curing, and the other by drying in a well-ventilated shed.

While many independent farmers grew tobacco on their own farms, there were also several large plantations operated on a share-tenant basis. The system which developed after the abolition of slavery is comparable in many respects to the cotton sharecropper system in the United States. However, as I described conditions in 1946, the *partidario* system, as it is called in Cuba, involves somewhat more responsibility and capital on the part of the renter than does the sharecropper system in the United States. Usually the tobacco partidario owns his own oxen, other livestock, and farm equipment, and he is of course responsible for performing the hand labor necessary in growing the crop. As is true in the cotton sharecropper system in the United States, the company furnishes the land and the dwelling-house, for which no rent is charged.

63

Some of the features of the organization of the tobacco-growing industry may be illustrated by a description of one of the large operating companies in Pinar del Río, the Cuban Land and Leaf Tobacco Company. It is an American-owned company with extensive holdings in the Vuelta Abajo region [visited by the author in 1946]. Both shade and sun tobacco are grown. There are a total of 81 partidarios, 19 of them growing shade tobacco and 62 sun tobacco. In addition, there are 3,300 wageworkers composed, in part, of members of the families of the partidarios. The contract between the company and the partidarios is different with respect to shade and sun tobacco. For shade tobacco, the crop is divided on a 50 per cent basis, as are also the following expenses: chemical fertilizer, cheesecloth, cost of fire curing (both labor and material), and the cost of grading the tobacco. The company provides manure free to the shade partidarios and also advances credit for the payment of wages without charging interest.

In the case of the partidarios growing sun tobacco, the company receives one-fourth of the crop but the partidarios must pay all of the costs of the chemical fertilizer, three-fourths of the manure fertilizer, and three-fourths of the cost of grading the tobacco. The company furnishes free to all of the partidarios, without additional charges, land, dwelling-house, tobacco barns, irrigation water, and medical care. A doctor is on duty every forenoon in the clinic which the company maintains, and, in addition, a male nurse is available at all times at company expense. For the wageworkers, a dwelling-house is provided, rent free, as well as a piece of land for growing vegetables, water for domestic purposes, and medical care, as with the partidarios. Contracts are written, each one being an original typewritten copy executed by a notary.[19]

The incomes of the tenants on this vega were surprisingly large, some of them amounting to as much as $18,000.[20]

At the same time I visited another tobacco farm in the same area. Part of this farm was operated by the proprietor and the balance was rented. About a fourth of the total area of 1,000 acres was planted to shade tobacco. The renter paid the owner 30 percent of the crop in return for the use of the land and dwelling (including repairs and maintenance), irrigation water, and water pipes for irrigating. The renter had the use of land for growing vegetables and corn or other field crops, and for grazing his oxen, milk cows, and hogs. The owner also supplied credit for current living and operating expenses, for which he charged 8 percent interest, even though the debt might be paid off within a few months. The tenant had to meet practically all the other expense of making the crop, including fertilizer and the tobacco plants, which were grown in a central nursery until ready for transplanting. There were also labor costs, which in the case of shade tobacco were especially great. On this farm there were about five hundred wageworkers who earned $2.36 per day. The workers were also permitted to plant gardens for themselves, but the proprietor said they usually planted tobacco on their assigned plots and sold it to the company, thus deriving additional income of from $60 to $300 per year.

The Coffee Farm

Coffee was grown on 19,721 farms in Cuba, according to the 1946 census of agriculture, and on 9,131 of them it was the major source of income. The system of tenure was somewhat similar to the one used in tobacco farming, in that a large cafetal was divided into small tracts which were rented on a share basis to tenants. There was also a considerable number of small proprietors who engaged in commercial coffee production. The industry was not a thriving one during the republic but it was on the upturn when the revolution took over. Practically all the coffee in Cuba is grown in the mountains under shade trees. Coffee production bears some similarity to sugar insofar as the treating of the coffee bean in preparing it for market is a specialized and centralized process. That is to say, the tenant on a cafetal depends upon the central processing plant for shelling, drying, and marketing, a process that is under the management and control of the *cafetalero.*

Like sugar and tobacco, coffee has been subject to severe competition. At times in the history of this crop, domestic needs could not be supplied and importation was necessary. Exports were possible from 1941 to 1945, but production then fell off and imports of some volume were needed during the years 1946 to 1952, after which exports again mounted.[21]

The Family Farm

A family farm consists of a tract of land devoted to the production of crops and livestock on which most, if not all, the labor is performed by the operator and his family. It is ordinarily a small farm. In the agricultural census of 1946 almost two-fifths of Cuban farms were less than twenty-five acres, while an additional 30 percent were twenty-five to sixty-two acres. In short, nearly three-fourths of all farms were so small that, taken together, they occupied only 11 percent of the total land.

The census of 1946 further revealed that only a little over one-fourth of all farms employed wageworkers and that only 10 percent of those were less than twenty-five acres in size. Family farms occur in all type-of-farming areas of the island. Near the cities there are dairy and truck garden farms supplying the city market, and there are small units to be found in the tobacco, coffee, sugarcane, and diversified farming areas. As of 1946, the farms were poorly equipped. Some had steel walking plows, while others used the primitive forked-tree type. The ox was the main source of power. What tractors there were in Cuba were found on the larger farms. Hand labor, using the shovel, pick, hoe, ax, and crowbar, was the common condition. The most universal tool was the machete, which hung from the worker's belt and was used for a multitude of purposes such as harvesting sugarcane, clearing the land of brush, and weeding. The almost total lack of off-farm employment meant that workers on these farms were often unemployed or underemployed. Women scarcely ever worked in the fields, but since the families tended to be rather large there were ordinarily two or more male workers per farm.

The Livestock Ranch

Cuba has a long history of livestock production. During most of the colonial period, hides and tallow were among the most important exports. Indeed, livestock raising was almost the only sensible way to use the land. Cultivation was limited to producing subsistence crops, especially before sugarcane became important. Moreover there were extensive areas of natural pastures where cattle and smaller animals could graze. Even today Cuba is a country with a relatively low population density and can afford to allow areas to be used extensively in the grazing of livestock.

Cattle are by far the most important animals in the livestock industry. Hogs take second place, with horses, mules, and donkeys still numerous but of declining importance. Sheep and goats make up a smaller, although significant group.[22]

Especially since World War II much emphasis has been given to the improvement of cattle and hogs. In order to develop breeds which can adjust to the tropical climate and at the same time improve the milk and meat production per animal, crossbreeding of cattle has been widely practiced. The native or *criollo* cattle, descended from the stock brought over by the Spaniards, were crossed with such breeds as the Aberdeen Angus, Shorthorn, Hereford, and later the Charolais to improve meat production. The Zebu or India Brahman was crossed with Holstein, Brown Swiss, and Jersey cattle to increase milk production. Santa Gertrudis, a breed developed by the King Ranch in Texas, proved to be well adapted to Cuba and by 1958 there were twenty-eight breeders registered in the Santa Gertrudis Breeders International, reporting a total of 6,872 head.[23] Since the Zebu was the main breed, the largest number of breeders specialized in producing them. There were reportedly on December 31, 1958, 20,000 head of cows, 16,000 calves, and 20,000 bulls of purebred Zebu registered in Cuba. In 1956, 1957, and 1958 "exports of pure-bred Zebus reached 3,000 head, with an approximate total value of $1,200,000."[24]

Cattle were reported in the 1946 census on 75 percent of Cuban farms, but on only 18 percent were they the major source of farm income. The near-universal occurrence of this animal on farms is largely accounted for by the fact that oxen were the major source of farm power at that time. The commercial cattle herds, other than dairy cows, were found on relatively large ranches in the eastern provinces. Exact figures on the number of cattle in Cuba do not exist. The only count was taken early in 1946 and reported 4,115,733 head, including 811,090 milk cows. A cattle census of 1952, made by the Ministry of Agriculture and said to have been incomplete, reported only 4,000,000. An estimate for 1958 placed the number at 6,000,000.[25]

The crossbreeding has always aimed at achieving two objectives: (1) the development of a dual-purpose animal which would have a high meat yield per carcass and at the same time produce more milk than the Zebu; and (2) the development of an animal able to adapt to the tropical environment. The primary emphasis was on the production of meat. Cuba was surpassed only by Argentina, Uruguay, and Paraguay in the per capita production of meat. Unfortunately, according to the IBRD mission (1950), records of cattle breeding were poorly kept, and most often there were no records at all. Nevertheless, much improvement in upgrading the cattle population took place, especially during the 1950's.

Milk production was always a secondary interest in Cuba, at least until 1950, and most of it came from the beef-cattle herds. Production per cow was extremely low, usually no more than two liters per day. Only in the Havana milkshed and around other cities did dairying take on a specialized aspect. And only in the larger cities was there a market for whole fresh milk. Throughout the major cattle-producing regions of Las Villas, Camagüey, and Oriente provinces, milk was sent to processing plants for manufacture into butter, cheese, and condensed or evaporated milk.

An example of a dual-purpose enterprise was visited by the author in 1946. This was a farm located near Sancti Spíritus, consisting of 2,200 acres and operated by a man and his four sons. There were 500 head of cattle on the farm, of which 240 were milked in the month of May. About 35,000 liters of milk a month were sold to a condensed milk factory, an average of about four liters per day per cow. The average daily production in the springtime was about four liters a day, but during the rest of the year it was only two.[26]

As stated earlier, the consumption of fresh whole milk was limited mainly to the cities, particularly the Havana area. There was an under supply of milk during the war years, although the records show that Cuba actually exported dairy products in 1940 and 1941. However, the country was a rather heavy importer of condensed and evaporated milk during the 1950's; imports reached a peak in 1955 and declined rather abruptly to 1958. Imports of dairy products from the United States amounted to $3.2 million in 1957 and $2.2 million in 1958. Apparently milk production was again approaching the point of self-sufficiency. During the period immediately after the Korean War, there was an apparent substantial increase in the consumption of whole milk. Cuban experts in exile report that in 1957 total production amounted to 959,946,000 liters,

65 percent of which was used for direct consumption, 10 percent for butter, 11 percent for cheese, 9 percent for cattle feed, and 1 percent for powdered milk. Total production thus equaled 1,947 liters per capita per year, and for whole milk a little over a fourth of a liter per day, assuming a population of 6.5 million people.[27]

Expansion in the quantity and quality of livestock and dairy production inevitably created a need for better pastures and better quality feed. The IBRD mission called attention to the fact that the livestock industry had suffered because of the lack of pasture improvement and fodder production. Much attention was given to the planting of imported grass varieties, especially *pangola,* which by 1958 was estimated to cover over 200,000 hectares or about half the total pasture surface.[28] Livestock production was encouraged by the fact that after 1952 and the end of the Korean War strict quotas on sugarcane were again imposed. Thus capital could be diverted from sugar to other phases of agriculture and much of it was devoted to pasture improvement. Renewed attention was also given to the possibility of finding suitable fodder crops, especially some with high protein content. The IBRD mission pointed out that pangola was deficient in protein and suggested experiments with alfalfa and Kudzu. Molasses was already being used in various ways as a supplementary feed.

As we have noted earlier, Cuba has an enormous demand for lard, most of which has to be imported. There was an obvious need for the expansion of hog production, but less progress was made with swine than with cattle. Hogs were reported on over 80 percent of the farms in 1946, with a total for the country of 1,344,000. The livestock census of 1952 reported that the number had declined to 1,285,000, although an estimate for 1955 showed an increase over 1946.[29] Hogs were kept mainly in small numbers on farms, and there were few specialized hog-producing units. Many hogs were poorly cared for, being allowed to run free and scrounge for their feed. Moreover the improvement in breeds was slow, although purebred Hampshires, Poland Chinas, and Duroc-Jerseys were being imported. The great need in Cuba has been for lard-type breeds, but these are not as well adapted to the tropical environment as the lean-meat type. Further, as the IBRD mission pointed out, the tendency has been

69

to slaughter hogs before they reached the optimum weight of 200 to 225 pounds.

Sheep and goats have been fairly common on Cuban farms, but they are not raised in commercial herds. Milk-producing types of goats are practical because they eat things usually shunned by other animals and at the same time provide a source of milk for the family. Poultry flocks were common on most farms; eggs as well as the meat are highly prized items in the Cuban diet. Chicken and egg production, like dairying, came to be specialized in commercial units. In 1961, 674 medium- and large-size enterprises were reported.

Summary

The production of livestock, especially beef cattle, has ranked first or second in economic importance since the beginning of Cuban colonization by Spain. The great expansion of sugarcane during the late nineteenth century diminished the prime importance of livestock, but the latter continued to be a major sector of Cuban economic life. Much progress was made in improving the quality of cattle after World War II as well as in the improvement of pastures and in the increased production of both meat and milk. There were times when both meat and dairy products were in sufficient supply to permit exports; the latter in 1941 especially and the former in 1957. Generally the growth in population and dietary improvement more than kept pace with production and imports have been necessary.

Farmyard animals — hogs, sheep, goats, and poultry — were widely distributed on Cuban farms but were not usually raised in commercial herds and flocks. Much improvement in breeds of hogs as well as in their management and feeding remained to be made.

In the matter of crop production, developments between 1946 and 1959 included the following:

1. The area under cultivation increased about 18.5 percent, with most of the expansion in sugarcane and rice. The increase in rice production was spectacular and approached 50 percent of total requirements. The sugarcane increase probably resulted from the free production years during the Korean War.

Cuban Agriculture before the Revolution

2. Cuba remained a heavy importer of foods other than rice, although improved technology was apparently increasing yields per hectare on all crops. Most notable was the expansion in the use of fertilizer, along with insecticides and herbicides.

3. The mechanization of farm operations made some progress. The importation of tractors and trucks increased materially. Clearing land, plowing, and the preparation of seedbeds were largely done by tractor power. This was especially true in sugarcane where the hauling of the cane to the mill or railroad was also largely done by truck and tractor. Cutting and trimming the cane, however, remained unmechanized due to the opposition of the workers who feared loss of their jobs, but also because of very difficult technical problems.

4. The expansion of irrigated areas was also pronounced, an important factor in the increased production of rice.

To sum up, we may say that Cuba was possessed of an enormously productive sugar industry, although the potential could seldom be realized because of the thralldom imposed by the international quota agreements. The production of meat, poultry, and eggs was high in comparison with other Latin American countries, although milk production was inadequate and the consumption of commercially produced whole milk was limited largely to the major cities. As in so much of the South of the United States, dairy products were not traditionally part of the diet of the lower classes. Rice production was expanding phenomenally but still satisfied only little more than half of domestic needs. The importation of food was still a major economic requirement. Nevertheless, it has been claimed by the Cuban economists in exile that "from 1952 to 1956, Cuba was able to save approximately 90 million dollars in foreign exchange because of its increased domestic production. The process of agricultural diversification reflected itself in an increase in exports of agricultural and livestock products other than sugar . . . Value of agricultural and livestock exports other than sugar and molasses accounted for 8.9 per cent of total exports in 1952, and 16.4 per cent in 1956."[30]

71

Chapter 5

Agriculture
and the Revolution

After twelve years of "socialism," as Fidel Castro has called his program, it is possible to appraise the consequences to Cuba in general and to agriculture especially. Up to this point, we have summarized the events of the rebellion, described in a limited way the ordeal of the early years when the revolutionary regime took over and consolidated the powers of government, and summarized the events leading up to the political and economic isolation of Cuba from other countries of the hemisphere. We have also sketched in broad outline the historical development of the island, given a limited inventory of its resources when the revolution occurred, and finally elaborated the discussion of resources by describing the status of agriculture as it was before 1959.

The new government faced the problem of developing an entirely new agricultural and general economic policy, a policy that would be consonant with its revolutionary ideology. Old structures and institutions were swept away and substitutes had to be found. As new policies evolved, one can discern two stages, the first covering the years 1959–1964 and the second from 1964 to the present time. The earlier period was marked by the acquisition of property which we have already described, but more importantly by the development of a first policy of economic development, up to the crucial change in late 1963. The second stage was marked by a return to agriculture as the primary resource in economic development.

Two programs that were set in motion by the revolution, in combination with a severe drought and one of the most destructive hurricanes in the history of the island, brought ruinous results to Cuban agriculture during the first four years. The two programs were the Agrarian Reform Laws of May and October 1959 and the anti-monoculture scheme. The latter involved the diversification of agriculture at the expense of sugarcane, along with accelerated industrialization. The four-year period of the first stage ended abruptly in the fall of 1963 when Premier Castro announced a return to agriculture as a matter of first priority in Cuban development.

The Background of Agrarian Reform

Of the two programs, the one with the most enduring influence on agriculture, as well as on the entire economy, was agrarian reform. It is important at the outset that the nature and significance of this policy be set forth. Moreover the historic background of its development requires a brief recital, since without question it was the most important single action taken by the revolution. Its instigation was anticipated although it was expected that there would be compensation for the expropriated owners as the Constitution of 1940 specified. Throughout the troubled controversy between Cuba and the United States, described in Chapter 2, the United States officially recognized Cuba's right to expropriate the property of foreign owners provided there was compensation. But it was a foregone conclusion that there would be some kind of land reform.

Agrarian reform was not an invention of the rebels, but it became a major rallying cry for them. Ever since the beginning of the republic and the astronomical infusion of foreign capital for the promotion of sugar production, many observing Cubans with a sense of responsibility for their country had lamented the passing of the period in their history when land was widely occupied by families farming it for their own benefit. The noted historian Ramiro Guerra y Sánchez (1880–1970) deplored the transition from what he termed an "agra-

73

rian society" to the kind built around the giant sugar central.[1] Cuban farmers largely lost control of their land during this period.

Agitation by reform groups during the 1930's was constant, and there was hope after the downfall of President Gerardo Machado in 1933 that some progress could be made not only in land reform but also in other much-needed reforms as well. The assumption of control by Batista resulted essentially in maintaining the status quo, except for the Law of Sugar Coordination of 1937. This law, as we have seen, provided for the distribution of the sugar among the mills, the colonos, and the wage laborers. The "right of indefinite occupation," which was guaranteed by the sugar coordination law to sugar colonos, was extended by Law No. 247 of July 17, 1952, to other leaseholders of less than five *caballerías* (a *caballería* equals 33.16 acres).[2] Eviction of any farmer was prohibited. Even squatters shared this protection. Laws also provided for the recovery of state-owned land which had been illegally possessed by private individuals, and this land was supposed to be distributed to landless farmers. Very little was ever recovered or distributed. The prosperity resulting from high sugar prices during World War II provided no incentive for governments to make drastic changes and upset conditions so favorable to themselves. Nonetheless, the laws of 1937 and 1952 represented significant advances in land reform.

The Constitution of 1940, adopted by a constituent assembly arranged by Batista, contained an article which proscribed latifundia[3] and authorized legislation looking to the development and protection of small farms. There was also a proposal for the limitation of ownership by foreigners. The provisions were not, however, implemented by law.

Fidel Castro's first commitment to agrarian reform was contained in the famous statement that he made during his trial before the Urgency Court of Santiago de Cuba in 1955. In a long address to the court he announced that if the attack on the Moncada Barracks had succeeded, the first revolutionary law would have been to "return sovereignty to the people," and a second would have "conceded the nonembargable and untransferable ownership of the land to the cane planters, leasees, renters, sharecroppers, and those who use land on loan, who occupy parcels of 167 acres or less. The state would in-

74

demnify the former owners on the basis of the income that they would receive as an average over ten year period."[4]

Later in his speech, Castro elaborated somewhat on the land question. After settling the 100,000 small farmers as owners of the land which they had previously tilled as tenants or otherwise occupied, the revolution, he said, in accordance with the constitution would establish the maximum amount of land a person could hold, given the type of farming involved. The excess over this maximum would be expropriated. Land stolen from the state would be recovered and swamplands would be drained for distribution to peasants. Nurseries would be planted and programs of reforestation inaugurated. The remaining land would be distributed among peasant families, priority being given on the basis of family size. Cooperatives would be promoted, and technical and professional assistance would be provided in farming and stock raising.

Although subsequent events cast doubt on Castro's sincerity in proposing to return sovereignty to the people, he has never ceased to have concern for land reform of some sort. A second important document, called the Manifesto of the Sierra Maestra, emanated from the rebels on July 12, 1957. The document covered a number of program proposals, including the following objective regarding land reform: "Establishment of the foundations for an agrarian reform that tends to the distribution of barren lands and to convert into proprietors all the lessee-planters, partners and squatters who possess small parcels of land, be it property of the state or of private persons, with prior indemnification to the former owners."[5]

The third document to come from the rebel headquarters — and the most important from our present standpoint — was issued October 10, 1958, and was designated as Law No. 3, "Concerning the Peasants' Rights to Land." The law was signed by Fidel Castro and Humberto Sori Marín, who is credited with drafting it.[6] The law specified that the land was to be given in ownership to those who cultivated it but set a limit of five caballerías (about 165 acres). Those then cultivating less than 5 cabs. were to be given two cabs. free with the state indemnifying the owners, and the latter were to offer for sale to the occupant enough land to bring his total to a maximum of 5 cabs. Indemnification of the owner would be based on the assessment for the last land tax before the agrarian reform took effect.

Properties acquired under provisions of the law would be heritable but not divisible among heirs. Land could be sold to the state or disposed of by other transfer authorized by the state. The state would provide credit, seeds, and implements and equipment for the new owners.[7]

The Agrarian Reform Laws

The so-called laws proclaimed by the rebel army headquarters in the Sierra Maestra were of course without force except in the area which it controlled at the time. After provisional president Manuel Urrutia and his Council of Ministers, acting as a legislative body, promulgated the Fundamental Law on February 7, 1959, the rebel laws could be applied to the nation. This law was, in effect, a constitution for legitimizing the new government. It followed in general the Constitution of 1940 with such amendments or changes as were considered appropriate.

The basic concepts for agrarian legislation contained in the 1940 constitution were incorporated in the Fundamental Law, with only one major change. This amendment provided that in case of expropriation "resulting from the application of Agrarian Reform it will not be indispensable to have a previous cash settlement. The law may establish other forms of payment provided they offer the necessary guarantee." It is of more than passing interest to note that Article 87 of the Fundamental Law guaranteed private property: "The Cuban State recognizes the existence and legitimacy of private property in its broadest concept of social function and without any limitations than those that for purposes of public or social interest may be established by law."

The part of the Fundamental Law that concerned agrarian reform was translated into the Agrarian Reform Law of May 17, 1959. Symbolically, it was promulgated from La Plata in the Sierra Maestra. In effect, the Council of Ministers amended the constitution by making the new law a part thereof, in order to avoid any conflict with existing text of the organic instrument. It is not essential here to undertake a detailed description of the law, but there are certain features which are of basic importance even though, as time has shown, several have become obsolete. Among the significant features are these:

1. A maximum of 30 cabs. (about 1,000 acres) was set for ownership by any one person or corporation; any excess would be expropriated for distribution to landless families. For rice or sugar farming the maximum might be extended to 100 cabs.; the same limit would apply to cattle ranches. Publicly owned land would be distributed on the same basis, but cooperatives yet to be organized would be exempt from the maximum.

2. The payment for expropriated lands was to be in the form of twenty-year bonds of the Republic of Cuba bearing interest at the rate of 4½ percent. Law No. 576 of September 1959 authorized the first issue of $100 million, but there was no announcement that any expropriated owner received payment in this form.

3. The law established a "vital minimum" of 2 cabs. of land, a "homestead," the exact size to depend upon the fertility of the soil, whether irrigated or not, and the distance from a trading center. Such a homestead could not be mortgaged and was inalienable. Renters, sharecroppers, and squatters had first priority.

4. The farmers who were to receive land in the proposed distribution were of three types: cooperatives; renters who had been working a tract of land; and present owners of land, who would if circumstances permitted be given enough additional land to equal the "vital minimum."

5. The law established the Institute for Agrarian Reform (INRA) to administer its provisions. The institute was given sweeping authority to "organize collective cultivation of the land" and to regulate all agricultural production temporarily in the hands of private owners; it was charged with the direction of rural life including education, health, and housing. Its powers were so broad, in fact, that it was essentially a state within a state.

6. The country was divided into twenty-eight agrarian development zones, each to be governed by an appointee of INRA. Such of-

ficers were given authority over provincial and municipal officials and had complete responsibility for carrying out the broad program of INRA.

The agency began without delay to exercise control over property confiscated from *batistianos*. Large cattle ranches were taken over and managers appointed by INRA took charge. "Cooperatives" were organized to operate sugarcane plantations, the members to consist of the laborers previously employed. The manager, however, was appointed by INRA and was entirely under its control, not that of the cooperative membership.

The members received a daily wage of 2.50 pesos but each was to participate in the annual profits according to the hours worked. According to Andrés Bianchi, the Chilean economist who studied the agricultural situation in 1962, the "lack of accounting records prevented the determination of the profits and it was decided not to distribute any dividends."[8] The experience with the cooperatives was unsatisfactory and the cane farms were converted into state farms in August 1962.

Besides managing confiscated properties INRA absorbed all the autonomous agencies set up by former governments including the Cuban Institute for Sugar Stabilization, the Committee for Tobacco Production, the Rice Stabilization Administration, the Institute for Coffee Stabilization, and the Bank for Agricultural and Industrial Development. In fact, it took over all the functions of the Ministry of Agriculture.

Within a year after its establishment, INRA had acquired about half the land in farms. Added to the lands taken from the supporters of Batista were the cattle ranches, the 1,250,000 hectares of the American-owned sugar mills, and the 910,000 hectares of the Cuban-owned mills. In addition there were some large rice plantations which came under state management.

The private sector at this time consisted of farmers with less than 402.6 hectares (about 1,000 acres). Most of the holdings were actually much smaller than this and included little more than, if as much as, the vital minimum of 27 hectares. These farmers were mainly the former renters, sharecroppers, and squatters, who were made owners by decree, as well as those who had owned their farms before the revolution. The actual distribution of titles was very slow. Up to February 1961, according to Bianchi, only 32,823 had been granted.[9]

Bianchi's figure corresponds approximately with one obtained in 1962 by the Cuban economists in exile, who reported 35,000 titles. They also learned something about the nature of these "titles." At first they were in the form of "diplomas attractively printed and which improved the design of the old titles that had been delivered in accordance with the 1937 legislation. . . . After the first 35,000 titles were delivered, subsequent titles were simply mimeographed notifications which merely stated that the farmer had the right to a determined parcel of land provided he complied with INRA's regulations."[10] No further information is available about the precise nature of these titles. Presumably they included a description of the parcel but the nature of such description is not known outside. Were boundaries determined by a special survey and exact areas stated? (Traditionally, a farm in Cuba was described by the names of the farms which bounded it, but with the drastic rearrangements of farms that were confiscated it is difficult to see how the system could be preserved.) One would also like to know about the registration of the titles. One fact is certain about these "diplomas"; they were not deeds in "fee simple absolute."

If the law had been strictly observed, farms in excess of 402.6 hectares would have been reduced to that size and the balance would have been expropriated from the owners. Cattle ranches and other large farms up to 1,430 hectares would have been allowed, and all above that size would have been taken for distribution to the landless. There would have been in that case a considerable number of units added to the category of middle-size farms. But the law was not followed, and the large units were taken over in toto.

On December 31, 1971, in an address to the association of small farmers (ANAP), Castro revealed for the first time how land had been distributed. "The only deeds that were handed out," he said, "were those covering lands which had been divided into plots and were in the hands of small tenants and sharecroppers. The rest of the land covered by the agrarian reform was not divided into plots and was not given to anyone in particular. It was held as the property of the people." This statement belatedly confirmed what outsiders assumed to have been the case.

Although many expropriations were made of farmers living in areas like Escambray, where there was counterrevolutionary activity following the Bay of Pigs invasion in April 1961, the major act of appropriation did not occur until late 1963. The agrarian law of October of that year called for the nationalization of all farms of more than 67.1 hectares. It affected 11,215 owners and 2,102,860 hectares of land.[11] This brought the government into direct control of 6,006,160 hectares. There were 154,703 farms remaining in the private sector (those under 67 hectares) with a total area of 2,348,150 hectares. The operators were subject to regulations of INRA and were organized in an association known as ANAP (*Asociación Nacional de Agricultores Pequeños*). Its national president, an appointive officer, was a member of the central committee of the Communist party.

The reason for the second agrarian law and the expropriation of the middle-size farms was apparently a political one: the law's preamble "stated that such farms were in the hands of bourgeois proprietors who acted 'detrimentally to the interest of the workers by obstructing production of food items for the population, speculating with these products, or using, with anti-social and counterrevolutionary purposes the large income they obtain by exploiting the work of the people.' " [12]

As far as the land was concerned, this law and its application in extensive expropriations completed the changes in the structure and institutional arrangements of the revolution. Property was in the hands of the state or under its control. How was it to be managed to the productive ends that had been visualized? The purposes have been well stated by the Cuban economists in exile as follows: "a rapid increase of agricultural output, the adoption of technological progress in agriculture, productive diversification, the elimination of monoculture, the reduction of foodstuff imports, and the redistribution of income through a drastic change in the structure of land tenure. This was to raise the standard of living of the Cuban farmer and accelerate the economic and social development of the country."[13]

The Attack on Monoculture

Economically Cuba has been in a sense a victim of the rich natural endowment of soil and climate that made it the world's leading producer of cane sugar. This condition coupled with its lack of other endowments (in fuel especially, but also in other basic elements needed for growth in nonagricultural sectors) made it unusually dependent on its major product. Unfortunately also for Cuba, the world capacity to produce sugar (beet and cane) is so great as to create a constant threat to the world price. Cuban dependence on sugar made for severe fluctuations in the national income and in economic stability. Cuban leaders have for many years sought to bring greater diversification in agriculture and to promote industrialization in order to free the nation to some extent from the dependence on sugar. Some progress was made in both sectors during the 1950's, as we noted in Chapters 3 and 4, but it was far from sufficient.

To the revolutionaries, monoculture was one of many evils for which the United States investors were mainly to blame. Foreign and Cuban capitalists, the argument went, were too enamored with the profits from sugar to want to support other endeavors which might compete for available resources. Similarly, industrialization was retarded, they believed, because foreign capital did not want local industries competing for the Cuban market. The drain on foreign currency caused by large imports of food from the United States could be reduced if some of the resources devoted to sugar production were diverted to other crops. Moreover, the promotion of industry would provide jobs outside of agriculture. Such arguments are familiar and have been in the common dialogue in Cuba for many years.

The revolutionary leaders therefore decided to do something about both crop diversification and industrialization. With practically all the land of the island under their control, the leaders were in a strategic position to completely reorganize the cropping

81

system. However, time would be required, and indeed much more than time, including intelligent planning.

Following the practice of other socialist countries, the Cuban government created JUCEPLAN (*Junta Central de Planificación*) in March 1960. Agriculture was only one of six departments in JUCEPLAN, whose work covered the entire economy, but plans for food production were necessarily a major concern. With INRA gathering statistics from the entire country on production possibilities for individual crops and for livestock, JUCEPLAN would set official goals for performance, not for one year but for five. A five-year plan was projected for 1961–1965, but because of the difficulty of getting the needed data the plan was to begin in 1962 and thus became a four-year plan.

Nevertheless, during the last half of 1960, some ambitious goals were set for the production of food crops throughout the island in 1961. They were based on overly optimistic projections of local officials of INRA, and in the summer of 1961 Havana began to receive reports from the provinces of serious shortages of food items such as oils, meat, fish, chicken, and vegetables, including malanga, perhaps the most popular item of all.

The reaction to these reports was a call for a conference on production, the conferees to consist of the prime minister, the Council of Ministers, officials of JUCEPLAN and INRA, and provincial and regional representatives of industry groups, agricultural units, and the mass organizations. The conference was held August 27–28, 1961, with the prime minister presiding. After a review of the total situation, the delegates set forth a series of objectives to correct the difficulties, and in particular they made the following pledge together with the prime minister:

1. That, for the month of December, 1961, the capital of the Republic will have a full supply of chickens and on February 1, 1962, a full supply will be available in all national markets.

2. That, after January 1962, the production of viands will exceed the demands of the national market.

3. That, on June 1962, the production of fish will meet the demands of national consumption.

4. That, on January 1, 1963, present rationing regulations for the distribution of fat will be abolished.[14]

Agriculture and the Revolution

How such a pledge could work the necessary magic to bring forth nonexistent supplies in the limited time allowed is hard to understand; and why it was made is a greater mystery. The pledge did, however, reveal a startling situation in the nation, startling not only to the top officials but to people at all levels. Here was the first symptom that something was seriously wrong in the countryside. It seems likely that the men making the pledge were unable to believe that Cuba could be short of food and considered the problem to be one of distribution rather than production. (There had never before been rationing in Cuba, even during World War II.)

The Effects of the Diversification Effort

Full realization that there was a growing shortage of food forced the regime in March 1962 to impose a rationing system which was to become a permanent feature of the revolution. On April 10, 1962, Castro in a speech in Matanzas remarked: "This is a revolution which must be ashamed of itself because it is forced to ration *malanga,* and the imperialists are saying to the Latin Americans: 'There is your socialism: hunger, shortages, rationing . . .'"[15] Statistics on production will be presented shortly but first a word needs to be said about sugarcane.

The adverse impact of the revolutionary policy was not felt immediately in sugar. There were large crops in 1959, 1960, and 1961. This led some observers to think that land reform could be accomplished without a reduction in production. But the sugar harvests of 1959–61 came from plantings made in previous years. As Bianchi has pointed out, the 1959 crop was not affected by the land reform law of May 1959 because it was already harvested. The 1961 crop was influenced positively by very favorable weather conditions during the growing period of 1960; the diversification program which called for the diversion of 134,000 hectares of canefields to other crops and necessitated clearing designated areas of cane and sending it to the mills; and the "perennial nature of cane," meaning of course that the cane was there to be cut because of plantings in previous years. It has been estimated that there was sufficient area in cane for two crops of 5,500,000 tons each.[16]

The 1962 crop was the first to show the effect of the program. It produced only 4,815,000 tons of sugar, compared with 6,767,000 tons the previous year. The decline, according to Bianchi, was caused in part by a severe drought during the growing season of 1961, but also by the diversification plan which resulted in the plowing up of large areas of cane on the best lands.[17] There was also poor organization and management of the state cane farms, now operated by "cooperatives"; as a result productivity was low in spite of the "superior quality of the cooperatives' land and the preference they received in the allocation of capital and fertilizer." The 1963 crop, a real disaster, produced only 3,821,000 tons. This crop was severely affected by a hurricane in October 1963 but suffered also from the same inhibiting factors as the 1962 crop.

Estimates of the production of selected crops for the three years 1957–1959, compared with production for the same crops during the first full years of the new regime, are shown in Table 7. The plan for diversification, including increased production of essential food crops, not only was not realized but serious declines occurred. However, it was not the fault of the planners. "The people's farms," Bianchi reports, "would put 830,000 hectares — nearly one-third of their total area — under more than twenty-five different crops and *pangola* [pasture grass]."[18]

The decline in rice production was particularly unfortunate since rice is a universally consumed food. Malanga, another staple of the Cuban diet, also continued to be badly affected. The figures in Table 7 reveal few items that showed any increase or even held to previous levels.

The FAO *Statistical Yearbook* for 1967 estimated that the total agricultural production, including sugar, exceeded the average for the prerevolutionary years of 1952–1958 only in 1959–1960, 1960–1961, 1961–1962, and 1964–1965; the production per capita in 1965–1966 was only 80 percent of the average for the years 1952–1956. Carmelo Mesa-Lago cites a report of the United Nations Economic Commission for Latin America to the effect that between 1961 and 1966 there was a decline in cereals of 33 percent; tubers and starchy roots, 6 percent; pulses, 6 percent; oil seeds, 64 percent; fibers, 34 percent; and other crops, 12 percent.[19]

Agriculture and the Revolution

Table 7. Physical Output of Selected Agricultural Products in Cuba
for Selected Years, 1957–66 (in Thousands of Metric Tons)

Item	1957	1958	1959	1962	1963	1964	1965	1966
Sugarcane	44.7	45.7	48.0	36.7	31.4	37.2	50.7	36.8
Tobacco	41.7	50.6	35.6	51.5	47.6	43.8	43.4	51.3
Coffee	43.7	29.5	48.0	52.2	34.7	32.0	23.9	33.4
Cocoa	2.8	2.8	2.8	2.4	2.5	1.2	2.2	2.0
Rice	261.0	253.0	326.0	208.0	204.0	123.5	49.9	68.4
Beans	35.7	23.0	35.0	29.1	17.5	14.3	10.8	11.3
Potatoes	94.3	70.6	63.5	...	85.8	75.3	83.5	104.0
Malanga	91.0	226.0	240.0	25.5	45.0	49.2	46.6	69.3
Sweet potatoes and yams	184.0	186.0	224.0	93.2	90.6	97.7	89.1	164.5
Cassava (yucca) ..	186.0	213.0	224.0	33.8	90.4	73.2	62.1	93.4
Tomatoes	43.9	55.2	65.0	44.7	92.5	111.6	120.0	132.9
Beef	185.0	184.0	200.0	147.0	143.0	170.0	165.0	177.0

SOURCE: Data for 1957–59 from Carmelo Mesa-Lago, "Availability and Reliability of Statistics in Communist Cuba," *Latin American Research Review*, 4, no. 2 (Summer 1969), p. 56; and for 1962–66, JUCEPLAN, Dirección Central de Estadística, *Boletín Estadístico 1966*, Table V.6. (This source does not give information for other years.) On July 26, 1970, Castro gave figures on beef production for 1968, 1969, and 1970 as 154.0, 143.0, and 145.0 thousand metric tons respectively.

Bianchi, a careful reporter on conditions in Cuba, has set down a number of factors that were responsible for the lessened production in 1962.[20] In the first place, there was the severe drought. A second factor was inadequate planning, not only in regard to the land area needed for a given production, but also in respect to the estimates of needs for equipment, fertilizers, seeds, insecticides, transport, and labor. He cites, for example, the preparation of 78,000 hectares for the planting of malanga although there turned out to be enough seed for only half that area. In Camagüey, he was told, 60 percent of the area planned for yams was never planted. The importation of farm machinery, he continued, represented a lack of balance. There were too many tractors and too few plows, harrows, and other associated implements. Poorly organized distribution and transport resulted in failure to get fertilizers to the right places at the proper time. Much of the fertilizer was wasted through inadequate packaging and lack of protection from the weather. The "inefficiency of the average manager" made administration difficult and ineffective. The managers of the people's farms were usually former

85

peasants, with little if any scientific training and with scanty knowledge of the new crops or of administrative techniques. These and other shortcomings of the early years of the regime have been remarked by others and even admitted by Cuban leaders in moments of self-analysis as recently as 1970, eight years later.

The revolution has been plagued by such problems and others since Bianchi made his observations in 1962. For example, after 1967 even the small farmers were asked not to sell any of their products to buyers other than the state agency, and production on their farms declined. They were formerly able to get higher prices for their products than the state would pay. In 1968 the small merchants who constituted their market were nationalized. Material incentives are generally discouraged by the regime in favor of such nonmaterial rewards as emulation, pennants, and plaques which, it is argued, will bring forth enthusiastic effort if the workers are truly committed to revolutionary ideals.

Livestock under Socialism

That there was serious depletion of the cattle herds of Cuba at the onset of the revolution, that is, between 1959 and 1963, has been confirmed by information from within as well as from outside the country. The ultimate confirmation from within, of course, was the severe rationing imposed in March 1962. The precise extent of the depletion is impossible to assess, but the fact that beef is still in short supply (as is also milk) would seem to indicate that the herds have yet some distance to go before they can provide the approximately 70 pounds per capita which they supplied in 1958.

The only official estimates of livestock in Cuba are presented in Table 8. They come mainly from *Boletín Estadístico 1966* of the statistical office of the national planning board (JUCEPLAN). The apparent decline in the number of cattle between 1946 and 1952 is accounted for by a decrease of more than 576,000 oxen during those years. In any case, the 1952 livestock census is generally regarded as incomplete.[21]

Assuming the number of cattle in 1958 to have been nearly six million, there was an increase of 600,000 by 1964. The five-year apparent gain, however, conceals the generally admitted heavy losses during 1959, 1960, and 1961. There are several explanations given for the decline of the herds in those years. In the first place, the forced departure of experienced owners and managers left control of the ranches in the hands of untrained individuals. At the same time there was apparently no central policy regarding conservation of the herds and no provision for training and supervising the new herdsmen. It is reported, for instance, that neglect in the matter of breeding resulted in very small calf crops. The control of diseases such as brucellosis and tuberculosis was also impaired.[22] There was also the question of caring for the pastures. It has been claimed that during the period of diversification pasture lands were plowed for planting to food crops. It is difficult to substantiate this claim, however.

A major factor in the destruction of the cattle herds was the excessive slaughter for current consumption. An increase in purchasing power and thus an increased demand for meat resulted from such governmental policies as reducing rents by 50 percent and providing nominal employment for many persons previously without wages.

Table 8. Estimated Numbers of Livestock in Cuba for Selected Years
from 1946 to 1966

Year	Cattle	Swine	Sheep and Goats	Poultry
1946	4,115,000	1,344,000	292,800	7,146,000
1952	4,042,100	1,285,800	355,600	. . .
1958	5,385,000[a]	. . .	. . .	. . .
1961	5,776,400[b]	827,600	. . .	15,380,000
1962	5,971,900	1,385,700	222,500	18,600,000
1963	6,378,000	1,539,900	213,100	19,500,000
1964	6,611,300[c]	1,746,400	240,500	21,900,000
1965	6,695,500[c]	1,810,000	257,800	21,400,000
1966	6,774,200[c]	. . .	. . .	11,400,000[d]

SOURCE: JUCEPLAN, Dirección Central de Estadística, *Boletín Estadístico 1966*, Table V.8.

[a] CERP, *Study on Cuba*, p. 526, citing the annual report of INRA for 1961. In addition to this figure, INRA estimated 940,000 dairy cows.

[b] Livestock census by INRA in 1961.

[c] From the compulsory livestock registry.

[d] State sector only.

To the extent that pastures were plowed, increased slaughter became imperative.[23] The early overkill of beef is confirmed in estimates given by Sergio Arana, a Chilean economist who spent eight years in Cuba.[24] According to Arana, in 1960 the kill was 1,200,000, and an inquiry made in 1961 revealed that, if the rate of kill during the first quarter were maintained during the remaining months, the slaughter would amount to 1,200,000 for that year also. This would far exceed the average estimated slaughter of 835,000 in 1958.[25] One would assume that the 1958 rate of kill represented an optimum number which the owners estimated would neither reduce their breeding stock nor allow it to increase beyond their pasture and forage capacity. If this assumption is correct, then the overkill in the two years reported by Arana would deplete the herds by about 750,000.

Further information on the excess kill is reported by Bianchi, who cites official data obtained in 1962 to the effect that in Las Villas province during the first quarter of 1961 the slaughter of cattle amounted to 41,587 head, compared with 17,267 for the corresponding period of 1959. Similarly, in Oriente province, 47,600 head were slaughtered in the first quarter of 1961, compared with 22,900 in 1959.[26]

The cattle population suffered also from the bad drought of 1961 and from the hurricane in 1963 which was one of the most destructive in the history of the island and killed many cattle. The government estimated cattle losses in Camagüey and Oriente provinces at 20 percent. The drought was also very destructive because no attention had been given to storing a supply of fodder against such an emergency. René Dumont of the Institute of Agriculture in Paris has been able to visit Cuba several times on the invitation of the government. A Marxist agronomist, he has nevertheless not hesitated to make critical reports on conditions he observed. During a visit in September 1963, just before the hurricane, he found serious conditions resulting from the drought and from poor management. On a ranch stocked with the famous Santa Gertrudis breed of cattle, he discovered that in the first half of 1962 the herd suffered a loss of 1,600 head and that calves from the 4,836 cows totaled only 1,500 for all of 1962. In another herd with more than 6,000 cows at Martires del Moncada, only 18 to 20 calves were born per month, compared with an average of 300 per month in 1963.[27]

Alvarez, who estimates the cattle numbers in 1964 at 4,500,000,[28] cites the heavy importation of cattle as evidence of the destruction of the herds. (He also is of the opinion that inadequate attention was given to obeying quarantine regulations and that certain unspecified diseases and a cattle tick were introduced.[29]) This importation came mainly from Canada, but also from other countries. It began in 1960 with 150 head of Aberdeen Angus, Hereford, Holstein, and Brown Swiss, brought by plane according to Alvarez. They were followed by three boatloads of 250 head each. Another cargo of 250 left Canada on June 22. During the summer of 1960, Alvarez states, the Cuban government purchased additional ships for the transport of cattle. Buying missions were also sent to Holland and Australia. Castro meanwhile announced that he wanted to buy 40,000 head of cattle for breeding experiments. He purchased two famous bulls in Canada (Rasafe Signet and Citation R) at prices around $30,000. One Canadian breeder reported that he sold 10,000 head of cattle to Cuba. Another Canadian farm sold to Cuba 600 bulls at $1,000 each.

All the facts regarding the cattle problem may never be known, but enough are available to indicate beyond doubt that the losses were severe. As Table 8 shows, by 1966 very little gain had been made in the herds over the number estimated for 1958, and this in spite of the fact that the ration imposed in 1962 allowed only 36 pounds of meat per capita (later reduced to 30 pounds in Havana and 25 in the rest of the country), compared with the 70 pounds per capita available in 1958. The ration, of course, does not represent total production, for the regime has exported beef.[30]

In an address on July 26, 1970, Castro confirmed the deplorable condition of the livestock herds. The production of beef amounted to 154,000 metric tons in 1968 and 143,000 tons in 1969; Castro estimated that the 1970 yield would be 145,000 tons. (See Table 7 for figures for earlier years.) At the same time Castro reported the number of cattle slaughtered as 485,000 in 1968, 466,000 in 1969, and an estimated 466,000 for 1970. For the latter year the slaughter would equal only 57 percent of that estimated for 1958. The yield per carcass was also low, the prime minister reported, and the calf crop was small, both facts indicating poor management of the herds.

The situation in milk production was equally bad. Production for 1970, according to Castro, was 25 percent less than in 1969. This decline, he said, meant that the government would have to import 56,000 tons of powdered milk from the dollar area at a cost of $12 million. After twelve years of the revolution, then, the story was one of a continuing deterioration of what was in 1958 a well-managed and productive industry.

The condition of the cattle population was so bad after the hurricane of 1963 that the government passed a law imposing a penalty of as much as five years in prison for the unauthorized slaughter of an animal, whether for sale or for consumption. In 1964 it became compulsory for an owner, even of a single animal, to register his livestock. Failure to do so would make him liable to severe penalty. In 1964 the government also decided to call for aid from the Food and Agriculture Organization. Under an agreement signed in April, the FAO supplied a mission of experts headed by Maurice Amiot of France to prepare a plan for cattle development. To facilitate the work of carrying out the plan, the Institute of Animal Science was established to conduct research in the fields of nutrition, animal genetics, biochemistry, pastures, and fodder crops. On March 2, 1969, *Granma* reported that the institute had a group of modern buildings located in a tract of 2,890 acres and a staff of 9 foreign specialists, 45 university graduates, 5 university students, and 75 graduates of technical schools. According to the same account, research was also being conducted on hogs, poultry, sheep, goats, and rabbits.

After the change in policy to favor agriculture that occurred in 1963, Castro gave cattle production a high priority, only slightly below that for sugar. In the plan for accelerating production, artificial insemination received major attention. Institutes for training veterinary technicians were established, and as rapidly as graduates were trained they were assigned to stations throughout the island. The problem of pastures and the planting of imported strains of grasses were given much attention. Pangola has been the most popular grass, though according to Dumont's report this variety is subject to a virus disease which has affected it in Surinam and British

Guiana and which may affect it in Cuba. Nevertheless, it seems to be the variety that will form the major part of the pasture resources. Dumont has estimated that 100,000 cabs. of pangola and other grasses on medium-quality soil but treated with fertilizer would produce all the pasturage Cuba needs.

There is no estimate of the number of swine for 1958, but it could hardly have been less, and was probably more, than the approximately 1.3 million reported in the livestock census of 1952. The decline to 827,600 swine in 1961 was undoubtedly due to the same factors that have been mentioned for cattle. The reported increase of some 558,000 from 1961 to 1962 is so remarkable as to make the estimates suspect.

Poultry has received special emphasis in the revolutionary program because of the popularity of both eggs and chicken meat in the Cuban diet. The fact that both items were still strictly rationed in 1971 means that production had not reached the levels so often announced and so often unrealized.

Industrialization

The second prong of the dual attack on monoculture was the acceleration of industrialization, meaning the building of factories of various kinds to provide increasing employment outside of agriculture. In a sense, it can be considered a phase of the diversification program, but the latter term is usually applied to the agricultural sector and the diversion of more acreage to food crops for local consumption. This program, as we have seen, was a failure. What happened in industrialization? The story is brief.

Shortly after Deputy Premier Anastas Mikoyan's trip to Cuba in February 1960, Ernesto Guevara, the minister of industries, visited the Soviet bloc countries and mainland China where he obtained large-scale credit and commitments to construct some seventy factories. Theodore Draper, citing an article by Guevara in *Cuba Socialista* of March 1964, lists the commitments as follows: from the USSR a credit of $100 million for a steel industry, electric plants, an oil refinery, and a geological survey; from Czechoslovakia, an automobile factory; from China, $60 million for twenty-four different

91

factories; from Rumania, fifteen factories; from Bulgaria, five; from Poland, twelve; and from East Germany, ten.[31]

It hardly needs saying that few of these promises were fulfilled. Factories which required the importation of raw materials proved to be impractical and uneconomical because the needed raw materials cost as much to obtain as the finished article manufactured outside of Cuba. In 1963 it was finally admitted that such accelerated industrialization had to be abandoned.

The Return to Monoculture

The first years were a medley of mistakes, misfortunes in the weather, and mismanagement. It was the mistake of amateurs to think it possible to establish almost a hundred industrial plants within the space of six or seven years and to train the necessary skilled labor to man them. It was also a mistake to assume that, in the uncertain political and economic environment, farmers would continue producing at their previous levels or that, when the previous managers of large enterprises had been expelled, new and inexperienced individuals could take over and operate them with equal efficiency.

The weather misfortunes were part, but only part, of the trouble. The main problem was the inability of the new government to organize — or rather to reorganize — society and make it function in all its disparate sectors under central control. The most over-worked word in the lexicon of the Cuban leadership was "coordination." A policy of instant diversification and industrialization could not work.

This is not to say that both aspects of the policy are not desirable. They are extremely desirable and must be developed in the future as part of the development of the nation. Monoculture remains a serious weakness of Cuba. There need to be other kinds of production to cushion the impact of ups and downs in the sugar market. Yet industries must develop in harmony with the physical and human resources of the country, as they were developing, however slowly, before 1958. The problem as to what industries will be economically viable in Cuba can only be settled through technical study by competent experts. For the foreseeable future, there is no alternative to an emphasis on agriculture.

Agriculture and the Revolution

In 1963, after so much damage had been caused, the regime returned to agriculture as the central project. The cane fields were replanted and drastic efforts launched to stem the decline in the livestock industry. The difficulties in restoration of these two basic branches of agriculture were many. Despite the great efforts put forth to increase sugar production, the goals have never been reached. In 1970 the regime failed by nearly a million and a half tons to wring from the soil and the people the harvest of ten million tons of sugar that had been set as a goal five years earlier. A much more modest production goal of seven million tons set for 1971 fell short by more than a million tons.

The extraordinary importance of the ten-million-ton crop stemmed from Cuba's growing indebtedness not only to the socialist countries but to countries of the free world as well. Under the five-year plan which was to culminate with the 1970 zafra, the Soviets agreed to purchase three to five million tons of sugar annually, mostly in barter for goods supplied to Cuba. Cuba set a schedule for production that would increase year by year until the production of ten million tons was achieved. However, as we shall see in the next chapter, with the exception of 1965 sugar production failed each year to reach the annual targets. For this reason tremendous national effort was made to achieve a harvest of ten million tons in 1970.

The Cuban leadership has aimed to use agriculture, especially sugar, to obtain mainly in the free world market the machinery necessary for eventual full economic development. The cattle industry, and indeed all food crops as well, are important not only because of possible exports for hard currency but also to offset imports of food which still constitute a heavy drain on the economy.

There are very impressive plans to bring the country nearer to the point of self-sufficiency. Increased areas have been planted to rice, cane plantations enlarged, and several thousand miles of roads and highways built or planned. New electric plants and fertilizer plants, along with many other projects, are all designed to impel a "big leap forward." One of the most important of the programs, in the mind of Premier Castro, is the construction of reservoirs to impound the water that falls on the island. Castro is determined to build enough dams so that "not a single drop of water will run off into the

93

ocean," a project that will help to mitigate the effect of droughts. Another program is the planting of windbreaks to reduce damage from hurricanes. These may or may not be effective, but at the least they will produce wood, which is another commodity in short supply.

After the passage of thirteen years, the struggle for survival goes on, and hope is pinned more and more on the future of agriculture to meet domestic food needs and for export. The struggle has both short and long term objectives. The all-important immediate goal is the production of increased tonnage of sugar to provide dollar currency and to meet obligations to the socialist countries. The long-term goal is economic development. To this end much investment has been made in the infrastructure.

Investment in the Infrastructure

The regime has been dedicating upward of 25 percent of its gross national product to development works, most of them directly or indirectly affecting agriculture. To this end, Premier Castro announced in February 1969 the creation of an agency for agricultural development known as DAP. Placed at its disposal was all the machinery needed for the construction of dams, land clearing operations, drainage systems, highways and roads, bridges, land terracing, and drilling wells for irrigation. The prime minister estimated that in 1969, 2,000 million cubic meters would be added to the water supply, half of it from wells and the other half from reservoirs. The government has reported that up to 1968 the capacity of all dams constructed was 862 million cubic meters.[32]

Land Clearing. Although precise information is not available, there is no doubt that large areas of formerly idle and waste lands have been cleared of brush and trees and made ready for planting. One objective of this work has been to rid the island of marabú. With drag chains drawn between two tractors or army tanks, not only small trees and brush but even larger trees have been uprooted. Dumont calls it "brutal" because not even a tree that could provide shade or serve other purposes was left. Meantime large areas were left unprotected from erosion.[33] On December 1, 1968, the newspaper *Granma* reported that the Trailblazer Brigade for land clearing

Agriculture and the Revolution

was organized into "battalions" of 20 machines (bulldozers, tractors, etc.) with 117 men each, and that 36 of these units were operating throughout the six provinces. They were under the direction of the army.

Roads and Highways. In his anniversary address of January 1, 1969, the prime minister reported that 120 brigades were at work building roads and highways in 115 different locations. By 1968, 5,475.7 kilometers had been constructed, 1,537.5 of which were paved. In addition, 124,746 kilometers of sugarcane roads were constructed or improved.[34]

Schools and Hospitals. Because of the emphasis given to education and health care, the regime has devoted considerable effort to the construction of schools and hospitals. The statistics available indicate that the number of schools has doubled since 1959, but it is known that many of these are renovated and remodeled structures previously used for other purposes. Some are former private residences. Perhaps the same can be said of the hospitals. The total number of hospitals reported in 1966 was 530, but the number of new ones constructed since 1959 was not given.[35] A radio announcement in 1970 reported that fifty hospitals with a total capacity of 1,500 beds had been constructed in remote rural areas. (See Chapter 11.)

Urbanization. Rural housing has been a crucial need in Cuba and the regime has recognized this. The ultimate objective apparently is to congregate all farm families — who now live on separate farms — into "urbanized" centers. The government reports having built 155 "communities" up to 1968.[36] One such community called Machurucuto in Havana province consists of six three-story apartment buildings containing two- and three-room apartments. Completely modern in every way, these apartments will house workers from the Niña Bonita Dairy and Genetics Center. The complex includes a graded school, polyclinic, cafeteria, and shopping center. Housing, incidentally, is free as are electricity and other utilities.

Some Major Plants. A very large investment has been made in a new fertilizer plant built in Cienfuegos at an estimated cost of $100 million. It will have a capacity of nearly 500,000 tons annually, enough to supply about 25 percent of the country's needs. It is expected to become operative in late 1971. A thermoelectric generating plant is also being built in Cienfuegos. It consists of two generators each with a capacity of 30,000 kilowats. Another electric plant, obtained from the USSR, is located at Mariel in Havana province. It has four generators each with a 50,000-kilowat capacity. Yet in 1972 there was a critical shortage of electricity.

Other major improvements include a grain elevator complex at Regla, Havana, with a capacity for storing 30,000 metric tons of imported wheat, soybeans, and corn. It should be mentioned too that a number of plants for mixing cattle and swine feed have been added to the basic capital of the country, along with a cement plant with an annual capacity of 500,000 tons. Although cement manufacturing facilities have been expanded, the total production had increased only slightly at the end of 1971.

Mechanization. There has been a large investment in bulldozers and tractors. As already indicated, the bulldozers have been busy clearing land, building roads, and constructing reservoirs, and for these purposes they are probably worth what they have cost. According to a statement of Premier Castro on November 6, 1969, the country had at that time 50,000 tractors, 10,000 of which arrived in 1969. However, the most needed machine is the one to cut sugarcane, and despite experimentation with models furnished by the USSR and some of local invention, a successful machine has not been developed. All of the 1970 crop had to be cut by hand. Rice harvesters have been obtained from Russia and Italy. Harvesters for this crop have long proved successful.

The transportation of cane by truck and tractor was a feature of the Cuban zafra before 1959. Earlier the harvest was largely transported by ox-drawn carts. Although the ox population has steadily declined as the tractor and truck took over, many individual farms continue to use oxen as their source of power. This is proving to be fortunate because only oxen can function well during the heavy rainy season, and most zafras of recent years have extended well beyond the dry period, January to April. In fact, the 1970 harvest was a year-long affair, rain notwithstanding. Accordingly, oxen were assembled in various areas where the fields were too wet for the machine.

Agriculture and the Revolution

The Fishing Fleet. It may well be that the most successful economic project of the first thirteen years has been the expansion of the fishing fleet. While fishing was a feature of the prerevolutionary period, it was not of great importance. Scarcely 25,000 tons were caught annually, and this mostly in Cuban waters. The regime has been able to obtain fishing vessels not only from the Soviet bloc countries, but also from the West, including Spain, Sweden, and France. In 1970 fifteen vessels were being constructed in East Germany. There are three fleets: the Caribbean shrimp fleet, the gulf fleet, and the Cuban fleet. The boats now have ocean-going capacity and fish in both north and south Atlantic waters. The number of vessels increased from 64 in 1963 to 249 in 1968, and the catch from 30,431.1 metric tons to 62,833.8 tons.[37]

The installation of requisite port facilities in Cienfuegos and Havana, including packaging and refrigeration units, represents a large supporting investment.

Cuba has also greatly enlarged its merchant marine and claims that there are now fifty ships totaling 407,000 tons. This compares with a pre-Communist fleet of fourteen ships and 58,000 tons.[38]

The Havana Greenbelt. One of the more spectacular projects of the revolution involves the almost total renovation and rearrangement of some 30,000 hectares around the city of Havana. The plan calls for most of the area to be planted to millions of coffee, citrus, and timber seedlings by upward of half a million "volunteer" workers. Vegetables will be produced on portions of the tract, and perhaps the largest area will be planted to pasture. It is contemplated that there will be enough dairies in the area to supply Havana with fresh milk. A planned botanical garden of 600 hectares will have plants and trees from every continent. Also planned is an Olympic stadium, a boxing arena, and a 1,300-meter waterway on which to hold regattas. To supply water for the area several reservoirs have been constructed or are planned. Actual achievements have fallen short of expectations. René Dumont reported in 1969 that most of the coffee seedlings planted between the rows of citrus trees had died and that only part of the trees had survived.[39]

One of Castro's hopes is that Havana city will not only be supplied with food from its province but will even be able to export some to the interior, from which it has always been a major importer. Like all of the other investments in development, time alone will tell whether the greenbelt will pay off in economic terms.

While these capital investments are not all that the regime has to report, they are indicative of the planned drive for accelerating economic development. The fishing fleet should begin paying off the mortgage almost immediately. Each boat is in reality a "harvester"; the "crop" was ready for "reaping." The boats should be able to pay for themselves.

Lamentably, the first dozen years of the revolution saw a steady reduction in agricultural production in absolute amounts. Meanwhile the population increased from an estimated 6,548,000 in 1958 to 8,553,395 enumerated in the census of September 1970. The production per capita is therefore much lower than the absolute decline in total amount. On July 26, 1970, the prime minister forecast no improvement in conditions until after 1975. He also emphasized as the limiting factor the number of persons in the labor force. While he was preoccupied with the size of the labor force, there is also another factor, namely, the incentives for workers to perform their tasks. We will give attention to both aspects in the next chapter.

Chapter **6**

Workers
and Peasants

"The learning process of revolutionaries in the field of economic construction is much more difficult than we imagined; the problems are much more complex than we had imagined; and the learning process much longer and harder than we had imagined." So said Fidel Castro on July 26, 1970. The inability of the revolution to equal the production rate of 1958, or even to prevent a steady decline from that level, has puzzled observers on the outside as well as the regime itself. The mystery is enhanced by the fact that after the disasters of the first four years, the government in 1963 committed itself to a rational program of agricultural production based upon the nation's fundamental resources of soil, climate, and people. By 1964, moreover, the government had weathered the Bay of Pigs invasion, the rebellion in Escambray,[1] and the missile crisis. Although disillusionment with the revolution was widespread, there was no organized opposition and the regime could feel itself relatively secure.

At the same time, the government had the advantage of almost complete control of the means of production, including land, factories, and shops. As for agriculture, it was logical to expect certain gains in efficiency. Since the island-plantation was subject to central management and planning, many advantages should have accrued. Resources could be allotted according to production plans; cropping systems could be imposed in accordance with the best scientific principles and without reference to previously existing farm boundaries.

New and improved agricultural methods could be introduced by simple decree without the necessity of persuading sometimes recalcitrant operators bound by tradition. Machinery could be moved from area to area as needed, again without persuading individual operators. In short, the entire island could be rearranged agriculturally as crops and livestock interests dictated, with the obvious advantages of improved adaptation.

The outlook was hopeful and Castro was not modest in making promises accordingly. As early as 1964 he announced that "in ten years the value of milk and beef produced [in Cuba] will exceed that of 10 million tons of sugar. Our production of milk will exceed that of Holland, and our production of cheese will exceed that of France." [2] René Dumont visited Cuba late in 1969 and said that after reading about a commitment by Castro to organize milk-producing herds totaling seven million head in two years, "my few remaining hairs rose on my head." Dumont then proceeded to show that it was mathematically impossible to reach this figure.[3]

No less unrestrained were the predictions in other branches of agriculture. "In 1971," Castro forecast on November 6, 1969, "there will be a surplus of hundreds of thousands of tons of rice after eating all the rice we want to eat." "What is scarce today will abound tomorrow" had been a recurrent theme in his addresses since he first used it on August 18, 1962. Yet scarcity is the rule in all foods and clothing, and items beyond the minimum needs for survival are nonexistent. Today more land is cultivated, more fertilizer applied, more tractors and their attachments and other mechanical aids utilized than ever before. Besides this heavy capital investment in agriculture, there has been since 1962 an extraordinary and ever-increasing infusion of human labor. Nevertheless, the results in production continue to fall short of the goals.

Trouble in the Labor Sector

Many observers of Cuba have been puzzled by the extraordinary effort to mobilize labor in agriculture on the one hand and the extremely modest productivity on the other. The latter situation has been illustrated by the comparison of production totals before and

100

during the revolution presented in Tables 7 and 8 in Chapter 5. However, to emphasize the point Table 9 shows the output of one crop, sugar, comparing the prerevolutionary year of 1952 with the seven years from 1965 to 1971. The year 1952 is used because it was a year when the release of production controls allowed relatively free rein to Cuba's production potential. It compares in this respect with the period of the 1960's when no controls were exercised. (It is worth noting in passing that production fell to a low point of 3,829,000 metric tons in 1963, one of the years not listed in the table.) We have observed earlier that unfavorable weather affected the crops in certain years; the sugar crop of 1966 suffered from drought during the growing season of 1965 and from excessive rain in 1966. Nevertheless, weather conditions bear only part of the blame; the main responsibility must be borne by labor and management.

Table 9. Sugar Production in 1952 and 1965–71

Year	Goal (in Metric Tons)	Production (in Metric Tons)	Length of Harvest (in Days)
1952	...	7,298,000	133
1965	6,000,000	6,156,000	185
1966	6,500,000	4,537,000	212
1967	7,500,000	6,236,000	241
1968	8,000,000	5,164,000	247
1969	9,000,000	4,459,000	242
1970	10,000,000	8,526,000	365
1971	7,000,000	5,924,000	242

SOURCE: The figures on production for 1952–69 were announced by Castro on May 20, 1970; those for 1970 and 1971 by Havana radio on July 25, 1970, and July 20, 1971. The length of the harvest in days is the elapsed time between the official beginnings and ends of the harvests.

The shortage of labor in agriculture has been heralded by the regime and remarked by every visitor to the island. Professor Wassily Leontief of Harvard University, a guest of the regime in 1969, made a generally favorable report on his visit, but added this comment:

One's first question about the present state of the Cuban economy, after one has seen the innumerable public posters, read the long articles in the daily press, and heard the interminable exhortations on the radio urging every inhabitant of the city — whether waiter in the restaurant or an important official in the Ministry or an SDS "escapee" living in the Habana Libre — to grasp a machete, and go to the country to cut sugarcane, is: why all the fuss? Why ten years after the glorious revolution? Why does Cuba have great and increasing difficulties in cutting six million tons of sugar now. When before it was able to harvest more than seven million without much trouble and without extracurricular assistance from people living in the cities? [4]

Leontief's answer to this enigma was that the skilled cane cutters were given their own plots of land to cultivate. These plots, he said, "provide them with secure and satisfactory livelihoods . . . [without] the necessity and willingness to engage in the backbreaking work of cutting sixteen hours a day without let up." This explanation, however, is not adequate. It would apply to relatively few, since the agrarian reform simply by fiat turned former tenants into owners of the land they had traditionally cultivated rather than distributing land to farm laborers, as we have already seen in Chapter 5. It was not the typical "temporary" cane cutter who became an owner. His "disappearance" from the cane fields must be otherwise explained, but such explanation is still lacking. The only experienced cane cutters remaining in the countryside were the small farmers who traditionally grew cane and who were not subject to agrarian reform. They cut as much as 28.6 percent of the sugarcane harvested in 1966 (the latest official figure).[5]

The Anatomy of the Labor Force

How many workers are available to the regime? It is not easy to answer the question because of changes brought by the revolution, but let us look at the 1953 census to get a general idea of the proportion of people of working age at that time. In 1953 the "economically active" population was 1,972,266 and constituted 35.3 percent of the total population. A comprehensive sample study of employment and unemployment was conducted by the National Economic Council covering fifty-two weeks from April 1956 to May 1957. It reported a total labor force of 2,204,000 or 34.8 percent of the estimated population of 6,500,000. If we go back to the 1943 census, we discover the labor force was 35.0 percent of the population. Thus the labor force has rather consistently amounted to about 35 percent.

In his July 26, 1970, address Castro discussed the labor force at some length because it was in part the basis for his estimate of future prospects for the economy. He estimated the 1970 population at 8,256,000, compared with an estimated population of 6,547,000 in 1958; there was thus a gain of 1,709,000. He defined the labor force as the age group 17 to 60 years for men and 17 to 55 for women. This definition is narrower than the one used in the 1950's, when the working force was considered to consist of all those 14 years of age and older. Even so, Castro estimated that 580,000 of the total gain in population was in the labor force. This proportion is slightly less than 34 percent but close to the percentages given above.

The census of September 1970 revealed a much larger population gain over the twelve years than Castro had estimated, amounting to roughly 2,000,000. (The total population count was 8,553,395.) Thirty-four percent of this gain would amount to an increase of 680,000 in the labor force. We may conclude, therefore, that the labor force in 1970 was proportionately the same as in 1957.

The magnitude of the population as revealed by the 1970 census was suprising even to the regime itself, which had underestimated the total by about 300,000. The steady emigration of more than 50,000 annually was thought to have brought the total population to an even lower figure than the official Cuban estimates. The United States Committee for Refugees (a private organization) has estimated that up to 1970 the Cuban migration to all countries amounted to 570,478. The most serious impact on Cuba of this migration was in its quality. As we shall see in Chapter 10, many of the emigrés were professional, semiprofessional, and managerial personnel, who were critically important in keeping the economy functioning. However, as the census figures show, there is still available a numerically large labor force.

Other Accretions to the Labor Pool

As a result of the drastic transformation of society wrought by the revolutionary government, there have been changes in the occupational patterns of the Cuban people. To the extent that fewer people are needed in certain nonagricultural occupations, we may surmise that the excess might be available for employment in agriculture.

1. One source of labor that could potentially function in agriculture, or release others to do so, came from the abolition of numerous occupations. Persons in insurance and real estate, brokers and middlemen of all sorts, rent collectors, travel agencies, tourist services in general, and many others, were no longer needed. Some tourist services remained, but since they were under monopoly control of the state, presumably fewer workers would be necessary. Besides, the tourist industry has virtually disappeared. Moreover, the abolition of the casinos and the national lottery released many people to the general labor pool. Prostitution was abolished officially and the practitioners assigned to trade schools to learn skills for productive work.

It is not possible to give a meaningful estimate of the number involved here, but certainly part of the 123,240 "salesmen and vendors" who were reported in the 1953 census and who would, of course, have been more numerous by the time their jobs were abolished in the 1960's, were released for other work. Private competitive retail establishments with adequate supplies of consumer goods on their shelves in 1958 would require many more salesmen than the same stores after 1962, when the shelves were emptied and practically all consumer items were rationed and distributed through state outlets.

2. While most of the large- and middle-size retail establishments were nationalized or "intervened" by 1962, there remained many thousands of small enterprises like coffee shops, bars, soft-drink stands, jewelry stores, laundries, dry cleaners, and other service establishments which continued in business. However, on March 13, 1968, Premier Castro declared a "revolutionary offensive" against them and in a few months an estimated 56,500 had been nationalized. Many enterprises such as bars, of which there were nine hundred in Havana alone, were closed permanently or placed on a two-day per week schedule. Where it was decided to continue some of the services provided by these businesses, the establishments were turned over to the Committees for the Defense of the Revolution to operate. Thousands of persons, deprived of their usual occupations, were urged to

take jobs in agriculture if they were physically able. Here was another minor addition to the labor pool.

3. Perhaps the major addition to the number of potential agricultural workers came through the incorporation of women in the labor force. Traditionally, Cuban women were not expected to work in agriculture. Thus the 1953 census reported only 10,054 female wage workers in this occupation. Of the remaining 240,000 women in the labor force in 1953, some 69,000 were domestic servants. Since domestic service was largely abolished by the revolution, most women in this occupation were released for other tasks. The other major group of 52,000 working women were engaged in manufacturing and crafts, and presumably most of them remained in those positions.

One of the most remarkable aspects of the revolution has been its attack on the old tradition that women do not work in the fields. This program is a phase of the "emancipation of women," something which has characterized other Communist states, although the latter were generally not faced with the same work tradition as was Cuba. It is reported that when Castro returned from his first visit to Russia in 1963, he told a meeting of the Cuban Federation of Women: "In the Soviet Union, women are a part of labor. Of course, Soviet women are very strong; and everybody, men and women, perform all sorts of work."[6] He strongly implied that Cuban women also should become more active in productive labor.

Even before Castro commented on his observations in the Soviet Union, a program was under way to enlist women for agricultural work. For example, in March 1963, the Cuban radio reported a meeting of 1,400 members of the Cuban Federation of Women in Victoria de las Tunas in Oriente province to discuss plans to "facilitate the massive incorporation of women into agricultural work . . . giving the combative Cuban women the opportunity to take an active part in the production process."[7]

The program is very active and pressure is applied by means of slogans, posters, radio and television propaganda, and meetings. During 1969 there were also 396,491 home visits, of which one in every four produced a recruit. According to *Granma*, difficulties in recruiting included "the weight of tradition," which said "the woman at home; the man in the street" or "a woman's career is marriage." Such attitudes were "hangovers from the past that still remain — and not only among women, but deeper in men, husbands, fathers and brothers."[8]

The goal for recruitment for 1969 was 100,000 women, and on January 15, 1970, the annual report of the Federation of Cuban Women noted that 113,362 women had been "incorporated" in the labor force, although not all of them were working at any given time. The report added that women were found to be "breaking old prejudices and incorporating themselves in construction of the new society."[9]

In part women are being employed to replace men in occupations which they can perform equally well. The men, in turn, are expected to join the agricultural labor force, attend trade schools to learn new skills, or accept unskilled jobs where they may be needed.

4. Another major enlistment of new workers has come through the Union of Young Communists (UJC). These are youth mainly of high school age who have been asked to constitute the Centennial Youth Column, in honor of the beginning of the war of independence in 1868. (The Castro regime relates its own revolution to the earlier one.) The program announced on April 23, 1968, called for the registration of youths 17 to 27 years of age to form a total "column" of 50,000 to serve for three years in Camagüey province. This province has had a major expansion of acreage for agricultural purposes; it also has a more sparse population and a greater need for labor from the outside than other provinces. As an inducement, the regime allowed the three years of work in Camagüey to take the place of compulsory military service. The youth were to receive a wage set by the Ministry of Labor, along with food, lodging, clothing, and some miscellaneous items.

On January 20, 1969, the head of UJC announced a plan to recruit 100,000 for the Centennial Column, but it was not made clear whether this was an addition to the original 50,000. The recruitment in this plan was for eighteen months instead of the three years originally called for.

Another 40,000 young people have been enlisted for two years on the Isle of Pines (now designated the Isle of Youth) to work primarily in livestock and citrus production. In all cases arrangements are made for the young people to continue their education.

5. In this address on July 26, 1970, Prime Minister Castro claimed there were 686,000 unemployed when the revolution took power. "A large number of them are working today; others have reached an age that makes them no longer fit for work; and there remain 75,000 who, neither housewives, students, nor disabled, simply do not work."[10] According to these figures, more than 600,000 were added to the labor force, less those who had retired.

It is not clear, however, where the figure of 686,000 unemployed came from. In the 1956–1957 study of employment and unemployment by the National Economic Council, 83.62 percent of the labor force was employed, and the strictly unemployed numbered 361,000 or 16.38 percent of the total force of 2,204,000. The group listed as "employed" included 154,000 "employed without pay by a relative." Another 150,000 were employed "less than 29 hours per week"; and another 27,000 were employed but without work at the time of the survey.[11] If these three categories are added to the 361,000 strictly unemployed persons, the total is 692,000, and this is probably the somewhat questionable method of treating the data that Castro's advisers have followed. At any rate, in 1958 the regime had an unused resource in the unemployed on which to capitalize, although there were clearly not as many as Castro claimed there were. It would be interesting to have an explanation as to what happened to the 600,000 persons added to the labor force, since the labor shortage persists. Above all, there would remain the question of how the labor force of 1958 with 31.1 percent unemployed was able to produce more than the much larger force employed in 1970.

6. For the first time we had in 1970 the spectacle of labor imports from abroad. More than seven hundred youths from the United States participated in cane cutting in early 1970. There was also a "brigade" of thirty-three from Rumania announced on March 9, 1970. Another brigade came from Bulgaria, along with groups from North Vietnam, North Korea, and other countries. These are relatively unimportant except for their propaganda value.

7. Finally we may mention another category of labor which, for want of a better term, we will designate "captive groups." There are

first of all the armed forces, consisting of perhaps 200,000 men and women. Some have been assigned to work in agriculture during critical periods. For example, an announcement in early May 1969 reported 40,000 at work in Camagüey province. The use of the armed forces is a clear addition to the pre-Castro labor force. It would have been an extraordinary situation indeed if Batista's army had been called upon to cut sugarcane.

Another such captive group is the school population from the fifth grade up, all of whom are subject to call for work in agriculture for periods of six weeks to two months. Then there are other institutional groups. Since the early years of the revolution, there have been labor camps for persons of varying degrees of disaffection toward the regime. Up to 1967 there were special works camps run by the army and euphemistically called Military Units for Aid to Production (UMAP). Some of the inmates of the labor camps are political dissidents; others are known to be religious objectors to the regime. There are also camps for sex deviants. Estimates of the numbers in camps of all kinds vary widely, ranging from a few thousand to eighty thousand. The latter figure may be far too high; official statistics are not available. We must add here also the thousands who registered for the "freedom flights" to the United States and who were immediately sent to agricultural work camps until they left. At the least, these groups worked for their board and keep. Even convalescing patients in hospitals may perform some simple tasks. A radio broadcast of March 12, 1968, announced that "inmates of the Psychiatric Hospital were working in the cane fields in Gabriel-San Antonio de los Baños region of Havana province. The doctors, nurses, employees, all are mobilized." These categories of workers cannot be combined for a total estimate, but it seems apparent that the total must far exceed the agricultural labor force of prerevolutionary Cuba.

Increasing Labor Output

Not only has the size of the agricultural labor force vastly expanded in the ways we have mentioned, but Cubans have been asked to work longer and if possible harder. The high labor standards of the old Cuba, won by the unions, have been voided. Workers are asked to put in longer hours, ten, twelve, or even more, and to forgo any extra compensation. Since 1967 union after union has taken a formal vote renouncing overtime pay. "The basic issue in the development of socialism," said Ernesto Guevara, "is the increase of production and productivity, even at the expense of sacrifice if necessary,"[12] and sacrifice seemed urgently needed in the early 1970's.

Productivity of the worker in capitalist societies increases usually by the introduction of labor-saving machines, better organization of work, and other methods. These, however, do not call for him to work longer or more intensely. The philosophy of the labor movements in such countries is based on the principle of maximum distribution of jobs among the supply of workers. For this reason, workers have resisted efforts to make them produce the maximum possible through their own strength and skill. But this arbitrary limitation of effort is precisely what the revolution opposes. It wants and urges workers to produce the maximum of which they are physically able. Says Mesa-Lago:

Before the Revolution the daily average for a sugar-cane cutter was 150 *arrobas* (one arroba equals 25 pounds). In harvesting the 1961 crop, cane-cutters working on state farms were exhorted to fulfill and overfulfill that standard. For the 1962 harvest, Ursinio Rojas, sugar-union leader, announced that "the cane-cutters must yield a daily average of 200 *arrobas*." During the 1963 harvest, the press hailed a "work hero" named Reinaldo de Castro, who had cut 1,900 *arrobas* of cane in a shift and had achieved a daily average of 1,280 *arrobas*.[13]

With such a vast increase in workers, regular and volunteer, men, and women, old and young, working longer hours, at an accelerated tempo, why has not production risen more rapidly? Despite the vast infusion of human labor, it has been difficult to achieve a production of sugar, for example, equal to that of the prerevolutionary years. The 1952 record of 7,298,000 tons was produced by 161 mills in an average of 133 days, with an average of "effective grinding days" of 117.[14] (The use of average days, it must be said, inevitably includes some centrals which required less and others that required more than the average.) Unfortunately, there are no such comparable averages for the period of the revolution. Nevertheless, the zafras of the years in which upward of five or six million tons were produced began in early November and continued into July of the following year. As we have already shown in Table 9, since 1964 the zafras have varied in length from 185 to 365 days.

The Distribution of the Labor Force

There are some justifiable explanations for the languishing agricultural production despite the enormous human resources that are being employed. In an address on March 13, 1969, Premier Castro gave a few reasons. "The effort devoted to road construction, hydraulic projects, and drainage, is gigantic and uses up much energy and time. It is true also that throughout the Spring, trucks and hoists were used in planting." He went on to emphasize the need to carry out "simultaneous plans — sugarcane, livestock, the 1969 harvest, and the 1970 harvest, the rice program and all the other plans."

It is no more than fair to say that the revolution has invested great effort in activities other than agriculture and the sugar industry, as we pointed out in Chapter 5. The list is an extensive one, but a few brief comments on the relation to the consumption of labor need to be made here.

1. Although the clearing and planting of new land occupied a considerable force, much of the work was accomplished with the use of bulldozers and tractors. On January 3, 1969, Castro announced that 6,138 machines were available for development, including bulldozers, earth-moving machines, power graders, power shovels, rollers, cranes, dump trucks, ditching machines, and oil-drilling rigs.

Castro might well have included the clearing of land along with road-building, hydraulics, and the other projects he listed as requiring a "gigantic" effort. Our point is that tasks so highly mechanized as these ought not to require a proportionate increase of human labor. Moreover, such land-clearing units as the Che Guevara Trailblazer Brigade were operated by the army. Further, army tanks were used in clearing brush and trees. It can hardly be argued that these activities called for a very heavy draft on the regular labor force.

2. On the other hand, the Havana greenbelt project certainly de-

manded a vast amount of human labor. Here, as elsewhere, the land was leveled and prepared for planting by machine. But the growing of millions of seedlings in large nurseries and their subsequent transplantation to the fields required enormous amounts of time from human beings.

3. The revolution has made a substantial investment in the construction of schools and hospitals throughout the island. Until a comparable census is taken, we will not know how much the number of construction workers has increased over the 65,000 reported in 1953. The number grew by 30 to 40 percent during the following years.[15] A 30 percent increase would equal 84,500. It is generally admitted that prerevolutionary construction was concentrated mainly in the urban centers and that such construction practically ceased after 1960. The rural areas are now being given priority, but admittedly not much rural housing has been built. Here were more workers for other tasks.

4. An effort has been made by the revolution to increase food production. The rice plan is part of this effort, of course, but rice is subject to more mechanization than such other crops as tomatoes, potatoes, or onions. These have called for much more hand labor.

5. Certainly among the major consumers of labor are the boarding schools, child-care centers, and numerous work camps. The logistics of keeping these units supplied and functioning must involve thousands of people beyond what was normally required before 1950, even though it must not be overlooked that prerevolutionary Cuba fed hundreds of thousands of people daily and that these services required a significant portion of the total labor force. Yet the transportation of thousands upon thousands of volunteer workers to the fields each day; the hauling of supplies of food and its preparation and serving; the maintenance of the dormitories; and all the other numerous tasks involved in operating such vast operations must require an enormous labor force.

In his address of March 13, 1968, Castro itemized some of the increases in the number of persons served meals: boarding schools, 389,300; public health and welfare, 108,500; recreation and sports, 16,800; fishing fleet and boat crews, 9,400; personnel for boarding schools, 50,500; sugarcane harvests and other mobilizations, 397,000;

and workers' dining rooms, 544,000. Castro noted that the total number of persons served meals daily outside their homes was 1,529,000 in 1968, an increase from 626,300 in 1965.

7. Livestock numbers may have been increased, but this industry is not a major consumer of labor. Only in the special breeding stations and in the expansion of dairy production would a significant increase in labor be required.

8. Several new production facilities have been constructed or are under construction, among them cement and fertilizer plants and electric generators. Similar work was under way before the revolution, however, and it is impossible to know whether proportionately more workers from the labor force are involved now.

9. The pouring of great masses of workers into agriculture, an unfamiliar industry to many, cannot fail to result in low average efficiency. There have been many complaints of inexperienced cane cutters damaging the cane for future growth, of workers failing to get the cane to the mill in time to prevent deterioration in the yield of sugar, and of fertilizer and other supplies delivered at the wrong time and then improperly cared for. Workers have been repeatedly exhorted to give better care to machinery.

10. The revolutionary government has undoubtedly made a substantial expansion of personnel in health and education, with a consequent increase in the burden on the labor force. In his July 26, 1970, address, Castro gave these figures on the increase of employment in social services:

	Health	Education	Scholarships
1958	8,209	23,648	15,698
1969	87,646	127,526	277,505

The figures are, however, misleading because they are not comparable. Before the revolution the public-health category included only personnel working in such activities as disease prevention, sanitation, registration of vital statistics, and so forth. The figure for 1969 included everyone engaged in health and medical care: doctors, nurses, technicians, hospital personnel, even the staffs of the three medical schools. All of these were included in the private sector in 1958. In public education the 1958 figure is obviously not comparable because numerous private schools have been omitted. The census of 1953 listed more than 38,000 persons who gave their occupation as "teacher," and this figure does not include education ministry personnel, janitors, and the like.

Indirectly Castro revealed in this July 26 speech that there were 200,000 persons in the armed services. (After enumerating those engaged in various services, he gave a total of 900,000 and said, "if we add the men engaged in the defense of our country, the figure goes over 1,100,000.") This would be nearly seven times the 30,000 men reportedly in the Batista army and constitutes a further draft on the labor supply. The increased number of scholarships takes some otherwise employable people out of the work force, but a large share of these are for the primary grades. Yet regardless of the noncomparability of the figures, the regime is undoubtedly using many more people in health, education, and defense than were employed in 1958.

In summary, then, we can reach certain limited conclusions about the size and distribution of the working force.

1. If the labor force in 1970 is considered to be 34 percent of the population enumerated in September 1970, then it seems clear that the Cuban government has proportionately as large a labor force as existed before 1959. In prerevolutionary Cuba, however, this labor force was not required to contribute unpaid labor, which in 1969 and 1970 added several hundred thousand man-hours to the work force.[16] This increase has been accomplished by voiding the gains in labor standards won by the unions under the capitalist regime which limited hours of work, provided vacation time, and so on. Furthermore, unused workers such as housewives have been recruited at great effort and with the application of social coercion.

2. One may reasonably assume that many fewer workers are required in trade and services than during the pre-Castro period. Food and clothing are distributed only on certain days and only through state outlets. Clothing is distributed just twice a year. The virtual disappearance of tourism has released thousands of persons for other tasks. Self-employed individuals, craftsmen of all kinds, small-store operators, and the like no longer exist. Farmers with more than 67 hectares of land were expropriated. Finally, it seems

113

doubtful that the regime is employing proportionately more personnel in construction than were used formerly.

3. In certain areas, the use of labor has been expanded. Cuba has a ballooning bureaucracy, both governmental and industrial. Certainly more people are involved in teaching school and servicing the boarding and semi-boarding schools and day nurseries. The health and medical establishment is probably using proportionately more labor than before. The armed services have been vastly enlarged by the revolution. The expansion of the fishing fleets and the merchant marine have also involved proportionately larger forces.

This numbers game, however, cannot be solved. We do not know how the large labor force is really being used, and how it compares sector by sector with the prerevolutionary structure. What is quite clear is that despite all the efforts of the regime to mobilize the nation's manpower, the goal of increased production has not been reached. It may well be that the French sociologist Raymond Aron is right in assuming that socialist regimes require great masses of labor. Speaking of the Russian Revolution, he has said: "It enlisted the masses and imposed forced savings, making a virtue of deprivation and overcoming inadequate techniques with the sheer weight of manpower."[17]

There is one further reason why the government is unable to harvest the sugarcane without mobilizing the entire nation. Returning to Leontief's question, "Why all the fuss?" — part of the answer is that the customary cane cutters "escaped" from the fields by joining the army or obtaining employment in the mushroomed bureaucracy. Those who remained became full-time workers for the state on the state farms. Since all the privately owned industries and enterprises were taken over by the government, there were infinite possibilities of getting on the state payroll. Peter Schmid, a Swiss journalist who visited Cuba in 1964, has described this remarkable growth in the bureaucracy:

The development of Cuba's bureaucracy strikes one as a flesh-and-blood confirmation of Parkinson's theory, according to which there is a cancerous increase of departments which must artificially create the tasks that justify their continued existence . . . [In Cuba] Czech and Hungarian experts worked out an organization chart for every

114

ministry and every industry, a kind of family tree with an immense number of inter-connected squares, each awaiting a name to fill it. No sooner was it filled than each square developed a chart of its own, officially requisitioning a house, in most cases taken over from a departed counter-revolutionary, obtained a car from the same sources, employed a number of secretaries, and occupied itself with the production of reports and order forms of newly nationalized industries. The most minute details of Eastern European procedures, no matter how absurd, were slavishly imitated.[18]

By 1967 it became clear to Prime Minister Castro that those sequestered in the bureaus must be driven or pulled out. "Everybody's lifelong dream," he complained on February 20, 1967, "is to land an office job." "There are factories, there are production units where the capitalist owner had three or four employees and we now have 25 or 40," he admitted. He also complained of the multiplication of business forms and, in apparent agreement with Schmid, said, "The forms represent one of the causes [of bureaucracy]. Thousands thought they were specialists in organization and started inventing forms." [19]

Lack of Incentive and Worker Morale

The disappearance of the professional cane cutters into the bureaucracy is only part of the story. There is also the problem of lack of incentive. In Fidel Castro's utopia there will be no money and no need for it. "In the future," Castro told the ANAP on May 19, 1967, "we will liberate ourselves from the ration books and from money in toto," the idea being that with an abundance of goods and services everything would be available without charge. But in order to achieve such a condition every citizen must work productively and he must work hard and long. He must do so, moreover, without material reward and only for the good of the whole society. This is the kind of citizen Castro visualizes as the "new man," free of selfishness and full of group consciousness, enthusiasm, and loyalty. Nonmonetary rewards are provided to the worker in badges of honor, in being designated as a "vanguard worker," or in being awarded free vacations or trips to other Communist countries. The Cuban worker, however, seems not to respond to such devices. High productivity is,

115

in short, not primarily a matter of numbers of potential workers in the population, but a matter of the workers' outlook on the future and what they aspire to do and to have.

The major incidence of absenteeism during the 1970 zafra raises serious questions about worker attitudes. "No one," noted Dumont in 1969, "has a direct interest in seeing that state enterprises are more efficient. This is very apparent. Even if, in general, the top managers have a lofty awareness of their national and revolutionary responsibility, at the same time they satisfy their thirst for power. As for the worker who suffers under a cruel sun and in badly ventilated barracks, he suffers even more when he gets complaining letters from his family, relating the multiple difficulties of daily life. At that point, he begins to feel he's had enough, and his production reflects it." [20]

There can be no doubt that worker morale is the basic cause of the faltering Cuban economy. The workers falter for many reasons. Some of them lack belief in the creed of socialism and faith in the system. Or, as the regime would say, they lack revolutionary *conciencia*. Others falter because of a general malaise after more than a decade of complete mobilization. They are weary of the sloganeering, the continual drumming of propaganda from radio, television, and loud speakers, weary of attending endless meetings. Many Cubans who once supported the revolution are disillusioned after years of worsening conditions and unfulfilled promises, of being denied the opportunity to work and accumulate goods and property for themselves and their families. Cuban workers under capable management built the substantial wealth which the revolution inherited in 1959. There is no doubt they are as ready as workers anywhere to work hard if they can see some chance of improving their lot.

The failure in production in 1970, not only in sugar but in other aspects of the economy, attests further to the low morale of the population. The analysis of the problem by the prime minister will be presented in the next chapter.

Chapter 7

How to Make People Work

On July 26, 1970, Prime Minister Castro delivered a remarkable address to the Cuban people. In what must have been an unprecedented speech by a head of government, Castro admitted to grave declines in many areas of production. He further confessed that he and other leaders of the government were in part responsible for the failures.[1] In comparison with the output during 1969, the prime minister reported, milk production in 1970 was down 25 percent; steel down 38 percent; fertilizer down 32 percent. The output of cement was higher than in 1969 but down 23 percent from 1968. Other categories of production had fallen short of projected goals: paper and cardboard, short by 5,900 tons; tires, 216,000 units short; batteries, 16,000 units short; leather shoes, one million pairs behind schedule and of deteriorating quality; textiles, short by 16.3 million square meters; soap and detergents, 32 percent short of plan; bread and crackers, in Havana 6 percent short of plan and 2 percent behind the production of 1969. Clothing of all kinds was in short supply, as were vegetables and fruits, both fresh and preserved.

There were a few brighter spots in the production picture. Castro reported that the manufacture of plastic shoes was on schedule and an output of ten million pairs was expected. The rice supply, the harvest of fresh fish, and the production of eggs for "indirect consumption" had all increased. Nickel mines were meeting their scheduled goals. Electricity production had increased 11 percent, but demand had risen by 17 percent and there were daily blackouts in the western provinces, due not only to insufficient generating installations but also to breakdowns.

Castro attributed this long list of failures to both "objective" and "subjective" factors. In the former category, he said, the chief problem was transportation, especially automotive transport. He blamed a lack of spare parts, which reduced the availability of machines, and a "high level of absenteeism." He went on to enumerate some of the consequences:

The following were the most important difficulties caused by internal transportation problems: delays in receiving trains with cattle from Camagüey and Las Villas, which resulted in a loss of weight in the cattle; nonfulfillment of the lard distribution plan and nonfulfillment of the plan for bringing milk bottles to the provinces. Practically all the beer, milk, and other bottles which are not imported are produced in the western part of the country, as is all the nonimported cloth. This requires shipping all this material east. Bottles for all the beer made in Oriente are produced in the western part of the country, in Havana.

Industrial goods pile up in the provincial warehouse of the Ministry of Domestic Trade in Havana. The plan for transportation of raw materials used for soaps and detergents, as well as the finished product, was not fulfilled. The transportation of silica sand for the production of cement and bottles, the transportation of steel bars, the transportation of fodder for the animals on state farms, and the transportation of bagasse for the paper factories in Las Villas were insufficient. There was a work stoppage in the nail factory in Santiago de Cuba due to a lack in the transportation of raw materials; and the national fertilizer production plan was not met because of low extraction of the finished product. There was a 36 percent drop in the number of railroad passengers, compared with 1969 in the January–May period, caused by the transfer of locomotives to the sugar harvest and the withdrawal of coaches from circulation due to lack of spare parts.

Castro then turned to the so-called subjective factors. "We must say that inefficiency, the subjective factor, is partly to blame for these problems . . . I am in no way trying to pin the blame on anyone not in the revolutionary leadership and myself."

How to Make People Work

In a speech on May 10 he had taken full blame for the failure to achieve the ten-million-ton sugar harvest: "In this matter of the 10 million tons," he said, "a basic fact is that the people have not lost the battle . . . We lost the battle. We, the administrative apparatus . . . We, the leaders of the Revolution . . ."

In a general sense it was true that incompetent management of the economy had led to the inability to reach production goals, and Castro correctly praised the workers for their own contribution to the zafra. Yet it was also true that the labor force had not put forth as much effort as it might have. Castro mentioned absenteeism in the transportation industry as a major cause of difficulties, and indeed there was widespread malingering, absenteeism, idleness, and dawdling on the job. A radio broadcast from Havana on October 26 reported that the problem of absent transport workers was a continuing one: "Due to absenteeism of transportation workers 554,000 persons were unable to travel during the month of September. A total of 1,847 trips were cancelled due to absentee workers."

The ideological aspect of the problem of indolence was set forth by Castro in two addresses in September 1970. "In a collective society, where man works for society," he told the Committees for the Defense of the Revolution (CDR) on September 28, "laziness must become a crime — a crime similar to stealing . . . The lazy person robs the people daily . . . This is one of the many problems affecting production. It disorganizes it — the lazy person, the absentee — he disorganizes it, complicates it, leaves the hardest part of the work for others to do."

Earlier, on September 3, Castro called the indolent the "new exploiters, because they do not work" although they receive without charge many goods and services produced by other members of society. A "rational and just society," he went on, had the "right to adopt measures of a coercive type" against such a minority.

Measures to Control Labor

At various times the revolutionary government has taken punitive action against workers who failed to give complete support to the regime. Laws passed in 1960, 1961, and 1962 gave the state complete authority over employment as well as control of the workers. These laws empowered the state to transfer workers from place to place and to decide what wages they would receive and what jobs they would perform. In late 1962 an identity card, the possession of which was compulsory, became an indispensable requirement for obtaining employment. Other forced registrations of workers were subsequently required.[2]

After August 1969 under the terms of Law No. 1225 every worker had to register in a "labor history file" and provide a history of his employment, an evaluation of performance for every job he had held, and detailed information about himself as a person. This file became a kind of visa for getting a job; it could be used, and it was used, as punishment by having the worker deprived of it.[3]

In order to increase the performance of labor, Law No. 1116 was passed in late 1964. This measure established severe sanctions against workers who failed to produce the amount set by the norms. As Carlos Rafael Rodríguez, the president of INRA, said in a radio interview: "Sanctions will be applied to correct anti-social attitudes, negligence, laziness, and to those that in some form or manner manage to work less than the eight hours established for all kinds of work . . . norms are only guides that should be adjusted to local levels by union leaders . . . and functionaries of the Ministry of Labor." [4]

Forced labor camps — the so-called Military Units for Aid to Production (UMAP) — existed from the early years of the revolution. Nine camps were identified and located on a map by the Cuban Economic Research Project.[5] Mesa-Lago and Hernández quote one section from a list of thirty-three derelictions that could result in a sentence to the labor camp for public employees and officials located in Pinar del Río in 1962: "(a) the negligence or inexcusable ignorance that might bring about the paralysis of an industrial plant; (b) the hampering of production or making impossible the fulfillment of the production goals established by the government; (c) the adoption of measures and decisions not oriented by the Ministry of Industry; (d) the employment of laborers without due authorization." The resolution added that after serving their terms "those punished for

120

violating the revolutionary norms . . . will be returned to their work or to new activities as determined by the Socialist State." [6] The UMAP as such were abolished in 1967 but forced labor camps continue.

A new approach to the problem of increasing productivity was outlined by Castro in an address to the Central Confederation of Labor on September 3, 1970: "We are going to commence the democratization of the labor movement. If the worker movement is not democratic, it does not serve. The worker that is truly elected by a majority, he comes as one with authority, not as some Don Nobody." Referring to this point again on September 28, Castro said, "The Revolution is entering a new phase in which a serious struggle will occur against the remaining vices, the old ones and new ones, the remaining weaknesses, and the remaining deficiencies, the mass organizations will also enter a new phase. Among other things they will also enter a new phase of democratization of the revolutionary process."

In making these statements, the prime minister was in reality recognizing that the party and administrative apparatus could not do the job alone and that responsibility would have to be decentralized. He warned that there would be "meetings, and meetings, and more meetings," which certainly proved to be the case.

The Law Against Loafing

The immediate implementation of the "democratization" process was a law against loafing (*vagancia*), first proposed as Resolution No. 425 by the Ministry of Labor on October 15, 1970. The resolution was used for discussion in meetings at approximately thirty thousand work centers throughout the country. The object was to hear complaints of workers and get their suggestions as to modifications of the proposal. These suggestions were the basis for the final legislation passed on March 15, 1971. But before final action was taken by the Council of Ministers, the proposed law was again discussed not only in the work centers, but also by all the mass organizations. This meant discussion by local units and members of the Federation of Cuban Women, the Committees for the Defense of the Revolution, the Union of Young Communists, the Centennial Youth Column, and the Association of Small Farmers, along with groups of students and members of the armed forces and the police. In all, according to the minister of labor Jorge Risquet, the law was discussed in 113,758 assemblies with a total attendance of 3,250,000.

The preamble of the law, as it was finally passed, observed that in contrast to the vast majority of workers there were those who attempted to live parasitically, without working, showing antisocial conduct, and setting a bad example for the new generation.[7] The preamble further declared that regular daily work was a social duty and one to be unavoidably fulfilled by men from age 17 to 60 who were physically and mentally able to work and women from 17 to 55.

Groups liable to disciplinary action under the provisions of the law were those who left their places of work for fifteen working days without justifiable cause, and those belonging to a work center who had been reprimanded at least twice by their work councils. The law spoke of such persons as *pre-delictivo de vagancia,* or predelinquent, and declared them subject to the following sanctions for a period of up to one year: (1) internment in a rehabilitation institution, doing productive work; (2) internment in a rehabilitation institution doing productive work at an outside job during the day but returning to sleep at the center; (3) home arrest while working under the supervision of employees at the delinquent's former work center and of the mass organizations near his home. (This would mean the Committees for the Defense of the Revolution or the Association of Small Farmers.)

These sentences could be suspended at any time by the labor organization that imposed them if the subject showed improvement in attitude and behavior. However, backsliders who had already been through the process of punishment were to get double penalties, that is, up to two years. Any individual or mass organization was authorized to complain to the police about persons whom they recognized as guilty of the "crime of loafing."

These features of the law applied to people already in the labor force. There remained the task of recruiting thousands of nonworkers. Presumably many if not all of these were identified when the census was taken in September 1970. It will be recalled that Castro

122

estimated that 75,000 of the "unemployed" group which existed in 1958 were not working. In addition, there were many teenagers who were not in school but who had not joined the labor force. In the fall of 1970 Castro estimated their number at about 400,000. A new regulation promulgated after the 1970 census required a continuous registration of all persons fourteen years or older and the reporting of any change in domicile to the police.

An observer finds it difficult to justify on economic grounds the time spent by 3,250,000 persons in discussions of the proposed law. At an assumed average of an hour and a half per assembly, the total time would equal well over five million man-hours. The regime, of course, was not figuring the cost economically, but rather as an educational investment. The issue was approached with caution, since there was a chance, considering the prevalence of absenteeism, that any measure that appeared too harsh would be self-defeating. As Fidel Castro warned in his September 3 address, "We must avoid at all costs simple solutions . . . We must act with political criteria, with intelligent measures." He noted that workers faced difficulties in connection with their employment; some, for example, had to travel great distances to reach their work centers. Other commentators have mentioned the delays caused by workers having to stand in line for meals at restaurants. For such reasons the anti-loafing legislation was broached with a degree of wariness in the hope that the extended discussions would cause many potential victims of the law to join the labor force voluntarily. This assumption was apparently borne out, because on the eve of the promulgation of the new law the minister of labor announced that some 101,000 persons had registered for work, about half of them new workers.[8]

The law provided the maximum penalty of the labor camp. Labor camps, as we have noted, were not a new feature on the revolutionary landscape, but a more extreme sanction was hardly feasible. The imprisonment of a delinquent worker would only mean losing whatever producing power the individual had. The logic of the situation suggests that the regime will continue to carry out the same measures that have been employed in the past, using exhortation and persuasion and, if these fail, public denunciation and the threat of the law. There are also other devices. Humiliation has been used. For example, during the 1970 harvest in Matanzas province some persistently absent workers had their names read over the radio and finally had their labor cards taken from them. During the search for suggestions for the law against vagrancy, one worker advised that the centers install beds and require absentees to sleep in the plant so they would be there in the morning. This suggestion amused Castro, who referred to it jokingly in one of his speeches, but as a matter of fact such a regulation was in a sense incorporated in the law. Persons attached to a "reeducation" work center who have jobs away from the camp are required to return each night.

Are Cuban Workers Prone to Loafing?

With such an enormous effort being devoted to solving the problem of idleness, laziness, and absenteeism, one may raise the question as to whether the Cubans are especially prone to such habits. There is a stereotype of the Cuban worker as somewhat casual, even lackadaisical, preferring to sit in the shade and strum a guitar. Some Cuban officials have projected just such an image. The Swiss journalist Peter Schmid quotes his Cuban guide as follows: "I don't understand these people . . . At the time of the Bay of Pigs invasion, these peasants took up their guns and enthusiastically hurried to their posts ready to lay down their lives for the Revolution. A few months later, I saw them dozing in the fields, shirking work. Why, I asked myself, are they ready to *die* for the Revolution but not to *work* for it?" [9]

In 1963 an American journalist on a visit to the land reform agency (INRA) in Havana was impressed by the "excessive use of slogans" to keep the revolutionary fervor alive. He told one of the officials that the slogans seemed "childish or sophomoric" and added, "If I were a Communist, I would not need them to do a good job." The official replied, "Ah, but you don't understand the Cuban mentality . . . If we don't keep goading our workers like this, they would go back to sleep. We have to keep needling them, reminding them that the work of the revolution is not finished. You may not need the slogans, but our workers do." [10]

124

Such comments may tend to reinforce the stereotype of the "lazy" worker but they do not validate it. The concept should not be used as an explanation for the current low labor productivity, which must be compared with the relatively high productivity during the pre-Castro years. Furthermore, Cuban exiles in the United States have proved themselves to be fully competitive in their new environment. It is possible, of course, to argue on historical grounds that the Cuban attitude toward work derives from an early Christian religio-economic tradition that regarded wealth as evidence of sin, in contrast to an essentially Protestant and Calvinistic tradition which exalted wealth as a sign of divine grace.[11] It would, however, be a mistake to give much emphasis to the Protestant ethic in seeking to explain low productivity in Cuba as compared with the United States.

The Significance of the Law

The main thrust of the 1971 law against loafing was to transfer responsibility for policing and disciplining reluctant workers from the government and the party to the local workers' councils in the factories and fields. Local labor unions were apparently strengthened for this task in 1970 by the first free elections of officers since the revolution took power. Instead of having to vote for a slate of officials who had been cleared in advance, union members were able to nominate candidates in an assembly. By the end of November 1970, for example, Radio Havana announced that 75,915 union officials in 16,745 locals had been elected from a total of 153,078 candidates.

It is unlikely, in my view, that the law will be harshly administered, although there is danger that in some work centers militants may press for the limit.[12] Moreover, even with increased vigilance the reluctant worker will find ways of evasion. Vagrancy, in its various meanings, exists in all societies. Capitalism has a builtin prophylactic against widespread vagrancy in the fact that workers are motivated by the prospect of "getting ahead," of making money and profits. But although the spirit of capitalism has powered production as no other system has done, it has not eliminated the unambitious

125

and the lazy. On the other side, Fidel Castro has committed his country to the creation of a spirit of socialism which he claims will excel capitalism in material and cultural rewards. In order to achieve this goal, he expects to form a "new man" through the process of education in all its aspects.

Chapter **8**

The New Man and the Old

While the economic achievements of the revolution have been disappointing, programs in the field of education have been conspicuously successful from a numerical point of view. The great literacy campaign of 1961 inspired widespread admiration, as did also the immediate extension of educational opportunity to practically all the children in the country. Both were noteworthy projects, planned and carried on during the crucial early years of the regime when many difficulties confronted it.

Education in Prerevolutionary Cuba

The need for improvement in education has been well documented. Many pages of my *Rural Cuba* were devoted to describing the forlorn conditions in the countryside as they existed in 1946.[1] Although the Cuban people have given the highest priority to education for their children, government leaders in the past repeatedly failed to provide adequate schools. Educational reform was a prominent topic in political discussions throughout the history of the republic. The first president, Tomás Estrada Palma, declared in 1902 that he wanted more schoolteachers than soldiers, but his political enemies did not grant him time and opportunity to realize his goal. Estrada Palma's policy was called to mind in 1946 by the remark of a tobacco sharecropper in Cabaiguán, who said, "I have never in my life had need for a policeman, yet I see them frequently hereabouts; but we do need a schoolteacher and one never comes." Incidentally, this man and his neighbors were privately paying an itinerant teacher to instruct their children.

Every political candidate for high office has paid lip service — and sometimes more, it is true — to educational reform. The Constitution of 1940, reflecting the deep-seated concern of the country, reiterated the long-standing requirement that all children from six to thirteen years of age attend school and that in schools operated by the state, province, or municipality tuition, books, and supplies should be free. Article 49 of the constitution further provided that the "nation shall maintain a system of schools for adults devoted particularly to the elimination . . . of illiteracy." With a naïve faith in monetary resources, the framers of the constitution specified that the budget for the Ministry of Education should "not be less than the ordinary budget of any other Ministry, except in the case of an emergency declared by law." The sad ineffectiveness of this provision was illustrated by the budget for 1946, which allocated to education nearly 30 percent of total expenditures. As it turned out, too little of the money found its way into the school system and too much into the accounts of corrupt officials.

A little calculation indicates that this budget figure would have been sufficient to provide an allocation of $35 per child if the five-year-olds were included or close to $50 per school-age child if they were excluded. This approximated the amount expended in several of the southern states of the United States, where primary school enrollment was more than 90 percent. In the school year 1942–1943, only 35 percent of Cuba's children attended school.[2] The tragedy of education in the prerevolutionary period was not the unwillingness of Cubans to support schools with their taxes, but the moral weakness of officials who betrayed the confidence which the electorate had placed in them.

But it would not be accurate to leave the impression that no progress was made in the years following World War II. The percentage of school-age children enrolled was 50.1 in 1945–1946, 58.7 in 1949–1950, and an estimated 56 in 1958.[3] There was thus actual retrogression in school attendance during 1957–1958, probably due in part to political unrest and actual warfare in parts of the country. It is important to note that the percentages for the years given were all less than those for 1907 (56), 1919 (61), and 1931 (71). Nevertheless, there was apparently some improvement in conditions between 1945 and 1960.

The rural school problem was complicated by the fact that Cuban farm people — like those in the United States — resided on separate tracts of land and were therefore scattered across the countryside. The one-room ungraded school was nearly universal in rural Cuba. Besides this fact, the predominantly urban-reared teachers were reluctant to accept rural teaching assignments because of the unsatisfactory living conditions, and few rural children were able to acquire the primary education which was a prerequisite to admission to a normal school. It was a vicious circle.

In an attempt to compel teachers to serve in rural areas, Batista created "sergeant-teachers," who because of their military status had to go wherever they were assigned. A rural normal school was specifically created to prepare them for their jobs. Batista must also be given credit for establishing some forty boarding schools where mainly rural children, including orphans, were provided with food, shelter, clothing, and medical care in addition to regular primary school instruction. These were prototypes for the numerous boarding schools of the Castro regime.

Another and more important problem was the centralization of responsibility for schools in the Ministry of Education. The founding Constitution of 1902 provided that the municipality should have primary responsibility for maintaining schools, but in the course of time this basic charge was eroded in favor of centralization in Havana. The consequence was a notorious neglect of the countryside. Had the responsibility and authority for elementary education remained with local elected boards of education, the history of Cuban rural schools would have been much more pleasant reading.

School Buildings. A condition which surprised an observer in 1946 was the apparent indifference of the government to providing structures in which classes could be held. Of the 7,516 schoolrooms reported in the census of 1943, only 198 belonged to the state and 49

129

to municipalities. Of the remainder, 1,249 were owned by individuals who granted them free for school purposes and 1,603 were rented.[4] As of 1949–1950 the IBRD mission reported a total of 7,579 schools, only a small increase over 1943. The number of state-owned schools had risen to 452, of which 172 were rural, but the vast majority of buildings were still rented from or provided free by individuals. At the same time, the mission reported that an additional 628 rural schools had been constructed under the Sugar Differential Fund.[5]

Information about school housing during the 1950's is scanty and comes from UNESCO's annual *International Yearbook of Education*. In 1951 thirty agricultural schools were reported in operation. In 1952 ten large six- and eight-room schools were built and "a number of" one- and two-room rural schools. In 1953 "many different kinds of educational institutions were built" and in 1955 "hundreds of pre-fabricated primary schools were erected in isolated rural areas." The report for 1956 announced a 20-million-peso construction program, and in 1957 there were "more than 60 school units [apparently urban], and 600 rural establishments." The first report of the revolutionary government in 1959 stated there were then 5,575 rural classrooms; 200 more were under construction along with 17 large city schools. Some progress in school construction was made during the 1950's, but clearly much unmet need remained.

Secondary Education. At the beginning of the republican period Protestant missions became active in establishing educational institutions, chiefly high schools. By 1956 there were ninety such schools with a total enrollment of 14,000.[6] The public secondary system included institutions which offered general pre-university education; teacher education; and vocational training. In 1958 there were twenty-one high schools with 37,248 students and teaching personnel of 1,180. The nineteen normal schools had a total enrollment of 8,899 and a teaching staff of 692. Of the vocational schools, twenty provided commercial training and twenty training in various trades and occupations. The total enrollment in these institutes was 15,698 with a staff of 1,377. In 1958 the 21 public high schools were supplemented by 108 private secondary schools sponsored by Catholics, Protestants, and nonchurch groups.[7] The high school offered a five-year course leading to the certificate of *bachiller.* The fifth year was devoted primarily to university preparatory courses in the student's chosen field of specialization. Few rural children were prepared for the university, and it was assumed they would enter trade or agricultural schools.

The Universities. There were four universities — three public and one private — in Cuba when the revolution came to power. The largest and oldest of them was the prestigious University of Havana, founded in 1721. It was the only institution of higher learning in Cuba until the founding of the University of Oriente at Santiago de Cuba in 1949 and Central University Marta Abreu at Santa Clara in Las Villas province in 1952. Both were authorized by Law No. 16 of November 22, 1949. In December 1950 further legislation authorized the establishment of private universities and the Catholic University of Saint Thomas of Villanova was founded by Augustinian Fathers from the United States.

The three new institutions were obviously only in the formative stages by 1959, but they represented an important development in higher education. The location of the two new state schools made university education accessible to more students than had formerly been the case. More than 25,000 students were enrolled in the four universities in 1958–1959. (All private schools, including the Catholic university, were abolished by the revolution.)

The University of Havana had thirteen faculties: philosophy and letters, education, science, engineering, agriculture, architecture, medicine, pharmacy, dentistry, veterinary science, law, social science and public law, and commerce. As in other Latin American countries, the most popular colleges were medicine, law, commerce, and education. The graduates of these colleges had the best opportunities for employment. Moreover, law and medicine carried high prestige. Law was a stepping-stone to political office, and medicine offered the possibility of private practice as well as governmental employment. The basic industry of agriculture, where engineering, veterinary, and agronomy graduates were most needed, suffered from shortages of trained personnel. Students who were able to meet the entrance requirements were usually not from rural backgrounds but from middle-class and largely urban families.

In summary, then, education in Cuba suffered from neglect during and after World War II, with the possible exception of higher education, where three new universities were established in the late 1940's and early 1950's. An impressive number of students was enrolled in the universities, but the emphasis on training for law and medicine to the neglect of agriculture and industry was a critical weakness. The gravest shortcoming of the educational system was at the rural primary and secondary levels. The generous financial allocations for education on the one hand and the poverty of educational facilities in the countryside on the other offer a doleful picture that was a disgrace to the government administrators responsible for it. The revolutionary government faced a major task in creating a better situation.

Literacy and the New Man

The aim of the revolutionary educational program, as we have mentioned, is the creation of the new man — the altruistic producer who works hard and unreservedly for the good of the whole society rather than to accrue material possessions for himself and his family. The great need in building the Communist state is a high level of production. Since the chief means of production are human labor and human ingenuity, the new man must be willing to work at whatever job the regime requires of him and to be educated for the range of tasks which must be performed. The economy is obviously in need of scientists who can solve the problems of production, of technicians who can apply the scientific solutions to the practical problems, and of a labor force to supply the brawn. Education is therefore geared to the production of the types of people required by society.

But there is also a moral, even spiritual, component of the "Communist man." Since he will be relieved of worry about providing his family with the necessities of life, he will be devoted to the ideal of cooperative labor for the good of everyone. As Castro has put it: "We work for ourselves by working for all, and we will be able to produce everything which we truly have the will to produce; everything that we need." The new man is thus (1) a productive worker willing to perform any task required; (2) an educated man trained for whatever technical or scientific field the regime may require; (3) a cooperative man imbued with the ideal of working for society rather than for self-aggrandizement; and (4) an obedient and loyal man who will respond to the calls of the regime.

Castro appears, without having said so explicitly, to be aware of the traditional distaste of many Cubans for manual labor. His expressed aim is to have every child know something about work.

[Our] schools will not resemble those institutions of days gone by where a minority of rich men's children went to study without gaining the least understanding of the meaning of work. And what reasons would they have had to know the meaning of work? If in that society work was done by the poor, if in that society the rich knew nothing of work, nor had any reason to know, it was because others did their work for them. Our children today will learn the meaning of work from the earliest age. Even if they are just six, and in first grade, they will know how to grow lettuce, how to produce a head of lettuce. Moreover, they will perhaps learn how to water a plant or care for a flower bed in order to make their surroundings more pleasant. They will do whatever they can, but the important thing is that they, as soon as they can reason, they will begin to develop the idea of how material goods are produced.

And they should also learn that such material goods do not just fall from the sky but must be produced through work. Thus they will acquire a noble concept of work, not the idea of work as something to be scorned, nor of work as a sacrifice, but rather as a pleasure, as something agreeable, the most ennobling thing a man can do, and which he needs to do. And this concept should not even include the idea that work is a duty, but rather a necessity, a form of investing our time in a worthy and useful manner.[8]

Clearly, if the new man was to be formed in the briefest possible time, it was indispensable to reach his mind through many avenues. The ability to read and write was, naturally, paramount. As we have pointed out earlier, Cuba had an excellent radio and television network and a very widespread distribution of receiving sets, but propaganda and indoctrination could not depend on the airwaves alone. It was also necessary to reach the adult population through the written word. "The struggle against the past," as the slogan had it, really meant a struggle against the values, aspirations, and ideology of the mass of adults in the population, who truly represented the past. If the old attitudes borne of life in a capitalist society were to be changed, adults would have to be taught to read the books and newspapers which could be used to alter their obsolescent point of view.

Making the new man out of the old was not a simple matter. In his address of July 26, 1967, Prime Minister Castro acknowledged that changing the thoughtways of the adult generation was the greatest task of the revolution. Referring to the assault on the Moncada Barracks, the anniversary of which was being celebrated, he enumerated other "fortresses" that remained to be attacked: the Moncadas of illiteracy, ignorance, economic underdevelopment, the shortage of technicians and resources of every type. "However," he added, "there remained the most difficult Moncada of all, the Moncada of the old ideas, of old selfish sentiments, of old habits of thinking and ways of viewing everything, and this fortress has not been completely taken."

It should not be forgotten that many generations and the entire generation living in our country at the time of the revolution was completely educated under the influence of capitalistic ideas, methods, and feelings. Many of these vices existed among our workers. Many of these concepts held sway. Logically, what Marx said was that in the historical process the workers and the exploited confronted the exploiters, that the working class was the class whose social function drew it together and made it capable of understanding and practicing socialism. That is absolutely true, but also absolutely true is the influence which these exploiting and ruling sectors exercised on the minds of the entire nation . . .

The Great Literacy Campaign

Illiteracy in Cuba had long been a major concern of responsible leaders. Rapid strides toward its eradication had been made in the early years of the republic and the percentage of literate Cubans increased from 43.2 in 1899 to 71.7 in 1931. Despite the political rhetoric that filled the air during every election campaign, little progress was made thereafter. The percentage of literates in 1953 was 76.4, only a slight improvement over 1931. The problem was mainly rural, for only 58.3 percent of the population in the countryside was literate in 1953.

134

The New Man and the Old

With power in his hands to do so, Fidel Castro announced in the fall of 1960 that the following year would be the Year of Education. Primarily, this meant a national campaign to wipe out illiteracy. Preparations had begun as early as April 1959 with the appointment of a literacy commission in the Ministry of Education. In the same year INRA, the agency which dealt with all rural problems, undertook some educational work in rural areas. Intensive preparations began with the creation of the National Commission in October 1960.[9]

Teaching materials were prepared, along with instruction manuals for the literacy tutors. In order to gauge the magnitude of the job, a census of illiterates was undertaken with the aid of teachers and volunteers. The aim was to discover all the illiterates who were fourteen years of age or older, especially those in the countryside. The census began in November 1960 and continued to the end of August 1961, by which time a reported 985,000 illiterates had been located.

The regular school term was cut short in April 1961 (a few days after the Bay of Pigs invasion), and teachers as well as pupils in primary and secondary grades were given two weeks of instruction before being sent out into the country. The student volunteers were called *brigadistas* and usually lived with the families they were assigned to instruct. They were organized in units of twenty-five to fifty under a local peasant leader, with a regular teacher to supervise their techniques of instruction.

In addition to the brigadistas, thousands of literate adults volunteered to instruct illiterates in their local neighborhoods. These volunteer teachers were called *alfabetizadores*. A third group, the *Patria o Muerte* Brigade, was set up in August, when it appeared to the Second National Congress of Education that the work was not proceeding as well as it should. This brigade was composed of 13,882 workers who were paid their regular salaries and sent into the rural areas to assist in the organization of the student brigadistas, provide them with supplies, and generally help in instruction.

Richard Jolly, using figures obtained from the "Official Report on the National Literacy Campaign," says that 271,000 persons were engaged in the campaign, divided into the following categories:

"Peoples' teachers," 121,000; Patria o Muerte Brigade, 15,000; professional schoolteachers, 35,000; and brigadistas, 100,000.[10]

The teachers of the illiterates ranged in age from ten years to over forty, but 87.5 percent were under twenty and 40 percent under fifteen. Fifty-five percent were girls. Of the total number of teachers, 52.2 percent were in the primary grades and 31.6 percent in junior high school. An important fact, to which we will refer to shortly, is that 88.2 percent came from an urban background.

When the campaign ended on December 21, the government announced the results that are presented in Table 10. After all the statistics had been assembled, the regime was able to report that of the 979,207 illiterates in the country, "707,212 adults have been taught to read and write. Considering that the population of Cuba is 6,933,253, and taking into account that, for various reasons, the benefit of alphabetization failed to reach 271,795 persons, a figure of 3.9% illiteracy in the total Cuban population is reached."[11]

Table 10. Results of the Literacy Campaign of 1961

Category	June 30	July 31	August 30	December 21
Illiterates				
Illiterates located	684,000	822,000	985,000	979,000
Illiterates involved in campaign in 1961	487,000	656,000	895,000	...
Persons studying	465,000	594,000	776,000	...
New literates: cumulative total	22,000	62,000	119,000	707,000
Remaining illiterates	...	...	...	272,000
Teaching Force				
Brigadistas	47,000	...	90,000	106,000
Alfabetizadores	145,000	...	178,000	174,000
Total teaching forces	192,000	234,000	268,000	280,000
Pupil/teacher ratio	2.4	2.5	2.9	...

SOURCE: Dudley Seers, ed., *Cuba: The Economic and Social Revolution* (Chapel Hill: University of North Carolina Press, 1964), p. 195.

Although the government has repeatedly claimed that the illiteracy rate is only 3.9 percent, the accuracy of this number may be questioned. For one thing, the figure for the total population of Cuba in 1961, used as a base of computation, was only an estimate.

No true census had been taken since 1953. One may further raise questions about the completeness of the "census" of illiterates taken by volunteers and about the degree of literacy achieved by the 707,000 new "literates." While the figures — for both population and the number of illiterates — may be approximately correct, the chance of error is great.

The Literacy Campaign in Perspective

The campaign was unmistakably a phenomenal national accomplishment. Its overall achievement has best been summarized by Richard Jolly:

In one of those massive mobilizations of whole populations seldom seen except in war, Cuba for 8 months mobilized over a quarter of a million men and women, schoolboys and schoolgirls, into a teaching force, transported half of them the length of the island, supplied them with 3,000,000 books and more than 100,000 paraffin lamps, and declared war on illiteracy. Before the campaign, the official rate of illiteracy was 21 percent. By December the government claimed that it was 3.9 percent. Some of the remaining illiterates continued to be instructed in 1962.[12]

Even if Cuba is not as free of illiteracy as has often been claimed, there were doubtless other advantages which accrued from the campaign. Both Jolly[13] and Fagen[14] have offered opinions on the impact of the experience. Both agree that the campaign had significance far beyond teaching 707,000 adults to read. It was above all a socially integrating experience for the nation as a whole. As Fagen puts it, "the literacy campaign, if not an overwhelming and unquestionable triumph from the scholastic point of view, was nevertheless seminally important in the evolution of the institutional life and political culture of the revolution."[15]

Fagen notes also that this was the first general mobilization of the whole population dedicated to the achievement of a specific goal. More such mobilizations were to follow, notably those for the annual sugarcane harvest. The regime learned how to organize such campaigns and especially how to utilize the mass organizations.

Jolly notes and gives examples of the political orientation of the

137

instruction book, *Venceremos,* and the teachers' handbook, *Alfabe-ticemos,* used in the campaign. This orientation, he correctly says, is in line with the announced policy of the revolution to use the educational system to promote its own purposes. Since the revolution expects to create the new man largely through education, it was inevitable that the illiterates would learn their letters in the idiom of the revolutionaries.

Considering the fact that illiteracy had long been regarded as over-due for elimination, it would be unjust to say that the campaign was solely politically motivated. The project was close to the center of the Cuban system of values and morally acceptable to practically everyone. But it was also a project which further enhanced the feeling of nationhood and was thus a stroke of political genius, whatever the results in raising the nation's level of literacy.

The justification for such a statement is to be found in the political condition of the revolution during the years 1960 and 1961. As we have related in Chapter 2, 1960 was an especially turbulent year, characterized by the heated controversy with the United States that culminated in the rupture of diplomatic relations; the domestic tur-moil arising from the confiscations of property; the flight of many thousand people from the island; and the steady drift toward com-munism which dismayed so many Cubans. Strong dissent, and even some pockets of armed resistance, continued in 1961 and there was also the fear of invasion. All these factors called for some action of a positive character, over and above the mere forcible repression of political dissenters. Such a positive project was the campaign against illiteracy. Its ostensibly apolitical character gave it superior political potency.

Thus after a period of instruction and indoctrination 100,000 brigadistas, mostly from the cities, went off to the hills and plains to live with families, work with them, and teach them how to read and write. The experience could not help being a socializing one for both sides. Fagen quotes a "perceptive Cuban educator" who very well summed up this aspect of the campaign:

Our campaign . . . has put the youth of Cuba in direct contact, on a daily and prolonged basis (for almost a year), with the peasants and mountain folk, the poorest and most isolated people on the island.

The New Man and the Old

. . . This extensive experience in communal life cannot help greatly increasing understanding among the various classes and strata of the population. . . . (During the campaign) the entire populace could participate in the tasks of the revolution . . . [which was] converted into a true mass movement.[16]

Elementary and Secondary Education

The literacy campaign directed mainly at adults was something of a crash program with tremendous propaganda value, but education of the children is in the long run of far greater importance to the regime. After it came to power the revolutionary government lost no time in preparing temporary schools in which large numbers of children could be accommodated as wards of the state, supplied with food, clothing, medical care, and given formal instruction. The school-construction program that had been launched in 1956 was continued and expanded. In 1959 the government reported in the *International Yearbook of Education* that it had under construction two hundred rural schools of one or two rooms with living quarters for teachers, and seventeen large city schools as well. The report also enumerated 3,200 private and 16,800 public classrooms but said that in order to accommodate the 1,600,000 children of school age it would be necessary to construct 2,000 urban and 10,000 rural schoolrooms. Former military barracks were reportedly remodeled to serve as schools, as were also many of the private residences confiscated from the wealthy exiles. The rapidity with which school enrollments increased is shown in Table 11.

Undoubtedly conditions approached the chaotic during the first two or three years as hordes of children entered the classrooms, many of them past the usual entrance age and perhaps most of them in school for the first time. Officials in the Ministry of Education faced an almost insoluble problem in finding space, teachers, and teaching materials. More than two-fifths of the pupils were in the first grade. Who would teach the extra 375,000 pupils in the primary grades? Many regular teachers had declined to teach because of the Communist orientation of instruction. Some had already chosen exile; others were to follow. Yet, as was done in the literacy campaign, the

Table 11. Number of Teachers and Pupils in Primary Schools, 1958–68

Year	Teachers	Student Enrollment	Number of Pupils per Teacher	Percentage of Pupils in Grade One
1958–59	17,355	717,417	42	27.9
1959–60	24,443	1,092,264	45	42.2
1960–61	29,924	1,136,277	38	39.6
1961–62	33,916	1,166,267	34	39.2
1962–63	36,613	1,201,286	33	37.9
1963–64	37,041	1,280,664	35	36.0
1964–65	38,473	1,323,925	34	31.9
1965–66	41,925	1,321,768	32	29.3
1966–67	43,056	1,363,899	32	26.2
1967–68	46,910	1,391,478	30	24.4
1968–69	47,876	1,444,395	30	...

SOURCE: Data for 1958–68 from JUCEPLAN, Dirección Central de Estadística, *Compendio Estadístico de Cuba, 1967*, unnumbered tables on pp. 32–35; and for 1968–69 *Granma*, January 12, 1969. On July 26, 1970, Castro reported 1,560,193 primary school pupils for the year 1969–70.

authorities called on high school or primary-grade students to instruct the beginners. There was an apparent potential reserve of teachers, inasmuch as the census of 1953 reported 38,815 individuals who gave teaching as their occupation. How many of these were really teachers and how many were *botellas* (sinecures) one cannot know. Neither can we know how many were primary teachers. Nevertheless, there were only 17,355 actively teaching in the primary grades in the year 1958–1959. This number was increased by some 7,000 the following year, according to the official figures, and the additional teachers were presumably available in the population.[17]

The Drop-Out Problem

Educational leaders soon discovered that it was one thing to put several hundred thousand additional children into schoolrooms and quite another to keep them there. Table 12 gives the figures on dropouts as reported by the government. The original data gave the enrollments by grade for six successive years. (Reports for the full six grades were available for only five years.) In order to present the material more simply, the number of sixth graders for the respective series was subtracted from the initial matriculation in the first grade to obtain the number of drop-outs from the groups that originally enrolled.

Table 12. Primary School Drop-Outs during the First Five Years of the Revolution

Year	Initial First Grade Enrollment	Sixth Grade Survivors	Drop-Outs	
			Number	Percentage
1958–59	199,922	75,910	124,012	62.5
1959–60	461,112	81,521	379,591	80.2
1960–61	449,416	91,211	358,205	79.8
1961–62	452,544	89,192	363,352	80.3
1962–63	454,976	99,000	355,976	78.2

SOURCE: Adapted from JUCEPLAN, Dirección Central de Estadística, *Boletín Estadístico 1966*, Table XII.3. Figures for the sixth-grade enrollment in 1962–63 were announced by Castro on December 12, 1967.

Every country has a drop-out problem, but in a crash program such as Cuba undertook the magnitude of the problem is greatly increased. The loss of 80 percent which prevailed over these five years was indeed extremely serious. Although there was an apparent improvement in the figure for those who entered school in 1962–1963, the difference is only a minor one. More pertinent in indicating a trend for the better may be the percentage of pupils who enrolled in first grade but who failed to reach the second grade, as shown in the accompanying tabulation. In this series we can use later figures and get a better perspective.

Year	*Percentage Failing to Enroll in Second Grade*	Year	*Percentage Failing to Enroll in Second Grade*
1958–59	.... 11.6	1962–63	.... 50.7
1959–60	.... 56.9	1963–64	.... 46.6
1960–61	.... 50.0	1964–65	.... 38.0
1961–62	.... 53.6	1965–66	.... 33.3
		1966–67	.... 30.9

The first year of education is obviously the testing time for student survival. The casualties for this crucial period were around 50 percent during the first five years of the revolution. If instead of basing the percentages on the previous year's matriculation, we were to base it on the total number of drop-outs over the five subsequent grades, the proportion of loss from the first-grade enrollments would run about 60 to 70 percent.

It is easy to understand the difficulties in retaining students during the early years of the regime. Many of the teachers recruited were younger than some of the students, and pupils who were two, three, or even more years older than the usual first-grade child would inevitably feel uncomfortable. In addition there were undoubtedly many parents who were reluctant to send their children to school because of the Communist-oriented curriculum. Poor teaching was inevitably another of the problems which contributed to the large drop-out rates of the early years.

The decline in first-year losses after 1962 may indicate a gradual improvement in the teaching personnel. It also reflects, no doubt, pressure on the students to work harder in order to obtain promotion from one grade to the next and, above all, to graduate from primary school. The government recognizes that the most important step is graduation from primary school since this achievement is a prerequisite for high school education and perhaps eventual entrance into the university or one of the technical institutes. Moreover, it is clear from the original data on which Table 12 is based that mere enrollment in the sixth grade does not mean automatic graduation. Of those who entered elementary school in 1958 and reached the sixth grade, for example, only 54.2 percent graduated. Nearly 73 percent of the next year's contingent graduated and in the following years about 80 percent of the sixth-graders completed their primary education.

The regime has been constantly concerned with the drop-out problem. Prime Minister Castro has seldom failed to mention the importance of school attendance in his addresses. Education and the elimination of illiteracy have been high priority interests from the first days of his government. Those among the drop-outs who failed to reach the level of literacy will be added to an untold number of those involved in the campaign of 1961 who have lapsed into at least functional illiteracy.

This is not to say that the drop-outs of the five first years of the revolution will never attain literacy. Without doubt many of those first graders were boys and girls in their teens who had never before been in school. As we have already noted, for social reasons they might not have wished to continue in primary school with children six and seven years old. Other educational programs are available which will enable many of them to continue studies in their places of work, at night school, or by correspondence courses. Moreover, practically all the boys and many of the girls who failed the first grade will eventually be inducted into the armed services, where they will be required to continue their studies. Through these and other programs, it is possible that most of the drop-outs will eventually become literate.

The pressure of the government on children and their parents to attend school is applied in many ways. The Ministry of Education has promoted the organization of parents' councils, the purpose of which is "to get parents cooperating in the work of the schools and actively involving them in political and mass organizations in educational work." "Through school councils," the official statement continues, "parents will be encouraged to keep close tabs on the conduct of their children in and out of school, their attitudes [and the] time they devote to their studies."[18] Another organization enlisted in the campaign for school attendance is the CDR (Committees for the Defense of the Revolution). There are reportedly more than three million adults in these vigilance committees throughout the country. They are asked to have representatives visit parents whose children are not in school or whose attendance is irregular.

It seems clear, however, that not only has illiteracy not been eradicated in Cuba, but that the hoped-for universal primary education has not been achieved. In March 1968 Castro reported that there were still 50,000 to 100,000 children between the ages of six and twelve who were not attending school.[19] There can, of course, be no such thing as instant grade school education. Yet it is also apparent that from a quantitative point of view, education has taken a great leap forward. Its magnitude is shown by the information summarized in Table 13.

The absolute figures are indeed impressive. However, it must be kept in mind that according to government estimates the population increased from 6,548,000 in mid-1958 to 8,205,000 in the corresponding period of 1969. When calculated in proportion to population, the

Table 13. Comparative School Data for 1959 and 1969

	1959		1969	
Category	Number	Per One Thousand[a] Population	Number	Per One Thousand[b] Population
Schools	7,567		14,726	
Elementary school students	717,417	109.5	1,444,395	176.0
Secondary school students	63,526	9.9	172,144	20.3
University students	25,599	3.9	40,147	4.9
All teachers	17,355		47,876	
Junior and senior high school teachers ..	2,580		10,499	
Higher education instructors	1,053		4,449	

SOURCE: Tabulated from information given by Castro on January 3, 1969, and reported in *Granma*, January 12, 1969.

[a] The total population in 1959 was 6,548,000.

[b] The total population in 1969 was 8,205,000.

enrollment figures for the elementary, secondary, and university levels of education are still impressive, but less so than the raw data themselves.

The Quality of Education

Observers from the United States have remarked the efforts of the regime to inculcate in Cuban children a feeling of hatred toward the United States and toward what they term "Yankee imperialism." Even reporters generally favorable to the revolution have commented on this aspect of education. As James Reston wrote in 1967, "the New Man of Castro's dream is getting an education in hate and violence. The Cubans are probably too friendly by nature to develop into a nasty little militaristic Sparta, but the propaganda and the expanding educational system seem to be going this way."[20]

Herbert Matthews has made a similar comment on the quality of the revolutionary education: "All boys and girls are now educated within a Cuban totalitarian system that glorifies the 'socialist world' and vilifies 'Yankee imperialism.' They and their professors are deprived of knowledge of the world outside Cuba and are given distorted or strictly limited pictures of life and events in other countries. Foreign books and magazines are scarce."[21] Leo Huberman has also pointed out that "there is justifiable criticism of the quality of instruction in the Cuban educational system — professional educators decry the low standards . . ."[22]

Dr. Erwin Roy John, an American physician, attended an international medical conference in Cuba late in 1965 and was permitted to travel freely throughout the island. Among the places he visited was the Camilo Cienfuegos School in the Sierra Maestra. While his general opinion of the revolution was favorable, he provides an interesting illustration of the political content of education by citing questions that were written on the blackboard in the infirmary classroom:

(1) What do we say when we are accused of exporting revolution? A. Revolution cannot be exported, only ideas.

(2) What can Cuba offer to other people? A. Ideas and examples on how to work and help the people.

(3) Where did our revolution come from? A. Our workers, farmers, and students.

(4) When is it necessary to make revolution? A. When conditions are like those in Venezuela, in Nicaragua, in Costa Rica.[23]

No discipline is free from political content in Cuba. Even mathematics can be used to promote the cause of the revolution. Fagen has provided a sampling of exercises from the arithmetic workbook used in 1962 as a basic text in the Cuban Schools for Worker and Peasant Education:

In the United States there are six million unemployed workers, of which three tenths are white and the rest Negroes. What part of those 6 million unemployed men are Negroes? . . .

Imperialism knows no other type of relations between States except domination and subjugation, the oppression of the weak by the strong. It bases international relations on abuse and threat, on violence and arbitrariness.

Between January 3 and June 10 in 1961, North American military airplanes violated Cuban air space 3 times in the month of January, 15 in February, 17 in March, 9 in April, 8 in May, and 10 in June.

145

What was the average monthly number of violations of Cuban air space by North American military airplanes?[24]

Conclusion

Education facilities were vastly expanded by the revolution, and an effort of heroic proportions was made in 1961 to eradicate illiteracy. The government claimed that some 700,000 illiterates were brought up to the first-grade level of literacy. Furthermore, adult schools for workers and peasants were established everywhere. Although the claim that illiteracy was eradicated may be questioned, there were doubtless other benefits in the social contacts between young people from the cities and the rural population.

There is nothing new in the virtues desired in the new man, except the emphasis on altruism, not as voluntary but as required behavior. Work for the good of society has always been valued highly in the Judaeo-Christian tradition and generously rewarded in public recognition. The difference is that in Western society the individual is allowed to work for his own material aggrandizement, something that is strongly condemned in the concept of the new man.

People in non-Communist countries are shocked by the brazen use of education as a means of propaganda, but the Cuban government claims that "education as an ideological super-structure is closely linked with the means of production," that "throughout the history of human society, education has been a product of the social classes which dominated at each stage," and that the "content and orientation of education are therefore determined by the social classes which are in power."[25] Now, it claims, the social classes in power in Cuba are the workers and peasants and it is they who dictate the content and orientation of education. One is constrained to add that the "workers and peasants" had little to do with the decision, but then, how does one answer the strange upside-down semantics of Communist theoreticians?

Chapter **9**

Neutralizing
the Culture-Conserving
Institutions

Education, as everyone is aware, is acquired by the child in many ways, and formal schooling is sometimes the least of the influences which shape his character and personality. The most important of these influences is, of course, the family. It is preeminently the institution that inculcates the values of the culture and the norms of behavior. In the process of growing up, the child learns informally from his siblings as well as from his parents and, very important, from his peers in the neighborhood. The school and family are supplemented and complemented by the church and various other community organizations and social institutions.

As the Cuban Revolution sought to alter an entire society, with its network of social organizations and shared values, it had to resort to drastic means. Cultural continuities had to be broken and the stream of tradition diverted from its old channel into new ones. In the long run this would be accomplished (if at all) through the school system, over which the state now had complete control, but for the immediate future it was necessary to reach the adults. The literacy campaign was the beginning of what the prime minister called the assault on the Moncada of ignorance.

147

Adults of whatever educational level are inevitably the special target for a regime which aims at nothing short of the complete transformation of a society and its values. It is the adults who are the carriers of the old tradition and who have been processed for life in the old system. Their children can be processed for the new system, but only if the parents can be persuaded or compelled to accept radical changes in the educational system. Hence the position of the adult group in a dictatorial regime aiming at radical departure from old cultural norms is one of the most unhappy and frustrating.[1]

In 1961 accounts circulated clandestinely of a proposed law known as *Patria Potestad* (state custody), providing that children from three to ten years of age were to be placed in child-care centers (*circulos infantiles*). These reports set in motion a flood of emigration of both parents and children, but especially of the latter. It is not certain that adoption of the law was really planned, though subsequent developments give credence to the possibility that it was. In any case, the regime found it necessary to set up restrictions on emigration and then in late 1965 to arrange a daily airlift that by the end of 1971 had carried more than 250,000 Cubans into exile.

The Demise of the Free Press

The attack on the Moncada of ignorance assumed specificity when the regime made its assault on the four culture-conserving institutions which provided hard-core resistance. These four were the free press, organized labor, the church, and the family. The first two were taken by force or attrition in the early days of the revolution.

Castro gave assurances during the early months of his regime that he had no intention of restricting the press. He justifiably outlawed the customary government subsidies on the ground that they were a form of corruption. The practice had given the previous government a measure of control over the press because no more than a handful of the twenty Cuban daily newspapers existing in 1956 were able to pay their way. From his headquarters in the Sierra Maestra, Castro condemned the practice of subsidization and the resulting censorship and promised complete freedom.

This was not the outcome, however. There were some fifteen daily newspapers in Havana when Castro came to power on January 1, 1959. By February 1961 only six survived. The withdrawal of subsidies and the loss of advertising due to the confiscation of retail stores and other ordinary advertisers made their continued publication impossible. The venerable *Diario de la Marina* was brought down by the workers themselves when they began writing footnotes to its editorials. One such "footnote" said that "the contents do not conform to the truth nor to the most elemental journalistic ethics." With the demise on May 11, 1960, of this widely respected newspaper, the regime was in full control of the press.

The broadcast media — consisting of 160 transmitters serving some one million radio receivers and 23 television stations — were used freely and without limit by Castro from the beginning of his regime. By September 12, 1960, when CMQ, the leading television and radio chain, was taken over, the airwaves were completely under the control of the revolutionary government. Newspapers, radio, and television were all turned to the service of the Communist propaganda machine. This was also true of the production of films.

The Attack on Organized Labor

It was not a workers' revolution in Cuba. On the contrary, the organized Cuban workers were strongly anti-Communist. Through their unions they had won many benefits, as we have previously noted. The right to strike was recognized. The worker had freedom of choice in regard to employment and employer. Other established benefits included paid vacations of one month for each eleven months worked and four paid legal holidays. Workers in pre-Communist Cuba were protected against arbitrary discharge by employers. The procedure for discharging an employee was complicated and often presented serious difficulties for entrepreneurs, but at least the worker had protection rarely enjoyed by workers in other countries.[2]

These and other benefits which the workers had achieved made them anxious to preserve the status quo of free enterprise rather than turn to the Communist system. Thus control of labor organizations was not a simple matter to accomplish, although it was an essential step for the leaders of the revolution. On the eve of the Castro takeover, the Central Confederation of Labor (CTC) was composed of thirty-three national federations of industries and six provincial federations. These federations had a membership of 2,490 individual unions and more than one million members.[3] At the time Batista took over in 1952, Communists controlled only 20 of a total of some 3,000 unions and had only 11 delegates out of a total of 4,500.[4] The CTC, it may be noted here, was originally organized in January 1939 under Communist leadership. This was during the first regime of Batista. Its control by Communists subsequently fluctuated as various administrations either sought or shunned Communist support on the basis of political expediency. The degree of influence which Batista's later opposition had on the Communists in the CTC is not recorded.

Unlike the attack on the newspapers, which was fought by attrition and mainly indirect methods, the fortress of labor required a frontal assault. Raúl Castro moved strongly into the labor situation during the Congress of the Cuban Confederation in late November 1959. He is credited with directing the strategy which resulted in the divorce of the CTC from the Inter-American Regional Organization of Labor, an anti-Communist group. This led to an invitation from Cuba to other Latin American groups to join in a "revolutionary labor confederation." Although the usual strategy of the Communists is to infiltrate the top echelons of labor organizations, they found stiff opposition in the CTC election in November 1959. Fidel Castro himself intervened to break down this resistance in the name of unity. The result was the pushing aside of three anti-Communist members of the executive board, two of whom represented the union of Catholic Worker Youth. Four of the thirteen members elected were either Communist party members or close followers of it. The important post of director of relations with unions abroad went to a party member and, most important of all, that of secretary-general of the confederation, went to David Salvador, an ardent supporter of Castro and at the time a suspected Communist. This suspicion was apparently unfounded for in the spring of 1960, after a violent argument with the minister of labor, Salvador tried to flee the country but was caught and imprisoned.

Thus, although a slate of directors originally backed by the government was rejected by the workers because it contained the names of known Communists, the influence of Fidel Castro's personal plea for unity resulted in effectively handing over control to the Communist regime. Castro's control was further consolidated by his appointment of a trusted associate, Augusto Martínez Sánchez, as minister of labor.

Instead of rising spontaneously against their presumed "oppressors," workers have proved to be a very resistant core of the old order. Castro admitted as much in his July 26, 1967, address. No doubt workers form a large proportion of the inmates of the forced labor camps.[5] There apparently remains a serious problem of "reeducation" of the workers and peasants, and only their ultimate replacement by the new men now being processed will solve it, if at all.

The Weakening of Marriage and the Family

Since it is the family more than any other social institution which acculturates and socializes the child, any plan to change radically the existing society must attempt to lessen if not eliminate its influence. Far from considering marriage as a sacrament, Socialists have always argued that the union should be simply consummated and registered. As for the children, they have reasoned that the sooner they could be taken from the parents the better. Why, it has been asked, should an ignorant parent be presumed to know how to rear children properly? Why not place them under the care of experts trained for the job?

Among the earliest decrees of Lenin after he attained power in Russia were two that concerned the family. On December 19 and 20, 1917, respectively appeared orders on "The Dissolution of Marriage" and "Civil Marriage, Children and Registration." These decrees did away with the obligatory ecclesiastical marriage ritual and with headship of the husband over the family. Marriage was to be a civil function and free. All that was required was for the couple to register with the civil functionary who kept the records. Illegitimacy was abolished whether due to the failure of parents to register or to simple cohabitation.[6]

The sweeping early decrees in the USSR may have been simply an expression of the hostility of the new regime to every practice that had grown up under capitalism. It certainly was an expression of hostility to the church. As later events proved, the Communists could not afford to destroy the family, since to do so would be to create social chaos. The family in any kind of society is a means of social control and an important factor in social stability. Even a revolutionary regime, which always has its beginning in chaos, must establish order very early if it is to consolidate itself.

Fifty years after Lenin's decrees, Cuba's regime announced similar legislation. Law No. 1215, dated December 8, 1967, required that a couple who desired to marry need only present themselves with two witnesses at the Collective Law Office and sign an affidavit. "That's all," reported Radio Havana, "you enter engaged and in a few minutes you leave just married." Before the revolution Cuban law required a couple to submit documents showing whether they were single, divorced, or widowed, but this requirement has now been waived.[7]

Cuba has weakened the family, however inadvertently, by various reforms, including the emancipation of women. Since women are now an important part of the labor force, including that of agriculture, they are mobilized for work in the fields in various places where they are needed, and sometimes far from their homes. The husband is likewise subject to volunteer work in agriculture and may be separated from his wife and family for considerable lengths of time. Moreover, if a man happens to be one of the more reluctant "volunteers," he may find himself in a forced labor camp for two years or longer.

Meanwhile, large numbers of children have been put in boarding schools and see their families perhaps only one month of the year. In many cases even children between forty-five days and six years of age are cared for in child-care centers. Thus there is not only frequent separation of husband and wife, sometimes for long periods of time, but also the separation of parents from their children.

Having separated husband and wife through the manipulation of the labor force, the state could easily assume the complete care of children as a corollary act. The boarding school (*internado*) is a favorite institution for this purpose. The official report (*Boletín*

152

Estadística 1966) showed 136,131 scholarships of this type (*becarios*) in 1966. In 1970 over 250,000 were reported. There were also semi-boarding schools for rural children, but only where a graded school was available. Such a school is the one at Cangre in Havana province. There rural children are transported from their homes by bus in the morning, given breakfast, lunch, and dinner, and returned to their homes for the night. Children in the full boarding schools are not only fed, but also clothed, housed, and provided with health care, along with instruction.

Youth in work camps such as those on the Isle of Pines (renamed the Isle of Youth) likewise have all their maintenance needs met and along with their work programs are required to take courses of instruction in formal classwork. Since the ability and willingness to do manual work is one of the characteristics of the new man, these youth camps are of special importance. In this connection the Centennial Youth Column should also be mentioned. This "volunteer" youth brigade, noted earlier, was recruited by the Union of Communist Youth to participate in the sugarcane harvest, particularly in the eastern provinces of Camagüey and Oriente. The Union of Communist Youth is an organization especially designed to facilitate the indoctrination of young people. Its counterpart for the earlier ages is the Pioneers. Great efforts are made to enroll all the eligible youth in these two groups. Parental objections are common but usually unavailing, as pressures come from various sources, including the Committees for the Defense of the Revolution (CDR).

The emancipation of Cuban women from the home and some of the responsibilities of child-rearing has been accompanied by a dis-emancipation of men, if one may use such a word. Male workers no longer enjoy the degree of freedom of choice they possessed before the revolution. We have indicated earlier the process of transition from free to regime-controlled labor. Many workers who resisted incorporation into the revolutionary system have been sent to forced labor camps and prisons.[8]

Most of the working men, however, are under the strict control of the unions to which they must belong. The CTC has the responsibility for mobilizing labor and getting it to the places where critical needs exist. The staffs of the bureaucracies are asked to operate on a

153

basis of one week in the field and three weeks on their usual jobs. Many are now asked to volunteer for a two-year stint, probably on one of the state farms. The regular armed forces consist of 200,000 most of whom are men.

The continual mobilization of men and women for special tasks and emergencies is hardly conducive to stable family life and the parental exercise of responsibility and authority for the children. Insofar as divorce is an index of family instability, it is relevant to report some statistics on marriage and divorce recently published by the government. While the data cover only the first eight years of the revolution, they are indicative of a trend. (See Table 14.) The fluctuation in the number of marriages is due to the efforts of the regime to legalize all common-law marriages, which caused a fictitious statistical increase in the years from 1960 to 1963 and again in 1964. At the same time, these fluctuations distorted the ratios in the final column of the table.

The effect of extended separation of husband and wife is always painful and sometimes devastating. One visitor in 1963 reported that many of the wives left in Havana had resorted to prostitution. An-

Table 14. Marriages and Divorces in Cuba, 1958–68

Year	Number of Marriages	Number of Divorces	Divorces per One Hundred Marriages
1958	30,658	2,551	8.3
1959	32,345	2,735	8.5
1960	65,037	3,472	5.3
1961	74,067	4,575	6.2
1962	60,799	5,877	9.7
1963	56,613	7,497	8.9
1964	47,368	7,933	16.7
1965	67,323	8,937	13.3
1966	46,084	9,347	20.3
1967	51,918	10,667	20.3
1968	84,620	15,357	18.1

SOURCE: For 1958–66, JUCEPLAN, Dirección Central de Estadística, *Compendio Estadístico de Cuba, 1967*, p. 13. Marriages are reported by the Civil Status Register (*Registro Estado Civil*). Divorce statistics are from the records of the Courts of First Instance (*Juzgados de Primera Instancia*). The data for 1967 and 1968 are from C. Paul Roberts and Mukhtar Hamour, *Cuba 1968* (University of California, Los Angeles, 1970), pp. 77, 80.

other more recent (1967) visitor interviewed a wife whose husband had been in a forced labor camp in Camagüey for more than a year. She worked to support their children. "It is hard for me," she is quoted as saying, "but my babies are the ones who suffer most. They have forgotten their father."[9] The disruption of parental care for the children is one side of the coin. The other side, and from the viewpoint of the revolution, the more important, is the "emancipation" of children from family influence before their "virgin minds," as Castro calls them, can be infected with the old culture.

The Neutralization of the Church

The famous dictum of Marx that religion is the "opium of the people" governs the policy of Communist regimes regarding the church. All regimes have attempted to suppress organized religious life. Although Cuba, like other Latin American countries, is nominally Roman Catholic, the Church has never been able to establish itself strongly there. One important historical reason is that in the War of Independence the Church was firmly on the side of Spain. During the republican era priests were mainly recruited from abroad and were not always of high quality. Relatively few Cuban youths chose the priesthood as a career.

Nevertheless, the Catholic Church was the most important religious organization. After Cuba's independence, Protestant missionaries from the United States established missions in the island. These were predominantly Methodist, Presbyterian, and Baptist. They made a major contribution to the nation through the operation of excellent secondary schools, conducted in such a way as not to arouse open hostility on the part of the Catholics. Indeed, the schools were often in effect supported as community schools and enrolled more Catholic than Protestant students.

In later years some of the newer sects gained footholds in Cuba. Among these the most important were the Jehovah's Witnesses. Also of increasing importance were various Pentecostal groups. The Jehovah's Witnesses penetrated areas where there were no churches and where priests visited only rarely, if at all.

155

The Roman Catholic Church. The revolutionary government was soon confronted with the outspoken opposition of the Catholic hierarchy, as the latter sensed the growing influence of communism, toward which it is notoriously hostile. The year 1959 was marked by Catholic support for the regime in the early months but a growing caution and skepticism as the year wore on. The Vatican recognized the new government early in 1959. The reforms proposed by Castro were praised by the hierarchy and applauded by the other religious leaders as well.

The Church had reason to hope its opinions and attitudes would be respected because Fidel Castro had received part of his education in Catholic schools. The Bishop of Santiago de Cuba, Msgr. Enrique Pérez Serantes, personally intervened in Castro's behalf in 1953 and saved him from execution. Thus the hierarchy doubtless felt they had some claim on him and were more and more distressed as they witnessed his steady shift to communism. By early 1960 it was apparent that communism was taking over in Cuba and the hierarchy began open resistance. In May Bishop Pérez publicly recognized the Communist danger and asked Cubans to "separate themselves from this implacable and oppressive enemy of Christianity." In succeeding weeks he issued additional pastoral letters attacking the spread of communism. In one of these he said: "It can no longer be said that Communism is at the door, because in truth it is within, speaking powerfully, as one who is on his own property." On one occasion, as the bishop read a pastoral letter, a squad of militia entered the church and began singing the Cuban national anthem. When he ordered them to leave, there was scuffling between members of the congregation and the militia; the police arrived and arrested not the militiamen but the church members.

In July a mass held at the Havana cathedral for victims of the revolutionary firing squads provoked another disturbance by a mob. As the worshipers left the cathedral, they were greeted with cries of "Viva Rusia," to which they answered, "Cuba, si; Rusia, no." The interchange of insults continued for several minutes and, according to Phillips, eventually the police arrested twelve women, six youths, and two priests. None of the hecklers who had initiated the encounter were arrested. Such heckling was reportedly common at numerous churches.

Church leaders had been loath to create a direct confrontation with Castro. In August, for the first time, the nine bishops of Cuba issued a joint pastoral letter. Conciliatory in tone in many respects, it endorsed agrarian reform; industrialization; reduced living costs; the construction of homes, schools, hospitals, and recreational facilities; and the effort to eradicate dishonesty in public administration. But the letter also strongly emphasized the opposition of the Church to communism. In response to the letter Castro took to the airwaves and during the course of a four-hour address charged that the revolution was being "provoked by a group of counterrevolutionaries who have wanted to seek shelter in temples."

On August 9 Cuba's second-ranking prelate, Msgr. Evelio Díaz, warned that unless there was freedom of worship without heckling religious services would be suspended.

This statement brought a vigorous retort from President Osvaldo Dorticós Torrado, and press and radio attacks on the Church were intensified. As the Vatican expressed "sorrow and concern" over church-state relations, Fidel Castro denounced the church's "provocation" as the work of "Scribes and Pharisees . . . serving Yankee imperialism and its partner, Franco." On December 6, 1960, Castro charged that Catholic churches and schools were making "criminal campaigns against the Revolution." After another pastoral letter from the cardinal and bishops, a bomb exploded in La Caridad Church. On December 8 Castro made his most severe denunciation of the Catholic Church, calling the priests Fascists and Falangists and repeating his earlier statement that to be anti-Communist was to be against the revolution. Promising the "destruction of everything old," he told the Church to stick to religion and philosophy and leave politics to him.

In 1961 the government seized all church property, including the schools, and accelerated the departure of foreign-born priests and nuns. The reason for taking over the parochial schools was given by President Dorticós: "The teachers today must occupy the trenches and positions of combat in education to defend the Revolution and

157

its culture" from those who use the schools for "criminal work against the Revolution." "The foremost counterrevolutionary enemy in this regard," he said, "were the Roman Catholic parochial schools of Cuba."[10]

In 1961 Christmas nativity scenes, Communist style, showed a Cuban *bohío* (hut) as the birthplace of Jesus. The three Wise Men pictured in the crèche bore a striking resemblance to Castro, Guevara, and Juan Almeida (chief of staff of the army). Among Castro's statements on the Church were these remarks: "Those who condemn the Revolution would condemn Christ, and they would be capable of crucifying Him because He did what we are doing." "To betray the poor is to betray Christ; to serve wealth is to betray Christ; to serve imperialism is to betray Christ." "The Church has lived with all regimes, why not with socialism?"[11]

The Protestant Denominations. While the Catholic Church bore the brunt of the Communist attack, Protestant groups likewise suffered. The government took over their schools as well as any income-producing property which they owned. There was some persecution of individuals. Fifty-three Baptists — forty ministers and thirteen laymen — were arrested as late as 1965 on charges of spying for the United States. The *Christian Century* (April 21, 1965), which reported this incident, also commented:

> While Castro was in the Sierra Maestra, Christians of all kinds — especially Presbyterians and Baptists — were wildly enthusiastic about the new deliverer, and gave him direct aid. After Castro came to power . . . and his leaning to the left began to show, Cuban Christians became ambivalent about him. Some remained loyal, some deserted him, and some praised his social revolution out of one corner of the mouth and damned his drift towards Communism out of the other. . . . Apparently Baptist leaders are now so thoroughly disenchanted with Castro that the government must consider them a threat to the present regime, whether or not the charges against them are true."

But undoubtedly the most indigestible group for the revolution has been the Jehovah's Witnesses. There were reputed to be 15,000 of them, although the sect does not report membership statistics. The Witnesses very early came under the condemnation of the regime for refusing to salute the flag, a problem which the United States has often encountered with them. According to *Newsweek* magazine, this refusal stimulated Castro to exclaim: "We cannot tolerate this irreverence to the Fatherland." He further accused the sect of being an agent of the CIA.[12]

The fate of the fifty-three Baptists whose arrest was reported is not known. Doubtless some of them were sent to labor camps. Paul Kidd, a Canadian reporter, was able to gain access to a labor camp without the knowledge or permission of top government officials. The camp contained 120 persons, none of whom "were either political prisoners or criminals; rather they were people who had been active in what is left of Cuba's shattered religious life — particularly Roman Catholics and Jehovah's Witnesses — or others loosely termed by the government as 'social misfits.' "

The Jewish Community. In 1958 the five Jewish congregations in Cuba reportedly included about 10,000 members. By 1969 only 1,000 remained. A rabbi who visited the island in 1969 reported, however, that all five congregations were still active and not subjected to any harassment. In summarizing his impressions, the rabbi reported:

> Speaking with many Jews of varying outlooks — some sympathetic to the revolution, some neutral, some hostile — I found unanimous agreement on one point: the revolutionary government of Cuba has been beyond criticism in its respect for and consideration of Jewish religious needs. In most cases, of course, the government has been neither interested nor involved, but in such matters as cemeteries, religious personnel, or ceremonial articles from abroad, some coordination has been necessary.[13]

The Relaxation of Religious Control

In the main, the regime has been able to achieve a large measure of control over the churches. However, such control is by no means absolute. Although parochial schools have been closed, worship in the churches apparently goes on without major hindrance. For example, during 1966 Dr. Erwin Roy John visited a priest of the Church of San José at Holguín in Oriente province. The priest told him that in the early period of the regime there had been some harassment; for a time the police kept a list of persons attending the church. In 1966 his congregation consisted of about 1,200 persons present for Sunday services. There had been more before the revolution, but some left "for economic reasons." The members were able to support the priest comfortably. Religious instruction was limited to the church and the home, since parochial schools were forbidden. Finally, the priest described the confiscation of church land as a severe handicap.

A report from the English author Graham Greene in 1963 also indicated the regime's toleration of religious observance. Greene characterized as "invincible ignorance" a statement by Bishop Fulton J. Sheen that the "church in Cuba was persecuted in the same way as the church in China." "Perhaps it is a fortunate thing for the world that Fidel Castro was educated as a Catholic," Greene commented, "for here in Cuba it is possible to conceive a first breach in Marxist philosophy (not in Marxist economics) — that philosophy as dry as Bentham and as outdated as Ingersoll." The English writer described a curious incident in connection with an anniversary observance of the 1957 attack on Batista's palace, which had been led by the deceased José Antonio Echeverría. The chairman of the occasion read as a tribute to Echeverría the latter's own political testament but omitted the sentence: "We are confident that the purity of our intentions will bring us the favor of God, to achieve a reign of justice in our land." This omission brought Castro to his feet and he based an entire speech on it, saying in part: "Can we be so cowardly, so mentally crippled, that we have the moral poverty to suppress three lines? What kind of concept is this of history? . . . Can such a manner of thinking be called Marxism? We know that a revolutionary can have a religious belief. It does not exclude anyone." [14]

What Castro has to say on the subject of religion is of course important, though his remarks are, to say the least, not always consistent. Perhaps more important is what actually happens. In this respect it is relevant to note a report in the *Christian Century* (May 29, 1963) of a meeting of the Cuban Council of Evangelical Churches, held in Camagüey and attended by one hundred Evangelist leaders. During 1962, it was announced at this meeting, the

160

Cuban Bible Society had distributed 27,000 Bibles, 35,000 copies of the New Testament, and 100,000 other pieces of Scripture. The council is composed of Methodists, Presbyterians, Friends, American Baptists, Free Baptists, the Salvation Army, the West Indian Mission, the Evangelical Theological Seminary at Matanzas, and the United Bible Societies.

A handbook published by the information department of the Ministry of Foreign Relations, undated but printed about 1965, stated that the official policy was freedom of religious activity of all kinds, with official cooperation to help the work of priests, ministers, and rabbis, and freedom for them to travel throughout the island and to attend meetings abroad.

One may conclude that once the state had demonstrated its superiority over the churches, eliminated religious control of education, and taken over church-owned property, there was little left for the regime to accomplish by further harassment. By reverting to a practice of toleration, with such exceptions as it might decide to make of individuals, the government could even benefit by allowing those who wished to do so to continue their religious observances.

The new generation, of course, will be weaned from religion as far as possible, and this is the major objective, but adults are likewise exposed to antireligious propaganda. An article in *Granma* (January 1, 1969) told of the "ideological struggle" among the peasants at San Andrés, one of the model communities. "One aspect . . . is the work directed toward the elimination of old religious beliefs and superstitions that have taken deep root, old concepts that tend to disappear as scientific knowledge is more fully understood and the people refute through their own intimate conviction old and harmful practices once they have at their disposal the formidable arsenal of the modern course of science."

Frank Soler of the *Miami Herald* (June 7, 1970), reviewing the condition of the church in Cuba, expressed the judgment that the church "has precariously survived . . . by maintaining a delicate balance between limited challenge and uneasy coexistence with the government. The price has been high. And the final result, despite the present apparent rapport, may still be eventual church annihilation. Not through blatant official repression but through gradual attrition."

The Outlook

There is scant basis for hope that the liberties of press, assembly, and religion will be revived. The press, having lost all semblance of freedom, mouths the tiresome propaganda of the revolution. Even good friends of the government describe it as bad; Leo Huberman says that "most of the magazines and all of the newspapers are of scandalously poor quality." [15] The labor unions are an arm of the administration and of the Communist party. Members are subject to rigid discipline and continuous indoctrination in Marxism-Leninism.

The two most important conservers of the old order — the family and the church — have both been weakened. Since the revolution the number of priests has declined from 723 to 238, although the population has grown by two million people. Without doubt, the churches will continue to experience the hostility that characterizes communism. Not only will there be no instruction in traditional beliefs in the schools, but children will be taught that religion is mostly myth and superstition.

No sensible observer can fault the regime for giving new opportunities to women, a reform long due, or for its provision of facilities for education and child care. For most Cubans, nevertheless, family life will continue to suffer. Relations between husband and wife have been undermined, and the family has largely lost control of the children. The divorce rate has risen spectacularly.

In summary, it seems that the main bastions — the main fortresses, to continue Castro's analogy — of the old order have been largely brought under the control of the government. The church, the family, and the other culture-transmitting institutions have lost much of their former strength. It is likely that they will go on losing power, and the government appears to want to accelerate the decline.

Chapter 10

Structural
and Organizational
Change in Cuba

In this chapter an attempt will be made to describe the changes that have taken place in the class structure and the social organization of Cuba. As we shall see, the old structure has been severely modified, as have the organizational institutions through which many social functions are carried out. At the same time the restructuring of the pattern of social stratification has brought a new leadership into control, with its own modification of the social organisms through which its power is exercised.

We begin the discussion of social stratification by referring to Karl Marx, who posited a two-class system consisting of the owners of the means of production and those whom they employed. This view was based on Marx's observations of capitalism in the Europe of the early nineteenth century, a place and a time in which workers lived in the utmost poverty, and men, women, and children worked twelve hours a day or longer at wages determined by the employer. The Marxian class concept led to the conclusion that if the owner group could be eliminated and its property turned over to the state, there would emerge a more egalitarian and much improved world for the workers.

163

But this class theory is quite inadequate. One does not need to be a professional sociologist to recognize that other factors affect the status position of individuals and groups in society. For example, within the so-called owner class there are many gradations of status, as there are in the employee group as well. And status or prestige on a scale from high to low is what class and social stratification are all about. Yet it is true that the economic dimension is of great importance. Thus we should add to the Marxian concept the dimensions of income, wealth, and occupation. In addition there are such further determinants of status as family background, education, ethnic origin, and power and authority. It is apparent to anyone that class or status is a phenomenon of many facets. It is, one hopes, also clear that social stratification based upon one or more of these dimensions is common to all social systems.

One more point should be made before we go on to specific discussion of Cuban society. This concerns the value system which controls, as it were, the functioning of these dimensions. Whether a given occupation has high or low prestige depends on how the members of a given society rank it on a vertical value scale from high to low. The value system motivates individuals to strive for those things which they perceive are given high rank on the value scale by their respective social systems. Some persons will succeed better than others in satisfying their desires because of variation in what Max Weber called their "life chances." This is not another determining factor, but a consequence of a combination of the dimensions already mentioned.

The Old Cuba

Cuba was formerly a capitalist country with an extensive range of occupations. All the factors or dimensions of social stratification we have mentioned were operating. There were visible gross inequalities in the distribution of wealth and income from the very rich to the very poor. This inequality was noticeable in both the urban and rural sectors. The social strata could be observed by noting the factors of occupation, level of education, style of life, obvious presence or lack of wealth and income, and even place of residence in the urban centers. Yet in attempting to categorize the population into the usual upper, middle, and lower classes in 1946, one found that the kind of work a person did was apparently the most important factor in classifying him. A person who worked with his hands, a manual worker, could hardly be considered a member of the middle, and certainly not of the upper, class even though his income might be greater than that of a salesman or accountant. This condition made it difficult to arrive at a general characterization of the social structure.

Moreover, it seemed impossible to lump both rural and urban segments together and treat them as a homogeneous unit, although they shared many common values and traditions. Churches, political parties, and other nationally based institutions had both rural and urban members, yet the hierarchy of classes and status positions differed in the two areas. Let us consider first the urban condition.

Urban Cuba

The society of Cuban cities shared many features with other urban societies of Western civilization. There were the usual extremes of wealth and poverty and a labor force engaged in the innumerable occupations involved in manufacturing, trade, finance, and services of various kinds. In Havana and to lesser extent in other cities of the island, there was evidence of great wealth in the luxurious residential suburbs; at the same time squeezed in among the grand houses were the *solares*, the urban slums where lived the domestics employed by the neighboring well-to-do. There was no problem in identifying the rich and the poor. What was troublesome was the classification of those ranged between the two poles.

The truly wealthy people lived according to an ancient tradition inherited from Spain. The conquistadores who came to the New World in search of gold had no intention of engaging in physical work. After the native Indians had been virtually annihilated during the first fifty years of settlement, Africans were imported as slaves to take their place in the mines and on the haciendas. But manual labor was something only the slaves were to perform, not the settlers from Spain. The hidalgo tradition forbade it.

165

In 1946 it was easily observed that this tradition continued and that it applied to the women as well as to the men. Upper-class women had the services of two or three domestics. As a rule there was a cook, a housemaid, and a nurse for the children. The wife was seldom seen outside the house, except when she went to church or was driven to the shops by the *chófer*. The same was true for the husband. He not only did not drive his car, he did nothing toward the upkeep of the house and lot. A gardener looked after the exterior, and if a light switch needed repair the chófer took care of it.

To a large extent this style of life was common to the professional group as well. Insofar as doctors, lawyers, judges, architects, and other professionals were able to afford it, they followed the same pattern. Even white-collar workers in the offices, salesmen in the stores, and other lower upper-class personnel tried hard to see that at least one servant was employed and that the appearances of an upper-class life style were maintained.

Ethnic Groups. The most significant group other than those descended from European stock was that composed of the descendants of the African slaves. Cuba always claimed that there was no discrimination on the basis of race, and it is true that the laws did not recognize skin color. Yet the fact remains that Negroes were not fully represented in the upper levels of occupations and were over-represented in such lower groups as domestic service and skilled and unskilled work. Inevitably, therefore, their incomes were less and their level of living accordingly lower.[1]

Another rather important group of non-Europeans were the Chinese. They were descended from the indentured workers imported into Cuba after the elimination of slavery in the nineteenth century. They were, as in so many other countries, engaged in the operation of laundries and restaurants, and in the growing and street-peddling of truck crops. Although not numerous, they occupied a special stratum in the urban structure.

The Middle Class

The major difficulty in describing the social class structure of the prerevolutionary period was in deciding whether there was indeed a middle class. Certainly, there were the professionals, the semiprofessionals, and the owners of small and medium-sized business enterprises who are usually designated as belonging to the middle group. In Cuba they tended to elude identification with those who did any manual work. One soon learned that income was an incidental factor, not a determining one. The consequence of the crucial factor of manual labor led the writer to decide there were only two main classes, the dividing line between them being the kind of work performed. The social class schema observed in 1946 was therefore as follows:

A. *Upper class,* consisting of all those who performed managerial tasks and clerical work and who were descended from upper-class families regardless of their current state of wealth and income.

1. *Upper upper,* consisting of the very wealthy, the top governmental officials, and some professional men who combined high professional prestige with considerable wealth and family tradition.

2. *Middle upper,* containing the majority of the professional group (doctors, lawyers, university staff, engineers), a number of the sugar *hacendados* and colonos, managers of sugar mills, medium to large landowners, proprietors of medium-sized businesses.

3. *Lower upper,* consisting of the smaller proprietors, elementary and high school teachers, bank employees at the clerical level, small colonos who owned their land, government workers at the lower professional level (but exclusive of those holding *botellas,* offices held which did not involve any actual labor), bookkeepers and accountants, small landowners.

B. *Lower class,* consisting in general of those who did manual work, and who were descended from families of this class.

1. *Upper lower,* consisting of many smaller shopkeepers, government employees of the non-civil service type, garage and other mechanics, bus and streetcar conductors and motormen, barbers and beauty parlor operatives, etc., small farmers, cash and share renters.

2. *Middle lower,* consisting in general of common laborers, domestic servants, agricultural wageworkers.

3. *Lower lower,* consisting of street vendors and beggars.[2]

No insistent claim is made for this arrangement, and certainly the writer would not expect that whatever validity the classification had in 1946 necessarily persisted to 1959. On the contrary, a case might be made for the gradual adaptation of the Cuban urban class system

167

toward that of the United States, with a tendency to give greater prestige value to manual work. There is much to be said for a three-way classification of Cuba, and in the further discussion of the matter we will use it, instead of the system worked out in 1946.

It is likely that the middle class increased both in number and in influence between 1946 and 1959. This is especially true if one includes in this class, as some Cuban writers in exile do, such occupational groups as professionals, artisans, small and medium merchants, commercial agents, colonos, managers and "high" employees (apparently meaning highly skilled), administrators, and proprietors. It has been estimated that in 1958 the middle class equaled 33 percent of the labor force.[3] The size of the middle class by the time Castro came to power impressed Ernst Halperin when he visited Cuba in 1961:

. . . about 15 to 20 percent of the populace may be said to have had, at the time of Castro's take-over, a living standard, if not an income, approximately as high as that of the average business or professional man in the United States. And the bulk of the numerous lower middle-class, and of the skilled blue-collar workers as well, were certainly no worse off than their counterparts in France and Germany. . . .

The Cuban middle-class is educated, moreover, and politically articulate. Castro's movement itself was, in its early stages, largely a middle-class revolt. Today the private sector in small and medium industry, in the crafts and in retail trade is still considerably larger in Cuba than in any country of the Soviet bloc, or, for that matter, in Yugoslavia.[4]

This estimate of the percentage of the work force in the more affluent categories, while less than that given above, could well be close to the mark. It may also be true that the stigma of manual labor has become less marked, so that skilled labor especially could justifiably be considered in the lower strata of the upper levels, as given in our model, and thus be included in a middle class as generally conceived. In sum, if we consider a three-class model for Cuba, the middle class apparently becomes a kind of residual group between the more easily recognized upper and lower classes. Its size depends on how one evaluates the various occupations given in the census, and only detailed studies in Cuba by competent authorities in the field of sociology could arrive at a more authentic classification.

Rural Society

The rural world offered a somewhat different set of problems in defining the social structure. First of all, in any comprehensive list of occupations farming would rate rather low, most probably in the lower class in the model presented earlier. For this reason it seemed necessary to discuss social stratification in the urban and rural sectors separately. People who tilled the land, in Cuba as elsewhere, were in a world which urbanites tended to regard as inferior to their own. Such workers were called *campesinos* (peasants) and given a low prestige rating. Often they were called *guajiros*, a somewhat more derogatory term. Nevertheless, within the farming complex there was much variation.

It appeared to be true in Cuba as in most rural societies of the Western world that prestige was closely associated with the relation a person had to the land, that is, whether he was an owner or not. In addition, income and wealth were highly important. As reported in the 1946 census, the tenure groups and the percentages in each were, in round numbers, as follows: managers, 6 percent; owners, 31 percent; renters and subrenters, 33 percent; sharecroppers, 21 percent; and squatters, 9 percent. Strictly in terms of tenure, this might serve as the model of stratification, but as we have indicated tenure is only one factor. Certainly land ownership was a highly important status-giving influence, because it provided values beyond economics in the element of security and of freedom to work according to one's desires and ambitions. It also provided a family home. These values, in part at least, were extended to nonowners by the Sugar Coordination Law of 1937 and the law of 1952 (discussed in chapter 5) which gave security of occupancy to the nonowners including squatters.

Within the owner group there were many variations. Some had access to capital which enabled them to purchase machinery, while others continued to depend on ox-power. There was also variation in the amount of land utilized and especially in the availability of other factors important in production, including not only machinery but livestock, fertilizers, improved seed, and the like.

169

Similar factors affected tenants as well. Some tenants, such as those in the tobacco areas, were able to enjoy comparatively large incomes. This was true also of the sugar colonos, many of whom became fairly wealthy although technically they were tenants. Part of their standing derived from the fact that they were not only assured permanent occupancy by the law of 1937 but were the possessors of the highly desired allotments under the quota system for the sugarcane area. For tenants such as these, outright ownership of land was of less value than it was to other tenants not so well situated. As far as the colonos and the estate managers were concerned, they might well be included in the middle class as we described it earlier. Many if not most of the colonos actually lived in the city, while the managers enjoyed a style of life in the country which approximated in most amenities that common in the urban middle class.

In summary, although the income factor cut across tenure lines, it did not nullify tenure as a status-determining factor but nevertheless became a conditioning influence. Size of operation, including the amount of land, labor, and capital employed, was also an important factor correlated with tenure.

At the very bottom of the rural hierarchy were the farm laborers. They constituted the largest single occupational group in the country, a reported 424,000 in 1946 and 568,779 in 1953.[5] Large numbers of them were migratory, employed mainly in sugar during the harvest season, but there were also considerable numbers in coffee and other crops. Their existence was precarious; they were often unemployed for half the year and were usually the most deprived in terms of education and health services.

It is important to note here that the social strata described were not fixed and impenetrable. On the contrary, Cuban society was what is called an open-class system, meaning that vertical circulation was possible. The major factor in promoting upward mobility was education. Even the poor, if they could obtain education — which was more difficult than for the better-off — were able to rise in the social scale. Education opened the way into politics and the rise to power. Batista offers an example. Largely by his own efforts he became a stenographer, which led to the position of court reporter and his rank of sergeant when in the army. His formal education was limited, but once in the military he was able to rise to the top through political machinations; it was however, the possession of a special skill which made this possible. Although most of the important leaders in Cuba had the benefit of university education, even a common unskilled worker could improve his position by increasing his knowledge and skill, whether through formal learning or by teaching himself and learning from his peers.

Social Changes under the Revolution

With this rapid review of the old social structure, we may proceed to describe the changes brought about by the revolution.

The Elite. The first group to be driven from their position of power and privilege were the large property owners. Owners of large tracts of land, factories, business establishments, and other forms of tangible property lost their holdings. Many, if not most of them, went into exile, leaving their real estate and personal property behind. Those who remained in Cuba received some compensation for their nationalized properties and enterprises in the form of monthly allowances based upon the value of the property.[6] It is easy to conclude that there will be no wealthy propertied class as such in Cuba as long as the revolutionary regime is in power.

The Middle Class. One of the ironies of the Cuban revolution is that while it was promoted, led, and largely supported by middle-class people, many of the latter soon found themselves outcasts and exiles. It will be recalled that Castro was the son of a large landholder and a graduate of the University of Havana law school. Ernesto Guevara, the Argentinian, was a medical school graduate. Nearly all the other leaders were from middle-class backgrounds. Many professional and other middle-class individuals who did not actually bear arms supported the campaign against Batista.

The middle class, doomed to disappointment of their hope for reforms under a restored and viable democratic government, watched the events of late 1959 and 1960 with fear and dread, until flight from the island seemed their only alternative. What began as a trickle in early 1959 became a veritable flood of human migrants

171

from Cuba through the following years. Cuba prohibited emigration as a result of the missile crisis in October 1962, but in December 1965 the daily airlift of exiles was authorized. The majority came to the United States. What is of special interest to us in this chapter is the occupational characteristics of the refugees, since this is the best indicator of class status. Richard R. Fagen, Richard A. Brody, and Thomas J. O'Leary, have reported that the incoming migrants up to October 1962 revealed a marked concentration of middle-class personnel (see Table 15).[7] These authors made two further analyses of registrants at the Refugee Center in Miami which showed trends in the occupational composition of employable migrants who arrived after the airlift began in 1965. A summary of all arrivals is presented in the last column of Table 16.

The tables clearly indicate the predominance of upper- and middle-class individuals in the pre-missile crisis period and, with some decline, its continuance thereafter. It would seem that the percentage of this group in the later migration has reached a plateau. This may

Table 15. Occupational Comparison of Cuban Work Force and Cuban Refugees

Occupational Group	1953 Cuban Census	Per- centage of Census	Cuban Refugees 1959–62	Per- centage of Refugees	Ratio: % of Refugees to % Census
Legal and judiciary	7,858	.4	1,695	3.1	7.8
Professional and semi- professional ...	78,051	4.0	12,124	21.9	5.5
Managerial and office	93,662	4.8	6,771	12.2	2.5
Clerical and sales	264,569	13.7	17,123	30.9	2.3
Domestic service, miliary and police	160,406	8.3	4,801	8.7	1.1
Skilled, semiskilled, and unskilled .	526,168	27.2	11,301	20.4	.75
Agriculture and fishing	807,514	41.7	1,539	2.8	.06
Total	1,938,228	100.1%	55,354	100.0%	

SOURCE: Richard R. Fagen, Richard A. Brody, and Thomas J. O'Leary, *Cubans in Exile: Disaffection and the Revolution* (Stanford: Stanford University Press, 1968), p. 19.

be due to efforts of the regime to persuade doctors, teachers, intellectuals, and others to remain.[8]

The class selectivity of the emigration is notable in the extraordinary rise in the proportion of skilled workers. This is especially worth remarking because in 1962 Maurice Zeitlin found that the group of skilled workers among the 202 whom he interviewed had a more positive attitude toward their work and were more favorable to the revolution.[9] The clerical and sales category, which constituted only 13 percent of the labor force in the census of 1953, has been consistently two and a half times that proportion among the exiles. The service group is about the same proportionately in the refugees as in the census.

Table 16. Occupational Comparison of Employable Refugees
for Selected Periods, 1962–70

Occupational Group	1962 (N = 27,419)	1966 (N = 17,124)	1967 (N = 14,867)	December 1, 1965, to April 30, 1970 (N = 74,393)
Professional, semiprofessional, and managerial	30.5%	21.2%	17.7%	18.2%
Clerical and sales	33.4	31.5	35.5	32.4
Skilled	17.1	21.6	26.0	25.8
Semiskilled and unskilled	8.3	11.5	8.2	10.0
Services	7.1	9.4	8.5	8.6
Agriculture and fishing	3.6	4.7	4.1	5.0
Total	100.0%	100.0%	100.0%	100.0%

SOURCE: For the years 1962, 1966, and 1967, Richard R. Fagen, Richard A. Brody, and Thomas J. O'Leary, *Cubans in Exile: Disaffection and the Revolution* (Stanford: Stanford University Press, 1968), Table 7.1, p. 115. The summary column was calculated from data supplied by the Cuban Refugee Program, Miami, Florida.

Obviously, not all of what must have been by 1959 more than eight thousand lawyers and judges in Cuba — not to mention the other professionals — left the country. The majority remained. How many were caught up in the early executions and how many are political prisoners is not known, but it is possible that most of them are presently working for the government. A substantial number of university professors went into exile, but most of this group obviously remained. The same can be said for the physicians, other professionals, and grade and high school teachers.[10] One must conclude that while the exodus certainly drained the professional group, it has by no means been entirely depleted, even granting that those who fled were among the most endowed.

The Petit Bourgeoisie. This group, which certainly contained many individuals who might properly be classified as middle class, was at first left relatively free from molestation. The medium-size enterprises, including the Cuban-owned banks and various merchandising establishments, had been nationalized on October 13, 1960.[11] Castro fretted a good deal over the continued expansion of small enterprises which sprang up spontaneously in response to a demand for soft drinks, sandwiches, and the like. In 1967 he condemned the operators as parasites who lived off the sweat of the workers, but he recognized they were meeting demands which the government itself was not prepared to supply.

Finally, however, Castro decided to act against them. On March 13, 1968, he announced that all private enterprises were to be closed or taken over by the government. The nationalized enterprises included bars, nightclubs, small groceries, hardware and furniture stores, barber shops and beauty parlors, photographic shops, quick-food and soft-drink stands, jewelry stores, and so on. On May 1 Raúl Castro stated that 57,600 such enterprises had been nationalized. As Fidel had said in his March 13 address: "Capitalism has to be dug out by the roots; parasitism has to be dug out by the roots; the exploitation of man has to be dug out by the roots." [12] Private enterprise and self-employment were thus eliminated with the exception of a group of private owners on small farms, described below. Plainly the kind of middle class which once existed in Cuba has ceased to be.

The Lower Classes. With the top levels of the prerevolutionary social hierarchy dispersed and deprived of private property and the privileges that went with it, there has obviously been a leveling downward. The status of the workers and peasants has been modified also, but here the leveling for the most part has been upward. The kind of economic and social disabilities which the workers in the sugarcane fields suffered in the pre-Castro days have been lessened or removed. As full-time permanent employees of the state, they no longer experience seasonal unemployment for several months of the year. Free medical care is available to them and free education to their children.

While these perquisites are available to other groups as well, it is the impoverished classes of the old regime who are most benefited. Formerly, only the upper classes and particularly urban residents had easy access to and could afford schooling and medical care. It has been a deliberate policy of Castro to favor the countryside over the city in bringing the benefits of the revolution to the population. Better housing for farm people is, however, still a matter promised for the future.

The skilled and semiskilled workers who were well organized had somewhat less to gain from the revolution. As we have noted heretofore, they have lost many of the benefits gained through their unions and are now asked to work longer and harder without receiving extra compensation.

Changes in the Rural Sector

Because the rural structure was discussed separately from the urban, it is necessary to consider the impact of the revolution on it separately as well. As we mentioned in chapter 5, the large and medium agricultural enterprises were confiscated and placed under state operation. There remain the so-called small farmers. Landlords were eliminated; there are no renters or squatters. Tenants who were operating farms of no more than 167 acres were made owners by decree. The nonowners of the old regime were thus raised to the new status of owners. Farmers who already owned farms of less than 167 acres were not disturbed, that is to say, they continued to farm as they had before the revolution. The total number of small farmers remaining after the agrarian reforms has been estimated at about 150,000, but only about 100,000 were considered large enough to be profitable.

In the case of the large enterprises, notably those engaged in raising sugarcane, rice, and cattle, the old organizations were replaced by state apparatuses. The sugar colonos no longer exist, although their duties as managers of canefields have to be performed by someone. Nothing is known on the outside about how the sugar industry is organized, but the same functions in the mills and the fields have to be performed now as before the revolution. The same is true throughout the agricultural industry.

The status of the new peasant proprietors is conditioned by the fact that they are subject to the general planning of the regime. They must depend on INRA for fertilizer and seed and for direction in what they are to grow, and they are subject to the requirements in regard to "volunteer" work. In short, their status as owners suffers from many restrictions imposed by the state.

Since those who were formerly tenants already had by law the guarantee of permanent occupancy of the land they were operating, they may or may not feel that the revolution has bestowed any great benefits upon them. The fact that their proportion in the refugee flights has increased (see Table 16) might be the result of growing disillusionment. After the middle-size farms were expropriated in 1963, Castro announced that about 30 percent of the land was still in the hands of the small farmers. There are increasing reports, however, that the percentage is declining. Castro has said many times that eventually all private farms will disappear. His program of "urbanization" calls for moving all farmers into small villages, a plan that can be achieved only through the elimination of the privately operated farms. Yet he has also committed himself to a policy of free choice for the farmers, leaving it to them to decide whether they want to move. On January 12, 1969, he reported again, according to *Granma*:

Any farmer who wants to live in town, to move into town with his family can do so. We have established several procedures: the farmer who wishes to remain isolated will remain where he is, living under the conditions he chooses. This is the process that has been followed with all the small farmers. And that's the basis on which this [urban] development is planned. The farmers will also see their financial problems disappear. There are farmers who have remained as individual producers; others have sold their land; and others rent their land to the projects. Frankly, we do not favor the procedure of buying. We have even preferred the procedure of renting the land. Why? Because the farmers feel more secure, more independent, and they can even participate in the work of the projects. These are the ways our Revolution has been finding and developing in order to make progress, to acquire the necessary technology, to overcome and defeat underdevelopment.

Without a doubt, this method of isolated production, working with one lone ox; where no machine can be employed; without the aid of machines or technology, electricity or anything else; and living under those conditions constitutes sheer backwardness. However, the fact that we believe it is a backward method does not imply that we believe it necessary for us to impose a solution to this problem. The fundamental principle of the Revolution's policy toward the farmers is based on the farmers' absolute freedom to accept or reject any measure adopted in relation to them.

Castro's statement was a very strong recommitment to the policy of noninterference, while at the same time it admitted that farmers were selling or renting their land to the government. There can be no doubt that the peasant-owner-operator is disappearing from the Cuban landscape and that eventually all farmers will be working for wages as employees of the state.[13] The matter is a rather delicate one for the revolution, as Castro by implication told Lee Lockwood in 1967: "It is very important to follow a correct policy toward the farmers, because the power of the Revolution is based on the intimate union of the workers and peasants." [14]

In sum, the short-run effect of the revolution was to provide for the lower classes a kind of festival of plenty, a consumer holiday, made possible by the large reserves accumulated under previous regimes. Money, suddenly plentiful as a result of reduced rents and utility rates and the placement of the unemployed on state salaries, created an artificial condition of plenty for all. This all came to an end with the introduction of rationing in early 1962. For a time there had been an apparent equalization among the classes as far as consumption was concerned, but in the longer term other conditions prevailed, including the rise of new privileged strata.

The New Class

The disappearance of the bourgeoisie did not mean that there would be none to take their place. Their position was immediately occupied by the new power elite. Privileges of many kinds are enjoyed by members of the new inner circle and dispensed to favorites as they wish. The ration book is a leveling factor, it is true, but those who "mind the stores" and those in charge of those "who mind the stores" have access to supplies denied the ones who stand in the long lines to reach the portals.

Money, curiously, is not much of a factor in status because there are few items available for purchase. At the same time, prices of food and other necessities are low and many services are free or inexpensive. Still, incomes are far from approaching equality, as the regime at one time promised. Salaries range from eighty-five to nine hundred pesos per month.[15] The importance lies in the differential, since meaningful comparisons cannot be made with prerevolutionary wages or with those in nonsocialist countries. Wage differentials, however, lose much of their significance in a world where there are few things beyond the necessities which can be obtained with money.[16]

That some Cubans are faring better than others is apparently no secret among the population. John Reed, a Canadian journalist who visited the island late in 1970, was told by several Cubans whom he interviewed that there "were many persons in Cuba with plenty of food and clothing, with large houses, cars, and even servants." One of his interviewees, an artist, was philosophical about the situation. In all societies, he said, there were some "who would take advantage of a position of power to better themselves materially. But we have faith that Fidel will correct this." [17]

Under capitalism the pecking order was based upon wealth, whether obtained through the practice of the Calvinistic principles of hard work, thrift, saving, inventiveness, and individual ambition and enterprise or by fraud, speculation, and corruption. That system of ranking has without doubt quite largely disappeared in Cuba and been replaced by a new order based not on wealth but on sheer political power — power attained originally through force of arms, consolidated by ruthless elimination of the old order, and maintained by suppression of all dissent and organized opposition. The tightening of controls over the country through what has been termed the militarization of the society is a development of recent years, notably since 1968. We will return to a brief review of this development shortly, but it is first necessary to describe the mass organizations through which that control is exercised.

The New Organisms

All the existing social organizations, large and small, were abolished at the beginning of the revolution. All the clubs, associations, political parties, and so on that exist in pluralistic democratic societies were suppressed. They were replaced by what the regime calls the mass organisms. These include the Central Confederation of Labor (CTC), the Federation of Cuban Women (FMC), the Association of Small Farmers (ANAP), the Young Communist Union (UJC) for Cuban youth, the Pioneers for grade-school children, and the Committees for the Defense of the Revolution (CDR).

The CDR constitute by far the most important organism of all. The reported membership on the occasion of the organization's tenth anniversary (September 28, 1970) was 3,222,145, equal to about 38 percent of the population of eight and a half million and a much higher percentage of the adults. Significantly, 500,000 were reported as "activists," apparently the trusted core of the membership or those regarded as loyal to the regime. The members are organized locally on a block basis in the cities. Each large apartment house has its CDR committee. In addition to its primary function of vigilance, the CDR perform a wide range of tasks for the government — among them have been taking a school and a livestock census, gathering empty bottles and flasks, and operating the distributive centers for food and other items.[18] The CDR were extremely active during the 1970 sugar harvest to prevent sabotage and report failure of workers to perform as they should. They cooperated closely with the Ministry of the Interior (police) and the armed forces in this job, as well as in guarding state property and frontier areas against invasion.

Similarly, all of the old government machinery was cast away. Abolished was the Congress, the independent judiciary, and all elective officials. Virtually, the only remnants of the previous government structure were the ministries (though radically changed) and the six provinces. These seem to have remained intact with few if any changes in boundaries. Not so with the next lower units of gov-

179

ernment, the municipalities. These numbered 126 in 1958 but were increased in 1966 to 321. In addition, a new intermediate unit of government known as the region was introduced. It is not clear why this new unit was created, but it probably serves to increase the control of the central power over the local. Each region contains a number of municipalities.

The Polarization of Power

The result of these changes has been the creation of a totalitarian form of government. At the pinnacle of power is Fidel Castro: prime minister, first secretary of the Communist party, and commander in chief of the armed forces. His brother Raúl is his deputy and designated successor. In addition, Castro is president of the two most powerful independent agencies: INRA, the land reform agency, and JUCEPLAN, the central planning board. As chief of government, the prime minister heads the Council of Ministers, which is the legislative body as well as the executive power. As first secretary, he presides over the Politburo and the Central Committee of the party, which in theory is the policy-making body.

Government and party have dual representation down through the provincial, regional, municipal, and local levels. The functions of these representatives are many because they are responsible for the provisioning of the population, including the operation of stores, bakeries, and other enterprises formerly in the private sector.[19] Members of the Central Committee of the party preside over the various mass organizations listed above, so that the reins of control are absolute and remain in the hands of Fidel Castro.

Toward the Garrison State

The drift toward what has become an absolute dictatorial regime was accelerated by the events of late 1967 and especially by action taken in 1968. For despite his hold on all the reins of authority Castro was facing failure in the fulfillment of the five-year plan. Production was lagging; his attacks on bureaucracy in 1967 and the transfer of thousands of so-called excess personnel out of the ministries, along with his exhortation for greater production and productivity, had

180

not had the desired results. On March 13, 1968, as we have seen, he declared a "revolutionary offensive" against the petit bourgeoisie, closing or nationalizing small private business. This action, along with other irritants, probably added to the restlessness of the country, and 1968 proved to be a year of extraordinary sabotage.

On September 28, 1968, the prime minister addressed the Committees for the Defense of the Revolution. If the speech of March 13 was upsetting, that of September 28 was even more so. The address followed a common pattern, with the first portion devoted to an enumeration of the achievements of the revolution and the bright prospects for the future. Then followed a listing of problems, with emphasis this time on sabotage. "The country advances visibly," Castro said, "but in our country there is not only the work of the revolution; there is also the work of the counterrevolution." He proceeded to enumerate fifteen major cases of sabotage and twenty-five of lesser importance; thirty-six school houses had been burned. "This is the work of the counterrevolution." After a long denunciation of "parasites," "loafers," and other enemies, he came down hard with the declaration: "Before this revolution can cease to exist, no head of a single counterrevolutionary will remain on his shoulders in this country. These are the rules of the game. Before they can destroy this revolution, the heads of all who may want to destroy it will roll." [20]

This is the language of a frustrated prime minister. He was frustrated by the knowledge that the five-year plan was not meeting its goals and that the youth, whom he had also denounced for immoral conduct in Havana, were ignoring the puritan norms of the revolution. Above all there was the obviously withering morale of the population. "In fact," K. S. Karol has noted, "he couldn't help noticing that the nation was rejecting the large dose of revolutionary medicine it was supposed to swallow. This recalcitrance had nothing to do with counterrevolution; it was simply that 'education through land work' proved too one-sided to form a social education to be truly salutary . . ." [21]

Several other significant events in the direction of increased social control occurred in 1968. In January one of the old Communists, Aníbal Escalante, and eight others were accused of "deviation" as a "microfaction," allegedly plotting against the Castro group. They were tried and Escalante was sentenced to fifteen years in prison. A further episode of this year involved the granting of the national poetry prize to Heberto Padilla by the Union of Cuban Artists and Writers. Literary officials reluctantly accepted the judgment of the jury but branded the book as "unfit revolutionarily." It was published with a lengthy introduction critical of its ideological content. This criticism was not adequate for the armed forces magazine *Verde Olivo,* which launched a vigorous campaign against intellectuals. This was the first indication of repression of intellectuals, who previously had been left relatively free.[22]

Padilla was arrested on March 20, 1971, and kept incommunicado for thirty-nine days, when he emerged to read a long "confession" of guilt for his offenses against the revolution which some of his friends regarded as a confession forced by torture. The publication of his letter brought a severe denunciation of the Cuban government from leading intellectuals of Europe, including such former friends of the revolution as Jean-Paul Sartre, Simone de Beauvoir, and Alberto Moravia.

With the evident disillusionment of a large part of the population in 1968, the pressure was on the CDR, the Ministry of the Interior (MININT), and FAR to step up their vigilance. Sabotage was to be prevented and the shoreline was to be guarded against incursions of exiles from the United States. Conferences among these three agencies were held to develop strategy. Meantime, government and party cadres and the CTC (labor organization) sought to find an answer to the malingering and absenteeism. Their efforts were not very successful since the lagging workers failed to meet the norms and the five-year plan ended in a failure in 1970. The new strategy to "make people work" came in 1971 as we have described.

Conclusion

This drive toward militarization of the country has introduced a new element into the social structure of the island. It has been referred to as "Stalinization."[23] The process accentuates polarization of the population. Despite the apparent moves in the early years toward a more equalitarian society, the fact is that gross inequalities existed in Cuba in 1971.

There remained the better-off and the less well-off, though the distance between them is not as great as that between the rich and the poor in the old Cuba. But those who suffer the least deprivation of material goods are those in the upper echelons of the military (MININT and FAR), the CDR, the party, and the bureaucracy. These enjoy the emanations of power and authority because of their proximity to the pinnacle. They are the true power elite. They are not limited by the ration book as to what they can have for themselves, be it food, clothes, housing, or such other symbols of status as the Alfa Romeo.

Below this are what the new elite refer to as the "masses." They are subject to the discipline of the government — and of the ration book. They include, in this sense, artists, writers, and intellectuals in general, most white-collar and all blue-collar workers.

Perhaps we are back to the two-level structure which we described in 1946, but this time it is not based on the kind of work, whether manual or not, but on the possession or absence of political authority.

This is not to say that the two levels are homogeneous; they are not, in any other way than the degree of access to scarce material goods. In any self-rating as to status, were it possible to conduct a survey in Cuba today, the result would show undoubtedly a considerable hierarchical stratification. The intellectuals would not rate themselves in the same class as common labor, nor the white-collar group with the campesinos, even though the latter may be much better fed. Yet, as a practical matter in a country where poverty is so widely distributed, the sharing of scarcity or relative abundance, as the case may be, cuts across other class determinants.

Chapter 11

On Balance

One undertakes an evaluation of the Cuban Revolution in full realization of the difficulties involved. Yet in the thirteenth year of its administration of the island, the revolutionary government is inevitably subject to such an assessment. It is in fact being judged, and rather harshly, by some of its most enthusiastic friends of earlier years. Writers of Marxist orientation, including the Americans Huberman and Sweezy, the French agronomist René Dumont, and the Polish-Russian-Parisian K. S. Karol, have passed judgment.[1] All of them have enjoyed the privilege of several visits to the country and, in Karol's case, lengthy interviews with the prime minister. These privileges were denied the present author but, unlike the writers mentioned, he did come to know the old Cuba during a year's study. Most of the early enthusiasts for the revolution had never been in Cuba and did not know it first hand.

All revolutions are matters of controversy; their achievements and even their justification are debated for generations after they happen. The Cuban Revolution, as the first socialist-communist one in the hemisphere, has been up to now more controversial than most for several reasons, but chiefly because of the relation the island holds to the two major powers of the world, the one capitalist, the other communist. The revolution is controversial also because of the extremes to which it went in abolishing private property and suppressing individual initiative. It was, indeed, an effort to create utopia; this sets it apart from other so-called socialist revolutions, which with

184

the possible exception of China could more properly be termed mixed socialist-capitalist.

The preceding chapters have presented the factual information that is available in regard to various aspects of the country. Numerous statements of Fidel Castro have been quoted to indicate the goals of the revolution. The kind of society that is to be established is one without any capitalistic taint, where everyone will work for the good of the whole society, where selfishness will be replaced with altruism, and where the abundance that will result from the enthusiastic hard labor of the producing masses will be shared equally by all and be free to all. Money, "that vile intermediary," will disappear. These are the major goals, but the underlying necessity for their attainment is the *formación* of the new man. Our tentative appraisal of the revolution will be presented under rubrics which cover its moral, social economic, and political aspects.

The Moral Reforms

The revolution has taken a puritanical attitude in the matter of morals. The logic is that immorality such as existed in the old Cuba was associated with capitalism, even caused by capitalism. Capitalism was the main target for destruction and with it all its evil concomitants. Besides, the necessity for economic survival made indulgence in time-wasting and energy-consuming vices, along with idleness and laziness, a kind of behavior to be forbidden.

Thus one of the early acts of the Castro government was to abolish prostitution. Practitioners of the oldest profession were taught new skills that would enable them to support themselves in a life of rectitude. Many societies have tried to suppress or control prostitution, with indifferent results, and reports from Cuba suggest that the effort has not been completely successful there. Lee Lockwood, in his interview with Castro in 1965, noted the continuation of the "Cuban institution of the *posada*," a slang word for a "motel-like place where couples go to make love, no questions asked."[2] While this is not prostitution, it is nevertheless sexual relations outside marriage. Other visitors to the country have noted the persistence of prostitution and Castro himself chastized some young people for engaging in this practice in his address of September 28, 1968. Notwithstanding the failure to achieve complete suppression, the regime must be given credit for its effort.

Gambling was likewise associated with capitalism, and because Americans were the major patrons as well as operators of the casinos, this evil was doubly contemptible to the regime. Another reason for abolishing gambling was the part it had played in the corruption of government officials, a practice which the new leaders were also determined to wipe out. Most people will agree that the elimination of gambling was a highly desirable action. It was condoned and approved as a tourist attraction, and tourism was a major source of income, yet its immoral concomitants, as well as gambling itself, are degrading to society.

The old Cuban institution of the lottery was also abolished. It had a history of dishonest administration and was used by politicians to enrich themselves. Thousands of poor people made a few pesos by selling lottery tickets, while other thousands purchased them by scraping together pesos and centavos which should have gone for more useful ends. It was not a social asset to the nation, and when the government decided to use the purchase of lottery tickets as a means of personal savings, instead of distributing the money in the form of winnings, most people again would applaud the action. Nevertheless Cubans soon lost interest in the project and it was scrapped. Cockfighting was also forbidden. This sport had long been a favorite recreation of the peasants, and previous regimes, under pressure from groups concerned about cruelty to animals, had tried to suppress it without much success.

But the most important moral reform occurred in the public offices when stealing from the government was made a capital offense. Much has been said and written about maladministration of public monies in Cuba by government officials. The practice has been condoned on the theory that Cuba lacked sufficient experience in self-government to develop standards of political integrity. Moreover, the existence of sinecures was often justified because the widespread unemployment in private industry made the government the only source of support for many persons. However, such arguments do not justify the excesses of most of the republican governments since the presidency of Tomás Estrada Palma.[3]

While nobody at all acquainted with Cuba is naïve enough to think that political integrity has been universally achieved, overnight as it were, the regime must be given high marks for effort. Although honesty in government had been given high priority by reform groups for many decades, Castro is the first leader since Estrada Palma to attempt to establish it as a norm.

Social Achievements

Education. The accomplishments of the Castro regime in providing schooling for the population must be considered as a major achievement. No other aspect of the revolutionary program has attained and merited such wide acclaim. The literacy campaign of 1961 was a spectacular event, though it was more important as a socializing process than in actually ridding the country of illiteracy. The regime itself maintained that the persons involved were brought only to the first-grade level and that only continuous study beyond that level could prevent a lapse into illiteracy again. It is to the credit of the regime that opportunities for adult education were provided by means of classwork at the labor centers, correspondence courses, and special scholarships for full-time attendance at regular schools for former illiterates.

Assuredly few would question the desirability of universal literacy among citizens of modern societies. But one may question the advantage of reading skills to Cubans whose reading matter is completely censored. The newspapers are now little more than propaganda leaflets, concerned chiefly with the glorious achievements of the revolution, the evil machinations of Yankee imperialism, and internal difficulties in the United States. Beyond the dreary press, Cubans are restricted to the works of Marx and Lenin and writers of similar persuasion.

The educational system is similarly geared to the production of a generation inculcated with the revolutionary point of view. This applies not only in political matters, where no criticism of the government is tolerated, but also in the choice of a career. An emphasis on technology and science pervades the curriculum. In his speech on September 28, 1968, Castro predicted that "in twelve years the number of intermediate-level technicians in our country will not be below 800,000. Some people will say, 'Is everybody to become a technician?' Yes, everybody will have to become a technician, because there will not be a single activity in the future which will not require solid training . . ."

In regard to higher education, a knowledgeable commentator who visited the island in late 1969 summarized the future as follows:

The régime contemplates nothing less than universal education up to and including university level. The three existing universities have been condemned as citadels of privilege and are to be abolished as such. They will be converted into institutes of advanced research while facilities for university-level studies, heavily slanted toward science and technology, will be provided at the main centers of work throughout the country — a system of apprenticeship on a national scale combining study with productive work. How this is to be achieved in terms of teachers, buildings and equipment has not been made clear, but nothing could be more egalitarian than the intention. The entire population is to pass through the same educational mill.[4]

The regime is able to regulate the number of students in any specialty through entrance examinations and the awarding of scholarships. A student who was in his fifth year at the University of Havana before he went into exile states that "government control of university affairs is complete. The Department of State Security (state police) has numerous agents in the University . . . All students are encouraged to join the Union of Young Communists. . . . Many students were expelled from the university when the UJC held public assemblies accusing groups of students of being counterrevolutionaries or homosexuals."[5] The government's extremely harsh treatment of homosexuals, it should be mentioned, is a demerit in the area of moral reform.

Health and Medical Facilities. The revolution has less to show for its efforts in the field of health care than in that of education, and for these reasons: (1) in 1958 Cuba already had a good program; (2) the revolution, by its policies, in effect encouraged the emigration of

188

about a third of its physicians, thus setting back the program which was already under way; (3) serious questions can be raised about the efficacy of the rural hospital construction program.

It must be admitted that rural people in the more remote areas of prerevolutionary Cuba were poorly provided with, or completely lacked ready access to, medical help. Cuban medical personnel, along with hospitals and other facilities, were highly concentrated in urban centers. Moreover, many of the rural population were too poor to afford medical care or even to get to centers where free care was available. Bad roads in remote areas also made it difficult to obtain medical attention. It is impossible, however, to estimate how much of the population was truly deprived of needed medical care because of poverty or isolation.

In 1958 Cuba had a rather complex system for providing health care. Physicians in private practice charged patients on a fee-for-service basis. But there were many doctors employed on salary by the widespread mutual associations. These cooperatives have had a long history in the island. In the late colonial period Spanish immigrants from various provinces of the homeland organized clubs for various purposes, including recreation, children's education, and the provision of medical care on a prepaid monthly basis.[6] Before long, the membership requirement was changed so that practically any person could be admitted regardless of the province of origin in Spain. By the late 1920's so many residents of Havana were receiving medical service through these associations that there was little opportunity for private practice. The doctors finally organized a strike.[7]

The population census of 1953 reported 6,201 physicians. Hernández cites an estimate of around 7,000 for 1958. With a doctor-population ratio of approximately 1 to 1,000, Cuba ranked fifth in the hemisphere, with only Argentina, the United States, Uruguay, and Canada showing better ratios. Cuban physicians received their training in the medical school of the University of Havana, which had at its disposal the 1,300-bed Calixto Garcia hospital. This was a free hospital for indigent patients.

While most hospitals were located in the urban centers, and above all in Havana, the overall ratio of beds to population could not be considered seriously inadequate (see Table 17).

Table 17. Hospital Facilities in Cuba in 1952, 1958, and 1966

Facilities	1952	1958	1966
Population	5,724,200	6,548,300	7,799,600
Hospitals and other			
medical centers	210	347	530
Public	60	87	
Private	150	250	
Number of beds	26,146	36,141	42,561
Public	11,754	21,141	
Private	14,392	15,000	
Beds per thousand			
population	4.5	5.5	5.4

SOURCE: For 1952 and 1958, Roberto E. Hernández, "La atención médica en Cuba hasta 1958," in *Journal of Inter-American Studies*, 11, no. 4 (October 1969), p. 553, Table 10; for 1966, JUCEPLAN, Dirección Central de Estadística, *Boletín Estadístico 1966*, Tables XIV.1, XIV.2.

The critical figures are the bed-population ratios. It should be explained here that for the 1952 data Hernández cites a publication of the United States Department of Commerce, *Investment in Cuba*, published in 1956, and for the 1958 data his source is Fulgencio Batista y Zaldívar, *Piedras y Leyes*, published in 1961. The accuracy of Batista's account may be questioned, although as Hernández points out the figures are similar to those reported in the United Nations *Statistical Yearbook* for 1958.

It should also be mentioned that the hospitals and other medical centers enumerated in the table included a wide range of institutions, most of them in Havana, which specialized in cancer, heart and circulatory diseases, tuberculosis, psychiatric illness, leprosy, orthopedic problems, obstetrics, and children's diseases. Also included were the first-aid stations (*casas de socorro*) and what are called dispensaries. This classification makes it difficult to evaluate the claims of the revolution. On December 22, 1969, a radio newscast from Havana, monitored in Miami, claimed a total of 188 hospitals, 48 of them rural, with a total bed capacity of 47,669. The commentator contrasted this with the 54 hospitals and total bed capacity of 25,730 which he said existed in 1958.[8]

While the bed-population ratio is an important index of the availability of hospital services, an even more important question is the rate of occupancy of the beds. Unfortunately, a census of patients is

190

not available. Especially in rural areas, the real problem is not the availability but the utilization of bed capacity.[9] We will return to this question later.

Since the conquest of yellow fever, typhoid, and certain other contagious diseases, Cuba has had a remarkably low death rate. Indeed, it is among the lowest in the world. And while other statistics on vital rates have been subject to serious question in the past, those regarding deaths are relatively reliable, because bodies cannot be interred without a death certificate. The general and infant mortality rates are shown in Table 18. Even though these rates have increased significantly since 1958, they are still very low in comparison with other countries of the world. The mortality rate in the United States, for example, was 9.5 in 1958 and the infant mortality rate 26.9 per thousand live births.

The revolutionary government claims that the general health of the people has improved.[10] However, with the important exception of polio, the data shown in Table 19 indicate a significant deterioration in the years immediately after 1958. There has been an apparent

Table 18. General and Infant Mortality Rates in Cuba[a]

Year	Total Mortality Rate	Infant Mortality Rate	Infant Deaths as Percentage of All Deaths
1953	5.8	37.6	...
1958	4.9	33.7	13.9
1959	6.6	34.5	15.1
1960	6.3	35.4	...
1961	6.6	37.2	19.6
1962	7.3	39.6	20.5
1963	6.8	37.6	20.1
1964	6.4	37.8	21.0
1965	6.5	37.7	20.3
1966	6.5	37.6	...
1967	6.4	...	...

SOURCE: Roberto E. Hernández, "La atención médica en Cuba hasta 1958," *Journal of Inter-American Studies*, 11, no. 4 (October 1969), pp. 543, 544; JUCEPLAN, Dirección Central de Estadística, *Compendio Estadístico 1967*; C. Paul Roberts and Mukhtar Hamour, *Cuba 1968* (Los Angeles: University of California, 1970), p. 44.

[a] The general mortality rate is per thousand inhabitants, while the infant rate is the number per thousand live births.

Table 19. Reported Cases and Rates of Infectious Diseases in Cuba, 1957–66

Disease	1957	1958	1959	1960	1961	1962	1963	1964	1965	1966
Reported Cases										
Brucellosis	4	2	8	5	16	35	37	53	625	359
Diphtheria	224	156	316	551	1335	1368	923	640	2012	1662
Gastroenteritis[a]		2784	2887			4157	2974	2525	8834	8977
Hepatitis					349	3615	4659	5249		
Leprosy	32	27	190	134	122	291	159	156		
Malaria	270	128	141	1290	3230	3519	833	624	127	36
Measles	184		684	728	31	1590	6799	2151		
Poliomyelitis	96	103	288	330	848	46	1	1	0	0
Syphilis		46	47	566	482	805	1691	1863		
Tetanus			274	311			358	332		
Tuberculosis	1832	1177	1849	1856	2625	2725	2768	3909		
Typhoid fever	457	331	865	1191	948	1007	420	1158	236	169
Rates (per 100,000 inhabitants)										
Brucellosis[b]			.1		.2	.5	.5	.7	8.2	4.6
Diphtheria	3.5	2.4	4.7	8.1	19.2	19.4	12.8	8.6	26.4	21.3
Gastroenteritis[a]		42.5	43.1			58.8	41.1	34.0	115.8	115.1
Hepatitis					5.0	51.1	64.4	70.6		
Leprosy	.5	.4	2.9	2.0	1.8	4.1	2.2	2.1		
Malaria	4.2	2.0	2.1	19.0	46.6	49.8	11.5	8.4	1.7	.5
Measles	2.9		10.3	10.7	.4	22.5	94.0	28.9		
Poliomyelitis	1.5	1.6	4.3	4.9	5.0	.7				
Syphilis		.7	.7	8.3	6.9	11.4	23.4	25.1		
Tetanus			4.1	4.6			4.9	4.5		
Tuberculosis	28.7	18.0	27.6	27.2	37.8	38.6	38.3	52.6		
Typhoid fever	7.1	5.1	13.0	17.5	13.7	14.2	5.8	15.6	3.1	2.2

SOURCE: Carmelo Mesa-Lago, "Availability and Reliability of Statistics in Socialist Cuba," *Latin American Research Review*, 4, no. 2 (Summer 1969), 70. Except as noted, blank spaces indicate that data were not available.
[a] The figures given are for the number of deaths.
[b] Rates for brucellosis were negligible in 1957, 1958, and 1959.

decline in the incidence of malaria and in deaths from gastroenteritis since 1964, but diphtheria, hepatitis, leprosy, measles, syphilis, and tuberculosis are still problems.

The government claims that it has provided, finally, fifty rural hospitals with fifteen hundred beds in "remote" areas. While the effort in behalf of the rural population in this matter is commendable, a few comments are justified. The precise location of these hospitals is not known to the present writer, with one exception. According to an announcement by Havana Radio on April 25, 1970, monitored in Miami, a twenty-bed, well-equipped hospital had been opened in San Blas, a small hamlet of twenty-one houses located in the municipality of Cienfuegos. The hospital personnel included seventeen individuals, among them a doctor, three nurses, two assistant nurses, a nurse in training, a laboratory technician, a radiologist, and a dentist. Presumably the balance were maintenance personnel. One can assume that suitable living quarters were provided, and this would require a special building or buildings. The staff doctor, according to the newscast, was serving the remainder of his two-year stint in rural service, required of all graduates of the three medical colleges.

In 1945, when I spent two days in the San Blas area, the hamlet was the center of a coffee-growing area located in a small valley of the Escambray mountains.[11] The village itself consisted of a couple of general stores, the residences of the storekeepers, and the headquarters buildings of a coffee plantation. San Blas was only 8 kilometers from La Sierra, the seat of the *barrio* or township of the same name. In 1943 the entire barrio of La Sierra had 3,640 people. According to the 1970 census the barrio, now called La Sierrita but presumably the same one, had a population of 6,779. (It is not known if the boundaries have been changed since 1943.)

In 1945 there was a small hospital at La Sierra (population 800), but no doctor or nurse was serving there at the time. San Blas is about 30 kilometers (18 miles) from Cienfuegos, one of the major cities of the island. What the people of San Blas wanted more than anything in 1945 was the completion of a hard-surfaced road from Cienfuegos to their location. With the completion of such a highway, medical care in Cienfuegos would be available as far as hospital cases were concerned. For minor ailments, for education in

193

health, particularly diets and sanitation, and for diagnosis, what was needed locally was a nurse and a doctor for at least periodical visits. Thus one can only wonder at the wisdom of investing the relatively large sums necessary to build, equip, and maintain a twenty-bed hospital in an area so sparsely settled.

One would expect that the local residents would have been consulted before an investment of this magnitude was launched. When we interviewed 742 farm families in various areas of Cuba in 1946, we asked them to indicate their major problems. The need mentioned most often was roads and highways (250 respondents), while next in order was education (188 respondents). Under the general heading of health and hygiene, 64 persons mentioned sanitation, 8 listed diet, and only 4 listed medical care.[12]

Good all-weather transportation would place practically every rural Cuban within a few minutes, or at most a few hours, of a city where hospital care is available. It would seem much better to take the comparatively few people who require hospitalization to urban centers than to bring entire hospitals to areas in which facilities are likely to be less than fully and economically used.

The Real Health Problem. As the International Bank mission reported in 1951, "Cuba is relatively free from diseases. One foreign official of long experience pointed out, no disease has reached epidemic proportions in the past twenty years and he could not remember even having to issue an unclean bill of health. . . . Plants managers, too, and others concerned with industry expressed the opinion that health was not a major problem *in industry,* except that the statutory nine days sick leave a year adds to the cost of labor." [13]

However, the report went on to point out that a problem of general health existed because of inadequate diets, poor sanitation, and parasites. The author, on the basis of his own observations in 1945–46, can bear witness to this fact. The remedy is not necessarily hospitals, however, but improvement of the diet (which is based too much on starchy foods) and education in sanitation. There is, of course, great need for better housing, which would go far toward improving health generally.

194

On Balance

The Revolution and the Economy

On July 20, 1969, Castro asserted: "The greatness of . . . the ten years that have passed lies mainly in the fact that it was necessary to start practically from zero, that it was necessary to do everything." Other observers, both Cubans and Americans, have made similar statements.[14] In previous chapters we have given the answer to these unfounded claims. Yet the progress of the revolution in the field of economic activity must be evaluated by what it had to begin with. Indeed, to be quite fair, the revolution should be measured by what development would have taken place without it. This factor is, of course, unknowable, but it should not be forgotten that an important pace of development was under way in the late 1950's.

While Cuba was not a fully developed economy, it was by no means the economic wasteland which the propaganda of the revolution tries to paint. On at least one commonly used index, Cuba in 1957 ranked 32 among 127 countries of the world, that is, in the upper quarter. It will be useful to summarize the economic position of prerevolutionary Cuba.

In 1958 the island possessed the largest cane-sugar-producing complex in the world, efficiently operated under trained and experienced managerial and technical personnel. It was rapidly becoming Cuban-owned. Of 161 centrals, 121 were owned by Cubans. The growers of sugarcane — the colonos and the owner-operators of farms — enjoyed relative security. The colonos paid a nominal rent, but enjoyed a security of occupancy practically equivalent to ownership. The major human problem in sugar production was the large unemployment of farm workers during half or more of the year.

Outside the sugar economy, other aspects of agriculture were advancing. Most notable in increased production was rice. From 1940, when imports amounted to 95 percent of consumption, production grew by 1956 to a point where only 44 percent was imported. Increase had been steady and doubtless would have continued. Livestock, notably cattle herds, supplied the nation with a per capita annual yield of around 75 pounds. Herds and pastures were rapidly undergoing improvement. Estimates of the number of cattle in 1958 vary, but there appear to have been around six million head.

A hotel-motel complex representing many millions of dollars of investment had been constructed during the 1950's throughout the island and several more were under construction. A national bank and a Bank for Agricultural and Industrial Development (BANFAIC) became operative during the 1950's. There was a growing development in private banking, chiefly among Cubans, whose banks in 1958 held 54 percent of all deposits. The country had no serious international balance-of-payments problem.[15]

Cuba was well stocked with supplies of all kinds in 1958. Warehouses were filled with goods because of unusually heavy purchases made in 1957 to escape the import tax which was to become effective the next year. Shelves of department and other stores were filled with goods.

Although Cuba's industrial plant was still underdeveloped, there were over 20,000 "industrial centers" valued at three and a quarter billion dollars.[16] Other resources included two highly developed nickel mines, three modern and efficient oil refineries, and excellent transportation and communication systems.

One important index of development is the percentage of a country's labor force in agriculture. It is true that Cuba in 1958 still had an estimated 39 percent of its labor force so engaged, a decrease of 2 percent since 1953. Nevertheless, this proportion was much lower than in most underdeveloped countries and the trend was downward.

On January 1, 1959, Cuba's rather substantial economic resources were taken over by a group of young men and women who had little previous experience in any form of management and who were especially ignorant about agriculture, the nation's basic industry; a group of young people full of utopian dreams, enamored of political power, animated by excessive hatred for the entrepreneurs whose leadership had brought the country to its present state of economic development, and with a patronizing attitude toward the workers and peasants who had furnished the brawn and skills in constructing the economy.

The consequence to Cuba has been an almost unmitigated economic disaster. "Almost" because there have been important, but often wasteful, investments in irrigation, roads, and other parts of

196

the infrastructure. But aside from fishing, there was not a single item in the range of agricultural and livestock products which after twelve years equaled or surpassed the per capita production of 1958. Even in sugar, after a year-long focus of effort of the whole population, production failed by a considerable amount to equal the per capita production of 1952. (In 1952 the estimated population was 5,300,000 and sugar production was 7,298,000 tons; the 1970 census showed a population of 8,553,395 and the sugar production was 8,500,000 tons.) The wreckage of the early years of the regime set back Cuba's economic development for years. It is a sad story, an unhappy story — unhappy for the more than 600,000 Cubans who left the country, were imprisoned, or served in labor camps. It is an unhappy story too for the people of the islands who have endured a decade of privation and hard labor and who have been fed on promises delayed of fulfillment.

The available evidence reveals that Fidel Castro's leadership in economic matters has been the major impediment to progress. He made three major mistakes and each time survived politically to continue making unwise decisions. The first mistake was his provocative behavior during the 1959–1960 controversy with the United States which led to the break in diplomatic relations. As noted earlier, not all the blame was Castro's, but to him belongs the major part.

The second error of major magnitude was the attempt at instant industrialization and diversification, with its consequent wastage of labor and capital resources. The third major misjudgment was the drive for the ten-million-ton sugar crop in 1970. All these mistakes have either explicitly or implicitly been acknowledged.

Beyond these misadventures, the prime minister makes day-to-day decisions without submitting them to his advisers for discussion. Castro's ego-involvement with the revolution is so intense that he feels he must make all major decisions and even many minor ones, and he cannot bring himself to delegate responsibility to others. This means that there are no opportunities for others around him to gain experience in managing the country. Castro's intense psychological need to be the sole decision-maker, whether the decision involves social, political, economic, or scientific matters, encourages sycophancy; only yes-men are tolerable. Castro's own judgment at this state of the revolution is that the economy is in a precarious condition, that austerity will continue, and that there is no hope of improvement until after 1975.

The Leader and the Masses

The political system created in Cuba does not allow the citizenry an effective voice in policy determination. Decisions are made at the top and communicated downward to the workers and peasants. Once policy decisions have been announced by Castro and sent down through the political channels, it is up to the representatives of government and party at the base levels to see that they are implemented. The workers and peasants are simply told what has to be done; they have no part in the original decision.

This is undoubtedly a major reason why the performance of the workers has been less than the regime had hoped for. Only after the failure of 1970 did the prime minister seem to realize what had gone wrong. In his speech of September 28, 1970, he spoke of "democratization," and there followed the almost interminable series of meetings to discuss the law against loafing. It was a comparatively trivial matter to justify such elaborate "participation" by the population. More significant was the permission granted to local labor centers to nominate and elect their officers. It would seem to most observers that much more is needed. Even in 1965 Lee Lockwood raised with Castro questions about some orderly structure, such as a constitution, which would provide a mechanism of a formal character. Rather vaguely, the prime minister indicated that something might be ready by 1970 to provide for a "continuous participation of the masses in the political apparatus." "The working masses," he said, "will be the members of the Party. The Party will be something like a combined parliament of the workers and interpreters of their will." [17] Castro appears to have lost interest in bringing this idea to realization.

"The building of socialism," warns Karol, "cannot be the business of one man or of a single group of men, however well-intentioned.

198

If the socialist ship is to come safely into harbor, everyone alike must take to his oars — a few men rowing up in front are not enough." Otherwise, the "result is bound to be apathy and a general flagging of political interest." [18] Castro seems to have taken heed of this advice in the modest gestures made toward labor in late 1970 and continuing in 1971. There has also been a proposal to reform the judicial structure which will allow the election of judges to serve on the people's courts.

However, it seems likely that the development of democratic structures to permit others to participate in policy formation will be difficult for a man of Castro's character. Matthews makes the comment that Castro "had no concept of the true meaning of freedom and democracy and was never to have one . . . that he had a complete blind spot in his mentality. He still does not realize it himself. It took a gradual unfolding of Cuban developments to make it clear that so long as Fidel Castro remains in power there will not be and cannot be democracy and freedom in Cuba." [19] Karol makes a somewhat different diagnosis of the Castro personality: "All his arguments betray an aristocratic spirit, a faith in the role of the elite," rather than trust "in the fruitful exchange of ideas between the rank and file and the leaders." [20] This analysis of Castro's temperament may be different, but the consequences are much the same as the ones stated by Matthews.

The Foreign Trade Predicament

It is axiomatic that unless production can be increased in all phases of the national economic life, the revolution is on a shaky foundation. A major difficulty stems from the change in trading partners. To be dependent on trade with Soviet Russia, several thousand miles away, instead of the United States, ninety miles distant, is patently absurd. Soviet oil tankers, after coming from the Black Sea, through the Mediterranean, and across the Atlantic, arrive every two to three days in a Cuban port. This bridge of tankers, spread over 6,000 miles of water, is the lifeline for the country since there is no other source of fuel. A tanker from Venezuela travels about 750 miles.

CUBA: THE MEASURE OF A REVOLUTION

The growing dependence upon Soviet financial and military support is the consequence of the mistakes made by the Cuban leadership, including among others the doctrinaire insistence on moral incentives for labor to which the workers have failed to respond. The flagging morale of the Cuban people, however, cannot be cured by any resort to material rewards, since there are no longer any desirable objects which increased money income could buy. The resort to a form of coercion is the only means now open to the leadership.

How deeply in debt is Cuba? Figures for the years after 1967 are not available. A summation of the annual values of exports and imports from 1959 through 1967 shows imports of 7,327.1 million pesos and exports of 5,647.4 million pesos, leaving a cumulative trade imbalance for these years of 1,679.7 million pesos. For the preceding comparable nine years, 1950 through 1958, there was a favorable balance of trade amounting to 539.3 million pesos.[21]

Roberts and Hamour, using official Cuban sources, have computed the export-import balances for the various socialist countries and for selected nonsocialist nations. Data for the years 1960 through 1967 show a total almost identical with the figures reported above for 1959 through 1967. The total cumulative trade deficit was 1,678.8 million pesos, of which 231.5 million were with nonsocialist countries.[22] Most of the socialist trade deficit is with the Soviet Union.

Various Cuban observers — Huberman and Sweezy, K. S. Karol, René Dumont — share the opinion that since 1967 the adverse balance of trade has been greatly increased. Huberman and Sweezy cite Soviet statistics which show an average annual deficit of 114.6 million rubles for the seven years from 1961 to 1967. (A ruble equaled $1.11 at the official rate.) For these years the total deficit amounted to 803.6 million rubles. The authors point out the "alarming" fact that the deficits during the last two of these years were much larger than the average: 174.6 million rubles for 1966 and 220 million for 1967.[23] If we assume the 1968 and 1969 deficits to be the same as those for 1967, the total for the nine years would be 1,243.6 billion rubles, equal to $1,380,396,000 at the official rate, owed to Russia alone. In addition, the USSR has supplied gratis military hardware estimated by Castro on April 22, 1970, to have a value of $1.5 billion.

On Balance

From 1966 to 1970 sugar commitments to Russia totaled 22 million tons. But Cuban production during these five years was only 28.9 million tons, and obviously the USSR has had to forgo much of the sugar promised by its Western partner. René Dumont estimated in 1969 that Cuba was 8 million tons short on its commitment to the Soviets. At 6.11 cents per pound, which the prime minister said in his address of May 20, 1970, was the rate paid by the USSR, the dollar value of the shortage would be $972 million.

These various sources indicate that the debt of Cuba to the USSR is not less than $1 billion and may be in excess of $2 billion. Indeed an estimate of $2 billion may be too conservative. In testimony before the Subcommittee on Inter-American Affairs of the House of Representatives on July 8, 1970, Robert A. Hurwitch of the state department said that "we estimate that Cuba has received $3.2 billion in economic assistance from the Soviet Union." He also said the estimated daily cost to the USSR was $1.4 million, which amounts to $511 million per year.[24] Whatever the true amounts of Cuba's trade may be, there is sufficient evidence to show that the country is in serious economic trouble.[25]

In 1969 the prime minister told a graduating class: "We have known the bitterness of having to depend on others and how this can be turned into a weapon against us." He referred, of course, to the United States, but the Cuban people now know what it is to be dependent upon the USSR. It is clear that the Soviets have a very expensive welfare client, and only they can decide whether the political dividends are worth the economic losses.

It is obvious, though, that Cuba's protector has begun to pay much closer attention to its client. The new trade agreement with the Soviet Union negotiated in late 1970 called for the creation of a joint Soviet-Cuban economic commission. This follows a pattern of relationships which the USSR has with other aid recipients. It most likely means a larger role of the Soviets in Cuban affairs.

Observers have also noted that the star of the old Communist Carlos Rafael Rodríguez appears to be rising. It was he who negotiated the new agreement for economic cooperation and he is chairman of the Cuban side of the new commission. Officials of very high level, along with numerous technicians and advisers, pour into Cuba as never before.[26] The technicians are no longer limiting themselves to advising their counterparts in Havana, but are spreading over the countryside as well.

Was the Revolution Necessary?

The question of the historical necessity of the Cuban Revolution is academic, of course, yet the issue of violent revolution as a means of social change is one for civilized people to ponder. It may well be that some revolutions are made necessary by what Brooks Adams calls the "mental opacity of the privileged orders." [27] Although he was speaking of the French Revolution, his observation can be applied to Cuba, where violence overthrew the "privileged orders." But the evidence to date is that while drastic changes were accomplished, the basic problems of the island remain.

Although Castro and his associates won the rebellion, they have failed to win the revolution. As we have pointed out repeatedly, the wonderful prophecies have not been fulfilled. Still suffering the deprivations imposed by the ration book, the Cuban people now discover they overthrew one dictator only to become subject to a new and more oppressive one. They have exchanged their historic association with the United States, ninety miles away, for a new and somewhat strange relationship with the USSR, some six thousand miles away. What has the revolution won for them?

Several writers have called the revolution "tragic." Irving P. Pflaum, a correspondent who saw the tragedy in the making in Cuba, wrote: "Evil and relentless forces seemed to be pushing Cubans and the North Americans into a mutually destructive, totally useless, needless struggle neither could win!" [28]

Many will agree with this verdict. It seems fair to say that, in general, revolutions of the violent kind are seldom necessary. Better results in the end can be attained by more peaceful means, even though they take longer. Revolutions are messy, bloody, irrational, and destructive — destructive not only of wealth but of people and often the most talented and productive ones. The result of such human wastage is a terrible time lag of chaos until new leadership arrives to fill the vacuum. Materially, a society which suffers a revolution loses its accumulated reserves in the chaos of transition during which the new inexperienced leaders try to learn how to operate a total economy.

Much to be preferred to revolutionary Cuba would be the old Cuba plus the reforms which the Ortodoxo party proposed to carry out. Let us take a look at the platform of the Ortodoxo party headed by Roberto Agramonte, who according to a December 1951 poll of *Bohemia* magazine was well ahead of the other two candidates. The principal planks were honesty in government; extensive reforms in education and health; an independent judiciary; free labor unions, to be reorganized on a democratic basis with officers chosen in free elections; agrarian reform, embodying the distribution of idle private and public lands to landless people, with compensation to the owners of expropriated land; long-range economic planning directed toward industrialization and the diversification of agriculture. In this last area, Agramonte proposed the investment of 30 percent of tax revenues in development. To encourage new industries, he proposed tax write-offs and some protection against foreign competition. These basic programs had been on the agendas of reform groups since the 1930's and had been aggressively promoted for several years by Eduardo Chibás, the founder of the Ortodoxo party. They were to be carried out within the democratic framework.[29]

This program, according to the *Bohemia* poll, was what most people wanted and expected. But something happened on the way to victory. The happening was the coup d'etat of Fulgencio Batista on March 10, 1952, and the canceling of the elections. Batista must be blamed for triggering the rebellion that was to overthrow him and for the revolution that followed. One is compelled in retrospect to agree with Castro that the coup was a crime against Cuba.[30]

Batista's act was especially unsettling to the middle class, that is, to those members who hoped that the country was developing some political maturity. For the fact is that there had been relatively free elections — as such went in Cuba — in 1940 and especially in 1944. The election of 1948 was peaceful, whatever else may be said of it, and the outlook was for a free election in 1952 with the prospect of victory for the Ortodoxo party and its reforms. Batista turned the clock back with his coup and probably ensured the death of democracy in Cuba for a generation or more.

Beyond Castro

Difficult as it is to imagine the Cuban Revolution without Fidel Castro, such a condition must be faced eventually. Not that he is in any immediate danger, as far as anyone outside can know. Indeed, the security measures invoked especially since 1967 against enemies, real or potential, provide a reasonable guarantee of the safety of the regime in general and of the prime minister in particular. Still all men are mortal, and dictatorships in Latin America have all been of limited duration. Granted that Castro's tenure has been one of the longest and that his particular regime is different from any others that have existed in the hemisphere, it is certain to finally terminate.

What might be the situation in Cuba without Fidel Castro, the man who made and has led the revolution for thirteen years? First of all, the naming of his successor may be critical. There are two considerations on this point: Castro has already designated his brother Raúl to succeed him, and there is no constitutional alternative procedure providing for succession. Since Raúl is minister of the armed forces, his chances of making good his succession should be favorable. Yet Raúl lacks the charisma and other personal qualities which have made his brother so effective. How popular Raúl is with the officers over whom he has command and how he is regarded by his associates in the Politburo and the Central Committee of the party are not known.

There are thus many imponderables. One of them is the extent to which loyalty that the armed forces personnel and particularly the officers have sworn to Fidel can be transferred to Raúl. The same consideration applies to party officials. The leadership potential in the military and the party is not known, but in case of a power struggle any latent leaders may well surface and challenge the Castro group. It can generally be assumed that a totalitarian leader who gains and maintains power by violence builds up a reservoir of hatred in the process. The Castros are unlikely to be exceptions.

On Balance

In regard to the military, it should be kept in mind that both personnel and equipment have been improved recently; specialized cadet schools were established in 1968 and Russia has been providing new armaments since that year. In addition, the police force has been enlarged and given extra training and more equipment. It is in itself a power to be reckoned with. Again, the loyalty of these groups to the regime in general is an important element.

Finally, should a power struggle develop, another major factor may prove to be the workers. The older ones have long since become disillusioned with the labor policies of the revolution. Any concerted action on their part to shut down operations might cause chaos in an already shaky economy.

Casting a shadow over any development in the future is the Soviet Union, with its vast economic and political investment in Cuba. Cuba's dependence upon it could give it veto power over any change, including the naming of Fidel Castro's successor.

In regard to post-Castro policies, we may venture two possibilities: first, a continuation of the Castro program, and second, some constrained adaptation in the economic area in the form of material incentives for labor in order to achieve greater productivity. On the first proposition, it is arguable that whoever the successor, and whatever the circumstances of his coming to power, there will be at first few if any changes in economic or political policies. It will be a waiting period, during which everyone identified closely with the revolution will be concerned above all with its preservation. There remains in Cuba a latent remnant of the old republican democracy which would like to see a return to representative government. Its strength is unknown, but it remains a threat of consequence to the regime. With their vested interests in the revolution, the present leaders must prevent a successful uprising of the old democracy, since they would in all probability suffer the same consequences that they inflicted on the ones they overthrew. There will be a period when, in spite of differences among them, the leaders will follow the admonition of Benjamin Franklin to another group of revolutionaries: "We must indeed all hang together, or, most assuredly, we shall all hang separately."

If there has been no improvement in the economic situation when the crisis comes — and Castro promises none before 1975 — the people will be as restless as ever and possibly even more ready to join in a complete overthrow. This is another reason for the successors to hold a tight rein.

On the other hand, a continuation of unrest and low productivity should suggest some changes in the direction of gradual relaxation of policy in favor of individual initiative. One would think small enterprises might be permitted, particularly in the service area. For despite the government's announced determination in 1968 to root out capitalism, Castro admitted the existence of a blackmarket on May 1, 1971. Peasants would be more enthusiastic producers if they were allowed — as they were in the early years — to market some of their goods privately. Labor would be stimulated if there were less emphasis on moral and more on material incentives. The USSR would hardly be likely to oppose such moves, since they are in harmony with its own practices.

No general uprising is to be anticipated, given the measures of control that exist. Civil war would not be possible, short of a major split in the armed forces, which is unlikely. Barring a complete overturn, another revolution, the more than 600,000 refugees face the likelihood of permanent exile. About one thousand acknowledge this probability monthly by becoming United States citizens. Nevertheless, if Cuba were "liberated" anew, as it were, and there was a return to a constitutional democracy, the call of the homeland would be strong. Moreover, those who have done well abroad because of their special talents and enterprise would be able to make an enormous contribution to the rehabilitation of Cuba. The erosion of time on the fortunes of the refugees is one of the most pathetic aspects of the revolution.

But to leave the rarefied air of speculation and return to the *tierra firme* of reality, Cubans must face the prospect in the immediate years ahead of continued hardship without hope of improvement. Unrest and discontent cannot fail to continue and increase. This leaves us with the uncertainty that anything can happen where there is deprivation, disillusionment, and increasing suppression.

Notes and
Selected Bibliography

Notes

CHAPTER 1. THE CUBAN REBELLION

NOTE: The story of the events that occurred during the rebellion and the "takeover" by the revolution is to be found best in the reports of press correspondents and other observers who were in Cuba during this period. I have relied especially on books by the following: Boris Goldenberg, a teacher for twenty years in Cuba; Jules Dubois, longtime Latin American correspondent for the *Chicago Tribune* but who left the island shortly after Castro came to power; Jay Mallin, for ten years (1952–62) the Cuban correspondent for *Time* magazine, who left the island after the Bay of Pigs incident; R. Hart Phillips, for twenty-five years resident correspondent of the *New York Times*; and Paul D. Bethel, press attaché at the United States embassy until the break in diplomatic relations in January 1961. Herbert L. Matthews, also of the *New York Times*, played a crucial role in the fortunes of Fidel Castro and wrote two books and several editorials in favor of Castro and the revolution. His colleague, Mrs. Phillips, was reporting the day-by-day development of the regime toward a "Communist" orientation (to her dismay) while Matthews was counseling patience, restraint, and conciliation. Other United States correspondents and observers visited Cuba early in the revolution. Among them were Theodore Draper, Paul Baran, Leo Huberman, Paul Sweezy, C. Wright Mills, Maurice Zeitlin, and Robert Scheer, all of whom published books describing the situation as they saw it from their varied points of view. Books are cited by title in the Notes with complete citations given in the Bibliography.

1. Ramón Grau San Martín was a physician and a professor at the University of Havana, where he was a leader of a radical group of students and professors who formed the *Directorio Estudentil* (Student Directorate). This was one of the groups who passionately opposed President Machado.

2. For example, former ambassador to Cuba Earl E. T. Smith told the U.S. Senate Subcommittee to Investigate the Administration of the Internal Security Act in August 1960 that the "United States, until the advent of Castro, was so overwhelmingly influential in Cuba that . . . the American Ambassador was the second most important man in Cuba; sometimes even more important than the President." This statement is unquestionably an exaggeration and it was ex-

tremely unwise for him to make it. Yet there is no doubt about the strong influence wielded by the United States in Cuban affairs.

3. Not surprisingly there is no objective study of Fidel Castro available. A man so controversial inspires either strong antipathy or fervent admiration. Mainly laudatory are the two books by Herbert L. Matthews, *The Cuban Story* and *Fidel Castro*; the lengthy interview with Castro by Lee Lockwood published as *Castro's Cuba: Cuba's Fidel*; Jules Dubois's volume *Fidel Castro: Rebel — Liberator or Dictator?* which covers events up to the takeover; and *Cuba and Castro*, the memoir of Teresa Casuso, an ardent supporter up to the time of her defection in mid-1959. Former associates of Castro such as Manuel Artime and Manuel Urrutia Lleó have offered more critical appraisals. Matthews has had more opportunity to study Castro at close range than has any other American writer, and one depends much on his works while recognizing his pro-Castro bias.

4. Lockwood, *Castro's Cuba: Cuba's Fidel*, p. 25.

5. Teresa Casuso, an employee of the Cuban embassy in Mexico and at the time one of Fidel's collaborators, describes a visit made by Fidel's mother in an unsuccessful attempt to prevent the burning of her field. Casuso also reports that after Fidel's triumphal entry into Havana in 1959 his mother neither came to see her son nor sent a message. *Cuba and Castro*, p. 130.

An older brother, Ramón, gave Fidel and Raúl some important help during their stay in the Sierra Maestra; he managed the family farm and was outraged when Fidel ordered the expropriation of the property and its conversion into a state farm. The youngest sister, Juana, who like her mother was embittered by the turn of events, finally defected to the United States and wrote and lectured against the regime of her brother. Although Herbert Matthews insists that with the exception of Juana the "Castro family has always remained close" (*Fidel Castro*, p. 19), there seems to be some evidence to the contrary. In connection with family matters, it needs to be recorded that on October 12, 1948, Castro married Mirta Díaz Balart, a philosophy student whom he met at the university. A son, Fidelito, was born to the couple in September 1949. Castro's wife divorced him while he was a prisoner on the Isle of Pines. She later remarried; to date he has not.

6. Suchlicki, *University Students and Revolution in Cuba, 1920–1968*, p. 54.

7. *Ibid.*, pp. 51–52.

8. *Ibid.*, pp. 52–53. The episode is important here because it reflects the atmosphere of violence and threats of violence which were part of the political climate of the late 1940's. On this see also Jules Dubois, *Fidel Castro: Rebel — Liberator or Dictator?*, pp. 17–23. As Latin American correspondent for the *Chicago Tribune*, Dubois was in Bogatá to report on the Inter-American Conference held under the auspices of the Pan American Union. For other accounts which consider this episode as evidence of Castro's early commitment to communism, see Nathaniel Weyl, *Red Star over Cuba* (Devin-Adair, 1960), pp. 1–38; and Mario Lazo, *Dagger in the Heart*, pp. 129–43.

9. Matthews, *Fidel Castro*, p. 23.

10. Suchlicki, *University Students and Revolution in Cuba*, p. 55.

11. *Ibid.*, p. 56.

12. Dubois, *Fidel Castro: Rebel — Liberator or Dictator?* p. 26.

13. *Ibid.*, p. 30.

14. *Ibid.*, p. 144.

15. The events leading up to his interview are recounted in Matthews's book *Cuban Story*, chap. 1; see also R. Hart Phillips, *Cuban Dilemma*, pp. v–vi. The interview was published in the *New York Times* on February 24, 1957, and is reprinted in Robert F. Smith, *What Happened in Cuba?* pp. 259–63.

Notes

CHAPTER 2. THE REVOLUTION TAKES OVER

NOTE: In compressing into a single chapter the events from 1959 to 1961, I have had to omit detailed discussion and documentation. But the purpose of this volume is not to dwell on this period except to chronicle the events which led finally to the tragic break in Cuban-American relations. The period has been covered in considerable detail by others. Of those authors mentioned in the Note to Chapter 1, especially useful are Phillips (*Cuban Dilemma* and *Cuba: Island of Paradox*), Bethel (*The Losers*), and Zeitlin and Scheer (*Cuba: Tragedy in Our Hemisphere*). The first two authors were in Cuba during the period and their books are in the nature of personal memoirs recording day-to-day events. Both are highly critical of United States diplomacy because of the failure to intervene. Zeitlin and Scheer in their scholarly and well-documented review of events also present a critical view of American diplomacy but for different reasons. Their view, from a prorevolutionary stance, is that United States failure consisted in not taking advantage of opportunities for reconciliation offered by the Cubans. Again, the books of Matthews and Goldenberg are very useful, as are those of Robert F. Smith. Finally the *New York Times* is the best single source for the record of events and for relevant documents. It has seemed unnecessary to cite it specifically for each event for which a date is given in the text, since an account would appear in the *Times* the following day.

1. Their success led — or more properly misled — Castro and his associate Ernesto (Che) Guevara to develop a theory of revolution to the effect that a small band of disciplined and well-trained guerrilla fighters could repeat the Cuban success in other countries of Latin America. The process would involve such a group moving into a rural area, developing rapport with the peasants, and recruiting them as collaborators after indoctrinating them with the hopes and aspirations of the revolution. As the number of recruits increased and revolutionary control spread over ever-enlarging areas, taxes could be collected and supplies obtained. The fallacy of the theory was fatally demonstrated by Guevara in Bolivia. The mistake was to generalize from a single experience, one carried out under unique circumstances. As Luis E. Aguilar has so well put it: "The myth theory . . . ignored a number of factors that were indispensable to Castro's victory. These included the support given to Castro by the middle class and parts of the upper class, because he represented himself as the leader of a moderate democratic movement; the demoralization of the Cuban army, rendered vulnerable to Castroite propaganda by the knowledge that it was propping up a corrupt and unpopular regime; and Washington's posture of neutrality between Batista and Castro — a stance adopted because of U.S. sensitivity to charges of having been overly friendly to a number of deposed Latin American dictators . . . See "Fragmentation of the Marxist Left," *Problems of Communism*, 19, no. 4 (July–August 1970), 7. On the Student Revolutionary Directorate and the Second Front, see Suchlicki, *University Students and Revolution in Cuba*, pp. 96–100; Matthews, *Cuban Story*, pp. 75ff.

2. Dubois, *Fidel Castro: Rebel — Liberator or Dictator?* p. 343.

3. A general strike called by Castro for April 9, 1958, failed badly. The labor leaders refused to go along with it, as did the old Communists. The latter publicly criticized it as ill advised.

4. In order to understand the choice of Urrutia as provisional president, it is necessary to know some historical background. In his Manifesto from the Sierra Maestra of July 12, 1957, Castro had called for all groups opposing Batista to organize a Civilian Revolutionary Front and to "select a figure to preside over the provisional government" (Dubois, *Fidel Castro: Rebel — Liberator or Dictator?*

pp. 168–72). The organization of the front was not undertaken until October 1957, when a group of distinguished Cubans in exile met in Miami. They drafted a long document declaring their determination to oppose the Batista regime and at the same time setting forth their proposals for the reform of Cuban affairs. They further proposed that Felipe Pazos be the provisional president. (Pazos was president of the Cuban National Bank from January 1959 until he went into exile toward the end of that year.) When this document reached Castro in the mountains, it brought forth a volcanic verbal eruption. Castro belabored the signers for attempting from their safe sanctuary in Miami to dictate the future of the revolution to those who were facing the guns of Batista and enduring the hardships of the campaign. He then proposed Manuel Urrutia Lleó as the provisional president. He left no doubt that revolutionary policies would be determined by the 26th of July Movement and made it equally clear that he was in charge of it.

5. Dubois, *Fidel Castro: Rebel — Liberator or Dictator?* p. 375.

6. Mallin, *Fortress Cuba*, p. 16.

7. Goldenberg, *Cuban Revolution and Latin America*, p. 188.

8. For a reporter's account of this trial, see Phillips, *Cuban Dilemma*, pp. 32ff.

9. International Commission of Jurists, *Cuba and the Rule of Law*, p. 259. Further conclusions stated that the accused were tortured during imprisonment, denied the services of a lawyer before trial, and not told of charges against them until the prosecutor put "forward his provisional conclusions."

10. Dubois, *Fidel Castro: Rebel — Liberator or Dictator?* pp. 198–99.

11. R. F. Smith, *The United States and Cuba*, p. 183. This outstanding authority has written three volumes which are indispensable to an understanding of the relations that have characterized the United States and Cuba since 1898. Smith's other works are *What Happened in Cuba?* (an invaluable collection of relevant documents beginning in 1783 and concluding with President John F. Kennedy's "Demands for the Withdrawal of Offensive Weapons from Cuba," October 22, 1962); and *Background to Revolution: The Development of Modern Cuba*. Although it is not our purpose to dwell on the history of Cuban-American relations, the interested reader will find valuable the following: Goldenberg, *The Cuban Revolution and Latin America*; Phillips, *Cuba: Island of Paradox* and *Cuban Dilemma*; C. E. Chapman, *History of the Cuban Republic*; the four-volume work by Herminio Portell Vilá, *Historia de Cuba, en sus relaciones con los Estados Unidos y España*; and Ramón Eduardo Ruiz, *Cuba: The Making of a Revolution*.

12. See Casuso, *Cuba and Castro*, pp. 207–12, for her account of the trip. Mrs. Phillips calls the trip a "triumphant tour. After five days in Washington and a short visit to Princeton, N.J., Castro was greeted rousingly in New York by 20,000 admirers. He held a news conference, toured Columbia University, conferred with Secretary-General Dag Hammarskjöld at the United Nations, visited Mayor Robert Wagner, addressed the Overseas Club, and held a Central Park rally which drew 30,000 people . . ." See Phillips, *Cuban Dilemma*, p. 72.

13. Nixon, *Six Crises*, pp. 351–52.

14. *Ibid.*, p. 352.

15. *Ibid.*

16. Matthews, *Fidel Castro*, p. 121. Matthews says: "The basic, unending antagonism toward the 'Yankees' was always there." He goes on to note a letter written by Castro in June 1958 to Celia Sanchez, his secretary, in which the rebel leader swore that "when this war is over, a much wider and bigger war will begin for me: the war that I am going to launch against them (the Americans). I am saying to myself that this is my true destiny." Theodore Draper, one of the most astute analysts of the Castro movement, which he calls "Castroism," also dismisses the theory that the treatment by Washington affected Castro's future plans.

Notes

His opinion is that "Fidel Castro and his inner circle have never been innocent victims of circumstances . . . A revolutionary leader does not betray the fundamental character of his revolution because American oil companies refuse to refine Soviet oil or because the United States suspends a sugar quota that has been attacked as 'a symbol of colonialism.' If he is really committed to a new social order different from capitalism or Communism, he does not resist the one by capitulating to the other with the speed of a push-button operation." See Draper, *Castro's Revolution*, p. 106.

17. Goldenberg, *Cuban Revolution and Latin America*, p. 182.

18. Javier Pazos, a veteran of Sierra Maestra and an official in the Finance Ministry of the first revolutionary government, who was a delegate to the Buenos Aires conference, states that "Fidel was very enthusiastic about his private Alliance for Progress scheme of $30 billion, which he put forward there. My impression then was that he was contemplating staying on the American side of the fence as a sponsor of this $30 billion scheme . . ." See "Cuba: Was a Deal Possible in 1959?" *New Republic*, January 12, 1963, p. 11. For the Goldenberg quotations, see his *Cuban Revolution and Latin America*, p. 183.

19. It would clearly have been impossible for any country to compensate in cash for property expropriated on the scale undertaken by Cuba. Payment in twenty-year bonds was the major means adopted in 1950 by the Italian land reform program, which involved but a small fraction of the national territory. On the other hand, had there been negotiation with goodwill on both sides, which there was not, some long-term payment program might have been arranged. That the regime, in offering or in suggesting bonds as compensation, expected the bonds to be of no worth was shown by the report by Manuel Artime of the "secret meeting" of high-echelon officials of INRA, in his book *Traición!* See also the discussion of this in Chapter 5 below.

20. R. F. Smith, *United States and Cuba*, p. 182.

21. Zeitlin and Scheer, *Cuba: Tragedy in Our Hemisphere*, p. 140, citing the *New York Times* of February 28, 1960. Their discussion under the subtitle "The Missed Opportunity for Reconciliation," pp. 138–42, lays major responsibility on the United States.

22. On the *Le Coubre* tragedy and Castro's funeral address at the Colón cemetery, see Zeitlin and Scheer, *ibid.*, pp. 143–49. In general these writers justify Castro's suspicion of United States involvement but point out that there is no evidence to prove it. For a different point of view, see the account by Phillips, who heard Castro's address: "It was an inflaming tirade against the United States, which he accused of sabotaging the vessel." *Cuban Dilemma*, p. 172. On the anniversary of the *Le Coubre* explosion, Havana radio annually reiterates the charge that it was the work of agents of the United States. On June 26, 1971, Castro referred to the explosion as "one of the most characteristic attacks perpetrated by the Central Intelligence Agency."

23. U.S., *Department of State Bulletin*, July 18, 1960, pp. 79–87. The quotation is on page 79.

24. The Eisenhower statement appears in R. F. Smith, *What Happened in Cuba?* p. 278. Phillips reports Castro as saying the quota reduction was a "blessing in disguise" because Cuba was now the "indisputable master of the world sugar market." See *Cuban Dilemma*, p. 225.

25. *Declaración de la Habana* (Matanzas: Suplemento de la Revista Museo, 1960), p. 6 of this nine-page pamphlet. Trans. from the Spanish.

26. Some of the ludicrous, unhappy, and unjust ramifications of urban reform in the lives of individuals are revealed by Mrs. Phillips, for example, the woman

213

who rented out a room in her house and suffered its dispossession in favor of her renter. Phillips, *Cuban Dilemma*, pp. 257–59.

27. On this point, see document no. 9, pp. 280–82, in R. F. Smith, *United States and Cuba.*

28. Robert F. Smith, though not regarding the United States as blameless by any means, has this to say about Castro: "He is blindly dedicated to a vision of the new Cuba . . . a fanatical idealist who never counted the costs of his action. This messianic self-righteousness produced an extremely hostile reaction to any hint of criticism or even neutralism. As a result he has heaped abuse on the United States and on Americans in Cuba which has provided ammunition for those Americans who look with disfavor on revolutions." *United States and Cuba,* p. 182.

29. It was not the revolution Castro had promised or that the Cuban people were led to expect. The detour from the original promise gave rise to charges of "deception" and "betrayal." See Theodore Draper, *Castro's Revolution: Myths and Realities*, especially chap. 1, "The Two Revolutions"; James Monahan and Kenneth O. Gilmore, *Great Deception*; and Andrés Suárez, *Cuba: Castroism and Communism.*

30. It is usual for American writers to speak of the Cuban press as "venal," "subsidized," and, as Herbert Matthews puts it, "responding to government and industry" (*Fidel Castro*, p. 346). The general impression given is that there was no freedom of the press or of expression. This is not true. It is true that newspapers were subsidized by the government, a practice at least as old as the republic. Yet there was a broad spectrum of opinion in the Cuban press, some supporting the government, some against it. For example, there was the conservative *Diario de la Marina*, the liberal daily *El Mundo*, and *Prensa Libre*, a leftist daily which was anti-Batista. Likewise, the famous weekly *Bohemia*, whose editor Miguel Angel Quevado, according to Goldenberg, "during the whole of the Batista period had openly proclaimed his friendship with Castro." Similarly, television and radio had differing attitudes toward the government. Eduardo Chibás spent hours every Sunday night criticizing the policies and practices of the government. During my year in Cuba, there was running criticism of the Grau San Martín government in the press.

CHAPTER 3. THE DEVELOPMENT
OF PREREVOLUTIONARY CUBA

1. On the plight of the natives during the conquest and the encomienda period, see I. A. Wright, *The Early History of Cuba, 1492–1586* (New York: Macmillan, 1916). For the origin and history of the encomiendas, see Lowry Nelson, *Rural Cuba*, chap. 5. I have drawn on this chapter rather heavily for the current writing.

2. See *Rural Cuba*, pp. 84–90, and Guerra y Sánchez, *Sugar and Society in the Caribbean*, pp. 31–81. It was interesting to fly over prerevolutionary Cuba and note on the landscape below the long sweeping arcs that were remnants of the boundaries of the original *haciendas circulares*. The circular grants appear to have been unique to Cuba. Such inquiries as I have made of students of other countries of Spanish America have revealed no similar instances.

3. There were also illicit sales to buccaneers, pirates, and freebooters.

4. Don Jacobo de la Pezuela y Lobo, *Diccionario geográfico, estadístico, histórico de la Isla de Cuba* (Madrid, 1863–66.)

5. For detailed information by industry group, see Cuban Economic Research Project (hereafter cited as CERP), *Study on Cuba*, p. 555.

214

Notes

6. CERP, *Study on Cuba*, p. 622. The reference is to Rostow's article which first appeared in the *British Economic Journal*. It has been often reprinted; see for example A. N. Agarwala and S. P. Singh, eds., *The Economics of Underdevelopment* (Oxford University Press, 1966), pp. 154–86.

7. Bruce M. Russet *et al.*, *World Handbook of Political and Social Indicators* (New Haven: Yale University Press, 1964), p. 155.

CHAPTER 4. CUBAN AGRICULTURE
BEFORE THE REVOLUTION

1. In saying this, I am by no means unmindful of the importance of other factors, including capital and management, but it was the land workers who toiled the hardest and for the most part received the least for their efforts.

2. The studies were made at the University of Miami under what was called the Cuban Economic Research Project (CERP). Among the published reports are the following: *Cuba: Agriculture and Planning, 1963–1964; Stages and Problems of Industrial Development in Cuba; Labor Conditions in Communist Cuba; Codification of Labor Law in Latin America: Cuba, a Case Study*; and *Social Security in Cuba*. In addition a summary volume, *A Study on Cuba*, was published by the University of Miami Press in 1965. This is an English language edition of *Un Estudio Sobre Cuba*, published in 1963.

3. International Bank for Reconstruction and Development (IBRD hereafter), *Report on Cuba*, pp. 94–95.

4. Nelson, *Rural Cuba*, pp. 260–61.

5. The total value of food imports from all sources amounted to $159 million or 20.5 percent of total imports of $777.1 million. Only "raw materials" exceeded food in value ($165.1 million) and percentage of the total (21.2 percent). See CERP, *Cuba: Agriculture and Planning*, pp. 57–58.

6. CERP, *Study on Cuba*, p. 536.

7. *Ibid.*, pp. 536–37. Table 381 gives rice production for 1946 as well as for other years to 1956, and Table 384 gives production for 1956–57.

8. *Ibid.*, pp. 563–64.

9. CERP, *Cuba: Agriculture and Planning*, p. 74.

10. CERP, *Study on Cuba*, p. 564.

11. CERP, *Stages and Problems of Industrial Development in Cuba*, p. 105. The reader will note that our previous comparison of the growth in cultivated area and in population included the years 1946–57 and also that an increase in land area is not the same as an "annual accumulated growth rate."

12. CERP, *Study on Cuba*, p. 574. The data are taken from the Bureau of the Census publication, *U.S. Exports of Domestic and Foreign Merchandise*, report no. FT410, part 2, 1941–59. See also CERP, *Cuba: Agriculture and Planning*, p. 68, which estimates 19,700 tractors in 1957–58.

13. CERP, *Study on Cuba*, p. 526, Table 362.

14. CERP, *Cuba: Agriculture and Planning*, pp. 75–76.

15. For a detailed exposition of the impact of this law, see CERP, *Study on Cuba*, pp. 339–52.

16. *Ibid.*, p. 523.

17. *Ibid.*, p. 362.

18. *Ibid.*, p. 531.

19. Nelson, *Rural Cuba*, p. 131.

20. I was interested in R. Hart Phillips's account of her visit to the Cuban Land and Leaf Tobacco Company some fourteen years after my own visit. In 1960, she reported, the property was valued at $2,600,000 and was operated by

seventy-five sharecroppers who received 80 percent of the crop and "made $15,000 to $20,000 a year." See *Cuban Dilemma*, pp. 168–69.

21. CERP, *Study on Cuba*, p. 533.

22. With regard to horses, it is important to note that Cubans have not used them as draft animals, a function reserved for oxen. But horses are highly prized for riding. Mules and donkeys were used for transport in more remote sections.

23. CERP, *Study on Cuba*, pp. 527–28. In its *Report on Cuba*, p. 887, IBRD lists the following types of crosses: criollo, criollo-Shorthorn, criollo-Hereford, criollo-Zebu, Shorthorn-Zebu, Brown Swiss–Zebu, and Angus-Zebu.

24. CERP, *Study on Cuba*, p. 527.

25. *Ibid.*, p. 526. A footnote to Table 361 on the same page quotes a report published by INRA (the land reform institute) in 1961 giving the number of cattle in 1958 as 5,385,000 plus 940,000 milk cows. This would bring the total to 6,325,000, which is probably too high.

26. Nelson, *Rural Cuba*, pp. 133–34.

27. CERP, *Cuba: Agriculture and Planning*, p. 298. The figures are derived from *América en Cifras* (Washington, D.C.: Pan American Union, 1960), whose authors also state that there was an "undeclared production amounting to from 18 to 20 million liters."

28. CERP, *Cuba: Agriculture and Planning*, p. 294.

29. CERP, *Study on Cuba*, p. 530.

30. *Ibid.*, p. 571.

CHAPTER 5. AGRICULTURE
AND THE REVOLUTION

NOTE: In regard to sources of Cuban statistics, it should be pointed out that during the revolutionary reorganization government statistical services were disrupted, and it was not until 1968 that a comprehensive and official report became available. The publication *Boletín Estadístico 1966* (Dirección Central de Estadística, Junta Central de Planificación), as its title indicates, brought statistics up to and including 1966. Although it was designated for "restrictive circulation," copies nevertheless were obtained in the United States. A somewhat less useful and more restricted report also became available, the *Compendio Estadístico de Cuba, 1967*. A disappointing feature of these reports is that they give data only from 1962, so that for the most part the first three years of the revolution are not covered. The material in these two government publications, plus additional data gathered in Cuba, has been published (in English) by the Latin American Center of the University of California at Los Angeles under the editorship of C. Paul Roberts and Mukhtar Hamour. This work, *Cuba 1968, Supplement to the Statistical Abstract of Latin America*, is an invaluable addition to the still limited sources.

Other sources are the annual reports of the United Nations and its specialized agencies, FAO, ILO, WHO, and UNESCO, as well as the reports of the Pan American Union, especially *América en Cifras*. Carmelo Mesa-Lago has rendered invaluable service in bringing together from these and other sources a comprehensive set of data on various aspects of the economy in his two-part article, "Availability and Reliability of Statistics in Communist Cuba," *Latin American Research Review*, 4, nos. 1, 2 (Spring, Summer 1969).

As I explained earlier, I have drawn heavily on the data assembled by the Cuban Economic Research Project (CERP), especially for the period before 1959, but also for the first years of the revolution. (See above, note 2, Chapter 4.) For the present chapter, I have found *Cuba: Agriculture and Planning* especially

Notes

helpful. For factual information, this report draws on official announcements published in the semiofficial daily newspaper *Revolución* and other publications still active in the early years. *Revolución* has ceased publication; the daily and weekly editions of *Granma* constitute the present medium for official announcements. The English language Weekly Review edition publishes all speeches of the prime minister in translation, and it is this edition of *Granma* that I have cited throughout. Castro is often the source of official statistics.

1. Guerra y Sánchez, *Sugar and Society in the Caribbean*, pp. 38–74.

2. It is not merely coincidental that both laws were passed during Batista regimes. While Batista is justly criticized for the corruption of his governments, he accomplished some good for rural Cuba, where he was born and reared in poor circumstances.

3. The word is used here to refer to the sugar plantations, which are simply large-scale capitalist agricultural-industrial enterprises. Latifundia such as existed in Chile and the Andean countries never existed in Cuba. The *fundo* in Chile is — or was — a feudal institution in which the *patrón* was complete master of the lives of the *inquilinos*. Social security legislation during the 1930's brought little improvement to the serfs, but it did define them as laborers entitled to the minimum daily wage. However, only a fourth of the wage needed to be paid by the patrón in cash. The balance was considered as perquisites consisting of a dwelling — such as it was — and three or four acres of adjacent land on which the occupant could grow what he wished for himself or for sale. According to old feudal custom, he also received some food each day: a loaf of bread and an allotment of beans, corn, or some other item. New land reform programs in the 1960's looked toward the breakup of the fundo and the distribution of parcels to the former inquilinos. But it should be made clear that there were no latifundia of this type in Cuba.

4. Fidel Castro, *Political, Economic and Social Thought of Fidel Castro*, p. 58. This is the English translation of the official version of "History Will Absolve Me" (*La Historia me Absolverá*) along with two other documents by Castro. Jules Dubois gives a slightly different translation in *Fidel Castro: Rebel — Liberator or Dictator?* pp. 69–70.

5. Dubois, *Fidel Castro: Rebel — Liberator or Dictator?* p. 170. Two words in this translation by Dubois are not accurately rendered. "Partners" is translated from *aparceros*, meaning more accurately sharecroppers or share tenants. "Barren lands" comes from *baldíos*, which means in this context idle, uncultivated, or unreclaimed land, such as swamps. For the original document, see Gregorio Selzer, *Fidel Castro: La Revolución Cubana*, p. 123.

6. Sorí Marín became minister of agriculture in the first cabinet, but he later found himself out of sympathy with what was happening; he was charged with counterrevolutionary activity and executed.

7. CERP, *Cuba: Agriculture and Planning*, p. 213. "There were 15 'whereases,' 4 chapters, 38 articles, three final provisions, and one transitory provision" in this law, which indicates a very detailed document. Sorí had obviously been working on it for some time. It was in effect a preliminary draft of the law finally passed in May 1959.

8. Bianchi, "Agriculture — Post-Revolutionary Development," in Seers, *Cuba: The Economic and Social Revolution*, p. 106.

9. *Ibid.*, p. 111.

10. CERP, *Cuba: Agriculture and Planning*, p. 220.

11. *Ibid.*, p. 234.

12. *Ibid.*, p. 234, quoting the law published in the newspaper *Revolución* for October 4, 1963.

13. *Ibid.*, p. 229.

14. *Ibid.*, p. 13, citing *Revolución* for August 29, 1961.

15. Goldenberg, *Cuban Revolution and Latin America*, p. 255, citing the newspaper *El Mundo* for May 10, 1962.

16. CERP, *Sugar in Cuba* (1966), p. 229.

17. In Seers, *Cuba: The Economic and Social Revolution*, pp. 131–32.

18. *Ibid.*, p. 129.

19. "The Revolutionary Offensive," in Irving Louis Horowitz, *Cuban Communism*, p. 80.

20. In Seers, *Cuba: The Economic and Social Revolution*, pp. 137–40.

21. CERP, *Study on Cuba*, p. 526.

22. Confirmation of the rise in the incidence of brucellosis and tuberculosis among livestock is shown in the increase of the same diseases in the human population (see Table 19, Chapter 11). Severo Aguire, who is considered by the economists in exile to be the best authority on livestock, published an article in *Cuba Socialista*, May 1963, in which he estimated the mortality among cows at more than 20 percent. On April 28, 1964, a story in the newspaper *Hoy* told of a mysterious disease which paralyzed and killed cattle in 48 hours. A visiting Soviet specialist, Alexander Alenkovich, after an investigation, estimated that "by reducing mortality and sterility, it is possible to increase production by 60 percent." CERP, *Cuba: Agriculture and Planning*, p. 300.

23. See Alvarez Díaz, *La Destrucción de la Ganadería Cubana*, p. 9. The author, now in exile, was minister of finance in the Prío administration and a professor at the University of Havana.

24. Sergio Arana, *La Revolución Agraria en Cuba* (Mexico City: Siglo Editores, 1968). The author is strongly favorable to the revolution.

25. CERP, *Study on Cuba*, p. 528.

26. Bianchi, in Seers, *Cuba: The Economic and Social Revolution*, p. 114.

27. As reported in CERP, *Cuba: Agriculture and Planning*, p. 303.

28. Alvarez Díaz, *La Destrucción de la Ganadería Cubana*, p. 11.

29. Evidence that a cattle tick was ravaging the herds came from a broadcast on July 12, 1962, from Radio Centro, which announced a nationwide campaign by the Combined Meat Enterprise to collect hides and leather. One of the slogans was "Make War Against the Cattle Ticks; Enemies of Meat, Milk, and Hides." The broadcast also urged the saving of the hides of dead animals. The crisis in the supply of hides was created by vast exports to the USSR. See Carmelo Mesa-Lago, "Unemployment in Socialist Countries: Soviet Union, East Europe, China, and Cuba," Ph.D. dissertation, Cornell University, 1968, p. 441.

30. *Boletín Estadístico 1966*, Table V.7, in reporting cattle purchased for slaughter, adds in a footnote "including cattle for export."

31. Draper, *Castroism: Theory and Practice*, p. 143. Seers, *Cuba: The Economic and Social Revolution*, pp. 384–89, gives a list provided by the Ministry of Industries of 94 industrial plants which were promised by various socialist countries to be completed by 1967.

32. See Roberts and Hamour, *Cuba 1968*, p. 165.

33. René Dumont, "The Militarization of Fidelismo," *Dissent* (September–October 1970), p. 418. (Excerpts in English from his book *Cuba: Est-il Socialiste?*).

34. Roberts and Hamour, *Cuba 1968*, p. 119. The number of kilometers of sugarcane roads appears somewhat exaggerated.

35. *Ibid.*, p. 109.

36. *Ibid.*, p. 166.

37. *Ibid.*, p. 148.

Notes

38. *Ibid.*, p. 120.
39. Dumont, "The Militarization of Fidelismo," p. 426.

CHAPTER 6. WORKERS AND PEASANTS

1. The Escambray rebellion should not be confused with the Second Front of Escambray, which participated in the anti-Batista campaign. The one referred to here was an anti-Castro movement. These rebels consisted of individuals who had become disillusioned with the socialist drift of the Castro regime and sought to organize a guerrilla movement against him similar to the one he had used against Batista. The group was not large, but given the widespread discontent throughout the island it might have become a serious threat had Castro not taken massive action against it. This action involved the mobilization of a superior force of militia, easily sufficient to overwhelm the rebels. Peasants who had supported them were subjected to expropriation and imprisonment. Some were imprisoned in the Havana area and some on the Isle of Pines. For illustrations of the character of these men, see Lockwood, *Castro's Cuba: Cuba's Fidel*, pp. 214ff.

2. CERP, *Cuba: Agriculture and Planning*, p. 301, citing the newspaper *Hoy* for March 2, 1964.

3. Dumont, "The Militarization of Fidelismo," p. 414.

4. *New York Review of Books*, August 21, 1969, p. 16.

5. *Boletín Estadístico 1966*, Table V.6.

6. Carmelo Mesa-Lago and Roberto E. Hernández, *Labor Conditions in Communist Cuba*, p. 38. In apparent recognition of the fact that Cuban women are not as "strong," the Ministry of Labor on March 8, 1968, issued Resolutions 47 and 48, the first setting forth 430 jobs, lighter, less risky, and more healthful which would be open to women, and the other listing 496 jobs more appropriate for men. *Miami Radio Monitoring Service*, March 8, 1968. Nevertheless, agricultural work was not closed to women.

7. Mesa-Lago and Hernández, *Labor Conditions in Communist Cuba*, p. 35n.

8. *Granma*, August 8, 1969.

9. *Miami Radio Monitoring Service*, January 15, 1970.

10. This address was, like all important Castro addresses, published in *Granma's* Weekly Review edition; it was reprinted in the *New York Review of Books* with an introduction by Lee Lockwood, September 24, 1970, pp. 18–33.

11. The figures are given in CERP, *Study on Cuba*, p. 430.

12. Mesa-Lago, *The Labor Sector and Socialist Distribution in Cuba*, p. 47.

13. *Ibid.*, p. 66. Similar achievements of cane cutters were given in *Granma*, April 6, 1969, reporting a meeting of local leaders in Camagüey with Premier Castro.

14. CERP, *Study on Cuba*, p. 478, Table 345.

15. *Ibid.*, p. 723.

16. Mesa-Lago, "The Economic Significance of Unpaid Labor in Socialist Cuba," *Industrial and Labor Relations Review*, 22, no. 3 (April 1969), pp. 339–57, estimates that unpaid labor in 1967 was the equivalent of at least 200,000 man-years and perhaps as many as 300,000. It might have been considerably increased in 1970 due to the special mobilizations. Mesa-Lago's article is the most expert analysis of the value of "volunteer" work that is available.

17. "The Promethean Dream: Society in Search of Itself," in *Britannica Perspectives*, vol. 2 (1968), p. 37.

18. Peter Schmid, "Letter from Havana," *Commentary*, September 1965, p. 57.

19. On reasons for the labor shortage, see also Mesa-Lago, *The Labor Sector and Socialist Distribution in Cuba*, p. 354, and his "Unemployment in Socialist

Countries: Soviet Union, East Europe, China, and Cuba," Ph.D. dissertation, Cornell University, 1968, pp. 415–37.

20. Dumont, "The Militarization of Fidelismo," p. 415.

CHAPTER 7.
HOW TO MAKE PEOPLE WORK

1. For reference to this address, see above, Chapter 6, note 10.

2. Mesa-Lago and Hernández, *Labor Conditions in Communist Cuba*, pp. 10ff.

3. These provisions are reminiscent of what a famous Russian scientist recently termed the "anti-worker decrees" of Joseph Stalin. See Andrei D. Sakharov, *Progress, Coexistence and Intellectual Freedom* (New York: Norton, 1968), p. 54. Mesa-Lago and Hernández provide an example of these decrees. One dated December 20, 1938, required any person seeking work for the first time to obtain a certificate from the block vigilance committee with regard to his antecedents. "No enterprise is permitted to employ any worker who does not present his identity card which should contain the following information: his past performance; transfers and reasons therefor; incentives and distinctions granted. Discharge due to absenteeism, if any, should be so registered on the identity card." *Labor Conditions in Communist Cuba*, p. 13, note 55.

4. CERP, *Cuba: Agriculture and Planning*, p. 241.

5. Mesa-Lago and Hernández, *Labor Conditions in Communist Cuba*, p. 16.

6. *Ibid.*, p. 18.

7. The main features of the law were announced by Havana radio on March 15, 1971, monitored in Miami, and distributed by the U.S. Information Service. An English translation of the broadcast was published in *Daily Report*, March 15, distributed by the U.S. Foreign Broadcast Information Service.

8. Not only was the anti-loafing law read and discussed in more than 113,000 meetings attended by 3,250,000 persons and publicized through radio-television shows and newspaper stories, but still more meetings and street demonstrations were held on March 17 to celebrate the law's enactment. The Rivera Funeral Parlor workers staged a symbolic burial of loafing. This "jubiliation" was followed by mass organizations' issuance of "communiques" in support of the law.

9. Schmid, "Letter from Havana," p. 57.

10. Mohammed A. Rauf, Jr., *Cuban Journal*, pp. 77–78.

11. This thesis in its historical aspects has been convincingly presented by R. H. Tawney, *Religion and the Rise of Capitalism* (New York: Harcourt, Brace, 1926), and by Max Weber, *The Protestant Ethic and the Spirit of Capitalism* (New York: Scribner, 1930). Nevertheless, there is no evidence in the current world that Catholics are any less acquisitive than Protestants.

12. I say this despite a radio announcement (monitored in Miami on March 19) by the head of the Central Labor Union, Hector Ramas Latour, who said that "the Cuban working class will be tough on shirkers. It will not have any qualms about enforcing this law. However, it prefers that the law's severity will only strike the few recalcitrant persons who, disobeying the social duty of working, defy the national will." In the four months after the law became effective on April 1, 1971, about 1,000 cases were processed, according to a Havana radio announcement on July 12, 1971. The total labor force is almost three million. Of these, 15 percent were persons with previous criminal records. The same announcement reported the termination of a 30-day course of training for 165 workers who were to function as judges of the labor courts. It appears that a great deal of time and effort has been required to find and punish 1,000 loafers.

Notes

CHAPTER 8. THE NEW MAN
AND THE OLD

1. The best overall review of conditions up to 1950 is contained in the *Report on Cuba* of the International Bank for Reconstruction and Development (IBRD), while the report by Jolly (Seers, *Cuba: The Economic and Social Revolution,* ch. 4) supplies data up to 1958–59.

2. Lowry Nelson, "Cuban Paradoxes," in A. Curtis Wilgus, *The Caribbean at Mid-Century* (Gainesville: University of Florida Press, 1951), p. 144; *Rural Cuba,* p. 227. The school year of 1942–43 was used because 1943 was a census year.

3. In making this estimate I have used the census of 1953 as the base. The official school-age group is 6 to 13 inclusive, but the census groups are 5–9 and 10–14 and thus do not correspond to our needs. The total in the two census groups was 1,380,640. A reduction of 20 percent, roughly to eliminate the 5- and 14-year-olds, gives a figure of 1,104,512, which was slightly less than 19 percent of the total population. The official estimate of the population of the country in 1958 (June 20) was 6,548,000. Assuming the school-age population to be 19 percent of this figure, we arrive at a total of 1,244,000, of whom 717,000, or 56 percent were enrolled in public primary schools.

4. For schoolrooms of earlier years, see Nelson, *Rural Cuba,* p. 236.

5. The Sugar Differential Fund was created when the Grau administration negotiated an agreement with the sugar producers which allowed the government to receive the difference between the price being paid for Cuban sugar by the United States and that offered in the world market. The sugar involved in this agreement was 300,000 tons. The funds thus obtained were to be used for school construction. The administration had promised to construct 1,500 rural schools, but as usual promises fell short of performance. According to testimony reported in IBRD, *Report on Cuba,* the 168 schools actually built were poorly located — mostly placed near the Central Highway as showpieces. Still, the location could have been partially motivated by the need to be near an all-weather road.

6. Wyatt MacGaffey and Clifford R. Burnett, *Cuba: Its People, Its Society, Its Culture,* p. 158.

7. *Boletín Estadístico 1966,* p. 140, Table XII.4; and CERP, *A Study on Cuba,* p. 427.

8. *Granma,* February 5, 1967. This eloquent tribute to the importance of physical work is a clear effort on Castro's part to counter the Latin tradition that only intellectual work is ennobling.

9. Richard R. Fagen, *Transformation of Political Culture in Cuba,* p. 38. This is the most detailed report on the literacy campaign in English. Another indispensable account is by Richard Jolly in Seers, *Cuba: The Economic and Social Revolution,* ch. 6.

10. Seers, *Cuba: The Economic and Social Revolution,* p. 197; see also Fagen, *Transformation of Political Culture in Cuba,* p. 47.

11. UNESCO, *International Yearbook of Education,* Vol. 24 (1962), p. 94.

12. In Seers, *Cuba: The Social and Economic Revolution,* p. 192.

13. *Ibid.,* pp. 195–205.

14. Fagen, *Transformation of Political Culture in Cuba,* pp. 54–68.

15. *Ibid.,* p. 55.

16. *Ibid.,* p. 59.

17. It is interesting to note that according to the 1962 revolutionary budget, as reported by Richard Jolly, two-thirds of the 31,258 primary teachers had received their training and were teaching before the revolution. Some 10,000 had

been teaching ten years or more. See Seers, *Cuba: The Economic and Social Revolution*, p. 423, n. 2.

18. *Granma*, April 14, 1968, p. 8.

19. *Granma*, March 24, 1968. This estimate may be too conservative. Radio Havana on October 14, 1970, quoted Armando Hart, a member of the Politburo, as saying there were 80,000 youths in Oriente province alone who were neither in school nor working, but they may have been over school age.

20. Reston, "Cuban Diary: Bringing up Castro's 'New Man,'" *New York Times Magazine*, August 13, 1967, p. 79.

21. Matthews, *Fidel Castro*, p. 268.

22. Huberman, "Revolution Revisited," *Nation*, August 2, 1965, p. 53. He comments, however, on the quantitative extent of instruction: "In adult education for the school year 1964–65 the Ministry of Education reports an enrollment of 839,325 . . ."

23. John, "An American in Cuba," *Nation*, March 14, 1966, p. 299.

24. Richard R. Fagen, *Cuba: The Political Content of Adult Education* pp. 66, 68–69. These two examples were selected from a long list merely to show how propaganda can be injected into any subject, and without serious regard to the veracity of facts. These questions and others were used also in the literacy campaign. On the politicization of education, see also Fagen, *Transformation of Political Culture in Cuba*, pp. 104–37, and Richard Jolly in Seers, *Cuba: The Economic and Social Revolution*, pp. 346–70.

25. *Cuba y la Conferencia de Educación, Desarrollo Económico y Social*, official report of the Cuban government to the UNESCO conference in Santiago, Chile, 1962.

CHAPTER 9. NEUTRALIZING THE CULTURE-CONSERVING INSTITUTIONS

1. For an excellent presentation of the adult education program, see Fagen, *Cuba: The Political Content of Adult Education*.

2. A carefully documented and dispassionate review of the situation of labor before and after the revolution is available in Mesa-Lago and Hernández, *Labor Conditions in Communist Cuba*.

3. *Ibid.*, p. 99. A footnote adds that a much higher proportion of the labor force belonged to unions in Cuba than in the United States.

4. *Ibid.* No comparable figures on Communist influence were given for 1958. Although Batista had enjoyed the support of the Communist party during his first administration, after his coup d'etat of March 10, 1952, he fought the Communists and suppressed the party by declaring it illegal on October 21, 1953.

5. Dr. Erwin Roy John, a friendly observer of the regime, visited the labor camp known as Boniato near Santiago de Cuba early in 1966. He estimated there were 5,000 inmates and expressed surprise that "many of the prisoners were peasants and workers"; he "had thought they would come predominantly from the middle class." "An American in Cuba," *Nation*, March 14, 1966, pp. 296–99. Similarly, Lee Lockwood, speaking of "internees" (actually political prisoners) in Havana, said: "The majority . . . are not, as one might assume, men of urban background, but *campesinos* — peasants of the mountains and the outlying areas . . ." *Castro's Cuba: Cuba's Fidel*, p. 210.

6. During the Civil War and for a period following it, marriage and sex relations deteriorated to a state of near chaos with promiscuity common in some areas. Reaction set in and Lenin himself spoke out against such behavior. See

Notes

Mildred Fairchild, "The Status of the Family in the Soviet Union Today," *American Sociological Review*, 2 (October 1937), 619–29.

7. Exiles told a reporter from the *Miami News* (January 18, 1968) that they considered this move a method adopted by the regime to check illicit sex relations of Cuban youth mobilized in labor and education camps. See Table 14 for the possible influence of this law on marriage and divorce rates.

8. No official statistics are available on the number of persons in camps and prisons. Reporters visiting the country have picked up estimates, presumably from persons somewhat hostile to the revolution. In 1967 the Italian journalist Marino de Medici reported an estimate of 80,000 in the Military Units for Aid to Production (UMAP), sometimes called camps for "reeducation," and 50,000 in the regular prisons. See "The Cost of Eight Years of Castro," *Reader's Digest*, July 1967. A Canadian reporter, Paul Kidd, in 1966 gave a report of 200 labor camps with a total population of 30,000. Another report estimated 70,000. Mario Lazo in *Dagger in the Heart* (p. 395) reports seeing an official list as of April 1967 containing 69,315 names of persons in jails, prisons, and prison camps. José Alvarez Díaz, *Cuba: Geopolítica y Pensamiento Económico* (p. 382n.) refers to a source giving a list of 93,631 in 1962. These numbers give an appearance of being authentic, but only the regime could make them so.

9. Marino de Medici, "The Cost of Eight Years of Castro," pp. 91–92.

10. This narration of the events connected with the confrontation of the revolution and the Roman Catholic Church is based in part on Edward B. Glick, "Castro and the Church," *Commonweal*, October 13, 1961, pp. 67–69. See also Mallin, *Fortress Cuba*, pp. 42–48; and Phillips, *Cuban Dilemma*, pp. 235–36, 243–44.

11. Glick, "Castro and the Church," pp. 68–69.

12. *Newsweek*, March 25, 1963. The same account gave the number of Protestants in Cuba as 85,222.

13. Everett Gendler, "Holy Days in Havana," *Conservative Judaism*, 23, no. 2 (Winter 1969), 15–29.

14. Graham Greene, "Return to Cuba," *New Republic*, November 2, 1963, pp. 16–18. Greene is the author of the novel *Our Man in Havana*.

15. *Nation*, August 2, 1965.

CHAPTER 10. STRUCTURAL
AND ORGANIZATIONAL CHANGE IN CUBA

1. Lowry Nelson, *Rural Cuba*, pp. 154–59.

2. *Ibid.*, p. 160.

3. Alvarez Díaz, *Cuba: Geopolítica y Pensamiento Económico*, p. 403.

4. Halperin, "Cuba's Middle Class," *New Republic*, August 7, 1961, pp. 9–10.

5. The figures are only roughly comparable. The census of agriculture taken in 1946 was more limited in scope than the general census of population of 1953. The latter would enumerate many town-dwelling farm workers which the agricultural census would miss. The point, for our purposes, is merely to show the large number of those engaged in agricultural labor.

6. Seers in *Cuba: The Economic and Social Revolution* (p. 394, n. 71) refers to *Cuba Socialista* of October 1962 for a report that 118,000 former owners of rental property were receiving life pensions which totaled $6,000,000 a month. This would average only about $50 a month per owner. Other accounts verify the existence of the policy and that the regime was making good on its promises in this matter.

7. Fagen, *Cubans in Exile: Disaffection and the Revolution*. It should be noted

that registration at the Refugee Center is not compulsory. Indeed, those who came in 1958 are not included. Fagen and his associates point out that these registrants for the years 1959–62 represented approximately only 77 percent of the total. Thus the actual number of middle-class refugees undoubtedly exceeds the number registered. An estimate by E. D. Martin, "U.S. Outlines Policies toward Cuban Refugees," *U.S. Department of State Bulletin,* June 24, 1963, gave a total of 215,000 Cuban emigrants from the latter part of 1958 to early 1963. Fagen, Brody, and O'Leary studied 165,000 registrants at the Refugee Center set up by the United States government for the period from January 1959 to October 1962, which is 77 percent of the Martin estimate. On August 31, 1971, the Cuban government announced the end of the airlift, which to that time had carried more than 250,000 persons into exile, but no termination date was set and the flights continued intermittently into 1972.

8. In regard to the intellectuals in 1968, see Manuel Mandonado-Denis, "The Situation of Cuba's Intellectuals," *Christian Century,* January 17, 1967, pp. 78–80, and Andre Schifferin, "Publishing in Cuba," *New York Times Book Review,* March 17, 1968, pp. 40ff. Since 1968, however, there has been increasing restriction on intellectual freedom.

9. Zeitlin, *Revolutionary Politics and the Cuban Working Class,* ch. 4.

10. Seers, *Cuba: The Economic and Social Revolution.* Richard Jolly reported figures from the 1962 budget showing that two-thirds of the 31,288 primary teachers "received their basic training and were teaching before the Revolution" (p. 423, n. 2).

11. See Andrés Suárez, *Cuba: Castroism and Communism,* p. 109.

12. *Granma,* March 24, 1968. The reasons for the nationalization were stated as follows: "These private businesses had become a source of irritation for their unfair practices, run-down condition, incessant violation of the revolutionary laws, and for serving in many cases as gathering places for parasites, antisocial and lumpen elements who utilized them as foci for their frankly counterrevolutionary or criminal activities."

13. This trend is confirmed by René Dumont, the French Marxist agronomist who visited Cuba in 1969 and reported in *Le Monde,* December 1969: "Small farmers are being expropriated, given compensation and 'integrated' into state production units, leaving each family with no more than a small plot for growing food." The trend is also confirmed by recent refugees. A tobacco farmer who arrived in Miami in February 1970 said he owned his farm in 1958 and had an annual income of between $3,000 and $4,000. His farm was "intervened" on April 15, 1968, and he was sent to cut cane. When he returned from the canefields he was informed that the state had expropriated his farm and that it would be operated by a cooperative along with several other farms. His tractor, his herd of cattle, and all other property were also expropriated. The cooperative was under military control.

14. Lockwood, *Castro's Cuba: Cuba's Fidel,* p. 62.

15. Dumont, "The Militarization of Fidelismo," *Dissent,* September–October 1970, p. 419. He notes as evidence of further inequality that the Che Guevara Trailblazer Brigade for land-clearing and construction work was operated by the armed forces and the members received 160 pesos per month plus food and lodging. Also, he says, "a young civil servant fresh from the university earns 300 pesos," and when on field trips receives free meal tickets worth 7 pesos each. He also notes that the army has "three messes: one for officers, one for noncommissioned officers and regular servicemen, and a third for the temporary recruits." The old order changeth not in the military.

16. John Reed spent a month in late 1970 in Cuba and reported one Cuban

Notes

saying jokingly that people were papering the walls with pesos. But the black market is a better measure of the depreciation in the value of money. Reed quotes these prices: one box of Chiclets, $5; a pair of nylons, $50; a bottle of liquor, "anywhere from $75 to $100." See "A Visit to Cuba: The Hard Life," *Boston Sunday Globe,* February 7, 1971, p. 11.

17. *Ibid.,* p. 11. Among the rewards lately granted to the faithful in government and party are, oddly enough, expensive Alfa Romeo cars. According to Reed, "The Alpha Romeo is perhaps one of the greatest bones of contention in Cuba today." This is understandable.

18. It is not necessary here to describe this organization in detail. For readers who want additional information, there is a highly commendable study — indeed the only one in English — by Richard R. Fagen in *Transformation of Political Culture in Cuba,* pp. 69–103.

19. A detailed list of these functions was given in *Granma,* September 10, 1967.

20. Quotations are from the version of this speech published in Foreign Broadcast Information Service, *Daily Report,* September 30, 1968.

21. K. S. Karol, *Guerrillas in Power,* p. 449. Karol, favorable to the revolution in its early period and still a "friendly" critic, has severely criticized the leadership in its drift toward military organization. He visited Cuba twice in 1961, again in 1967, and finally in 1968.

22. See n. 8 above.

23. See Karol, *Guerrillas in Power,* pp. 448, 525, 529, for examples. Karol, because of his familiarity with what happened in Russia, often draws parallels with Cuba.

CHAPTER 11. ON BALANCE

1. Huberman and Sweezy, *Socialism in Cuba;* K. S. Karol, *Guerrillas in Power;* René Dumont, *Cuba: Est-il Socialiste?* and the excerpts in English published in *Dissent,* September–October 1970, pp. 411–28.

2. Lockwood, *Castro's Cuba: Cuba's Fidel,* p. 123.

3. "There is hardly an incident of Cuban history since 1902 that is not a matter of controversy, but if there is anything on which there is even an approach to general agreement, it is that Estrada Palma was honest and incorruptible." Charles E. Chapman, *A History of the Cuban Republic,* p. 152.

4. Viator (pseud.), "Cuba Revisited after Ten Years of Castro," *Foreign Affairs,* 48 (January 1970), 318–19.

5. Luis Fernandez Verges, in an interview with Jaime Suchlicki, University of Miami, who kindly allowed the author to read it. Verges, who had been acting as an instructor, was expelled from the university when he applied to leave Cuba.

6. Some of these mutual associations are still functioning. Members continue to pay their monthly fees and are treated in special clinics by physicians who are still allowed in private practice.

7. For an excellent description of the entire medical care situation in Cuba before 1959, see Roberto E. Hernández, "La atención médica en Cuba hasta 1958," *Journal of Inter-American Studies,* 11, no. 4 (October 1969), 533–57.

8. To further complicate matters Batista claimed that "considering only government-operated hospitals and the municipal hospitals of Havana, the total increased . . . from 54 in 1944 to 97 in 1958. The total number of beds rose from . . . 13,625 in 1944 to 21,141 in 1958." *Growth and Decline of the Cuban Republic,* p. 107.

9. For an example in the United States, see Loudon Wainwright, "Help Wanted: Doctors Needed in a Real Nice Iowa Town with a Brand New Hospital," *Life,* May 29, 1970, pp. 48–52. The writer described a community of 4,000 in a rich

area of Iowa, serving a total population of 22,000. A new 89-bed well-equipped hospital, completed at a cost of $1.7 million, faced a shutdown because of low patronage.

10. Among the latest American authors to support these claims are Huberman and Sweezy, *Socialism in Cuba* (1969), ch. 3. On beds per thousand inhabitants they cite statistics from the Ministry of Health to show that since the revolution the ratio had increased from 3.3 to 5.4. They also claimed there were 7,000 doctors, "1,000 more than before the Revolution," overlooking the fact that there were 6,201 in the census of 1953. Even the chief of the Pan American Sanitary Bureau on his return from Cuba in late 1970 voiced to reporters similar unsubstantiated claims.

11. For a full account of this visit, see Nelson, *Rural Cuba*, pp. 12ff.

12. *Ibid.*, p. 249.

13. IBRD, *Report on Cuba*, p. 441. Emphasis in the original.

14. According to the Miami Radio Monitoring Service, radio commentator Pepe Aguero said on May 14, 1970: "The Revolution received as a heavy inheritance from the colonial and imperialist domination of our country, underdevelopment in all its aspects." Huberman and Sweezy (*Socialism in Cuba*, pp. 65–66) refer to "Cuba's grotesque underdevelopment and ruthless exploitation by United States imperialism — opposite sides of the same coin . . ." Finally, Herbert L. Matthews (*Fidel Castro*, p. 54), though conceding that Cuba "was relatively prosperous at the time of the revolution" and pointing out correctly that the "question of whether Cuba was and is an 'underdeveloped' nation is a matter of definition and depends in part on what statistics are used and who uses them," goes on to say: "So far as the Cuban revolution is concerned, the problem of [underdevelopment] is unimportant." With the last remark we would take issue.

15. International Monetary Fund, *International Financial Statistics*, 14, no. 5 (1961), 95.

16. CERP, *Study on Cuba*, p. 555.

17. Lockwood, *Castro's Cuba: Cuba's Fidel*, pp. 180–81.

18. Karol, *Guerrillas in Power*, p. 459. See his lengthy discussion of the political problem, pp. 451–70.

19. Matthews, *Cuban Story*, p. 163.

20. Karol, *Guerrillas in Power*, p. 489.

21. *United Nations Yearbook of International Trade Statistics, 1968*, p. 211.

22. See Roberts and Hamour, *Cuba 1968*, pp. 168–71.

23. Huberman and Sweezy, *Socialism in Cuba*, p. 200.

24. *Cuba and the Caribbean*, Hearings before the Subcommittee on Inter-American Affairs of the Committee on Foreign Affairs, House of Representatives, 91st Congress, 2d Session, p. 18.

25. A dispatch from Paris dated December 19, 1970, stated that the French–Latin American Chamber of Commerce considered the imbalanced foreign trade of Cuba "alarming"; that the debt to nonsocialist countries was $400 million; and that in 1971 the country would "reach its highest potential ceiling in foreign currency debt." Foreign Broadcast Information Service, *Daily Report*, December 21, 1970.

26. On April 21, 1971, for example, the vice-chairman of the USSR Council of Ministers arrived in Havana. He was significantly, also the president of the USSR Central Planning Agency, GOSPLAN. Several officials of the agency accompanied him.

27. Adams, *The Theory of Social Revolution* (New York: Macmillan, 1913), p. 143.

28. Irving P. Pflaum, *Tragic Island*, p. 28.

29. For further discussion of the Ortodoxo program, see Loree Wilkerson, *Fidel Castro's Political Programs from Reformism to Marxism-Leninism*, pp. 28ff.

Notes

30. Ironically, part of Castro's brief to the court in 1952 asking that Batista be tried as a criminal stated: "I resort to logic. I pulse the terrible reality, and the logic tells me that if there exist courts in Cuba Batista should be punished, and if Batista is not punished and continues as master of the State, Prime Minister, senator, Major General, civil and military chief, executive power and legislative power, owner of lives and farms, then there do not exist courts, they have been suppressed." Jules Dubois, *Fidel Castro: Rebel — Liberator or Dictator?* p. 29. Castro now holds all the essential offices he ascribed to Batista.

Weights and Measures

Officially the metric system has been adopted in Cuba, but certain traditional Spanish measures and weights are also in common use. Some of these measures with their equivalents are as follows:

Cuban Weights and Measures	United States Equivalent
Kilogram	2.204 pounds
Arroba	25 pounds
Quintal	220.46 pounds
Metric ton	1.1 tons
Meter	39.37 inches
Kilometer	0.62 miles
Hectare	2.47 acres
Caballería (13.4 hectares)	33.16 acres
Liter	1.057 quarts

Selected Bibliography

NOTE: There has been such a proliferation of books, monographs, chapters in books, and journal articles that no attempt has been made here to present a comprehensive list. This bibliography contains only the items which have been most useful to the author. It may be helpful to others, however, to list some of the more extended bibliographies:

Cuban Studies Newsletter, 1, no. 1 (December 1970–). Center for Latin American Studies, University of Pittsburgh. Contains items published since 1968.

Gilberto V. Fort, *The Cuban Revolution of Fidel Castro: Viewed from Abroad.* Lawrence: University of Kansas Libraries, 1969. Contains 839 annotated items.

Earl J. Pariseau, *Cuban Acquisitions and Bibliography.* Washington, D.C.: Library of Congress, 1970. Proceedings and working papers of an international conference held at the Library of Congress, April 13–15, 1970. Lists materials available in the United States, the United Kingdom, Spain, and Germany.

Fermín Peraza, *Revolutionary Cuba: A Bibliographical Guide.* Editions for 1966 (695 entries) and 1967 (911 entries) were published by the University of Miami Press, Coral Gables, in 1967 and 1969 respectively.

Jaime Suchlicki, *The Cuban Revolution: A Documentary Bibliography.* Coral Gables, Fla.: Center for Advanced International Studies, University of Miami, 1969. *A Documentary Guide to the Cuban Revolution.* Coral Gables, University of Miami Press, forthcoming.

Alvarez Díaz, José Ramón. *La Destrucción de la Ganadería Cubana.* Miami, Fla.: Editorial AIP, 1965.

————. *The Road to Nowhere: Castro's Rise and Fall.* Miami, Fla.: Editorial AIP, 1965.

————, A. Arredondo, R. H. Shelton, and J. F. Vizcaíno. *Cuba: Geopolítica y Pensamiento Económico.* Miami, Fla.: Economistas de Cuba en Exilio, 1964.

Artime, Manuel. *Traición! Gritan 20,000 Tumbas Cubanas.* Mexico City: Editorial Jus., 1960.

Baran, Paul A. *Reflections on the Cuban Revolution.* New York: Monthly Review Press, 1961.

Batista y Zaldívar, Fulgencio. *The Growth and Decline of the Cuban Republic.* Trans. Blas N. Rocafort. New York: Devin-Adair, 1964.

Bethel, Paul D. *The Losers: The Definitive Report, by an Eyewitness, of the*

Selected Bibliography

Communist Conquest of Cuba and the Soviet Penetration in Latin America.
New Rochelle, N.Y.: Arlington House, 1969.

Boorstein, Edward. *The Economic Transformation of Cuba.* New York: Monthly
Review Press, 1968.

Buell, Raymond Leslie, ed. *Problems of the New Cuba.* New York: Foreign
Policy Association, 1935.

Castro, Fidel. *History Will Absolve Me.* New York: Liberal Press, 1959.

————. *Political, Economic and Social Thought of Fidel Castro.* Havana: Editorial Lex, 1959.

————. *Fidel Castro Speaks.* Ed. Martin Kenner and James Petras. New York:
Grove Press, 1969.

————. *The Selected Works of Fidel Castro.* Ed. Nelson P. Valdés and Rolando
E. Bonachea, 3 vols. Cambridge, Mass.: MIT Press, 1971.

Note: Castro's addresses are published in *Granma* in the English language
Weekly Review as well as in the Spanish, usually the weekend following
delivery.

Casuso, Teresa. *Cuba and Castro.* Trans. Elmer Grossberg. New York: Random
House, 1961.

Chapman, Charles E. *A History of the Cuban Republic.* New York: Macmillan,
1927.

Conte Agüero, Luis. *Los dos rostros de Fidel Castro.* Mexico City: Editorial Jus.,
1961.

Cuba, Junta Central de Planificación, Dirección Central de Estadística. *Boletín
Estadístico 1966.*

————. *Compendio Estadístico de Cuba, 1967.*

Cuban Economic Research Project. *Labor Conditions in Communist Cuba.* University of Miami Press, 1963. Carmelo Mesa-Lago and Roberto E. Hernández
Morales are credited with the authorship and this work is so cited in the present
volume.

————. *Social Security in Cuba.* Mimeo. University of Miami, 1964.

————. *Cuba: Agriculture and Planning, 1963–1964.* Mimeo. University of Miami,
1965.

————. *Stages and Problems of Industrial Development in Cuba.* Mimeo. University
of Miami, 1965.

————. *A Study on Cuba.* Coral Gables, Fla.: University of Miami Press, 1965. Essentially a translation from the Spanish *Un Estudio Sobre Cuba* (University of
Miami Press, 1963).

————. *Sugar in Cuba.* Mimeo. University of Miami, 1966.

Draper, Theodore. *Castro's Revolution: Myths and Realities.* New York: Praeger,
1962.

————. *Castroism: Theory and Practice.* New York: Praeger, 1965.

Dubois, Jules. *Fidel Castro: Rebel — Liberator or Dictator?* Indianapolis: Bobbs-
Merrill, 1959.

Dumont, René. *Cuba: Socialisme et Developpement.* Paris: Editions du Seuil, 1964.

————. *Cuba: Est-il socialiste?* Paris: Editions du Seuil, 1970.

————. "The Militarization of Fidelismo." *Dissent,* September–October 1970, pp.
411–28. Excerpts in English from *Cuba: Est-il socialiste?*

Echevarría, Oscar A. *Agricultura Cubana, 1934–1966.* Miami, Fla.: Editorial Universal, 1970.

Fagen, Richard R. "Calculation and Emotion in Foreign Policy: The Cuban Case."
Journal of Conflict Resolution, 6, no. 3 (September 1962), 214–21.

————. *Cuba: The Political Content of Adult Education.* Hoover Institution

Studies No. 4. Stanford, Cal.: Hoover Institution on War, Revolution, and Peace, 1964.

———. "The Cuban Revolution: Enemies and Friends." In David Finlay et al., Enemies in Politics. Chicago: Rand McNally, 1967.

———. The Transformation of Political Culture in Cuba. Stanford, Cal.: Stanford University Press, 1969.

———, Richard A. Brody, and Thomas J. O'Leary. Cubans in Exile: Disaffection and the Revolution. Stanford, Cal.: Stanford University Press, 1968.

Fitzgibbon, Russel H. Cuba and the United States, 1900–1935, Menasha, Wis.: George Banta, 1935.

Foner, Philip S. A History of Cuba in Its Relations with the United States. 2 vols. New York: International Publishers, 1963.

Frankel, Theodore, ed. Special Cuban issue of Problems of Communism, 19, no. 4 (July–August 1970). Articles by Luis E. Aguilar, Edward González, Robert F. Lamberg, and Robert J. Alexander.

Glick, Edward B. "Castro and the Church." Commonweal, October 13, 1961, pp. 67–69.

Goldenberg, Boris. The Cuban Revolution and Latin America. New York: Praeger, 1965.

González, Edward. "Castro's Revolution, Cuban Communist Appeals, and the Soviet Response." World Politics, October 1968, pp. 39–68.

———. "Castro: The Limits of Charisma." Problems of Communism, 19, no. 4 (July–August 1970), 12–24.

Guerra y Sánchez, Ramiro. Sugar and Society in the Caribbean: An Economic History of Cuban Agriculture. New Haven: Yale University Press, 1964.

———, et al. Historia de la Nación Cubana. 10 vols. Havana: Editorial Historia de la Nación Cubana, 1952.

Guevara, Ernesto (Che). Che Guevara on Guerrilla Warfare. Ed. Harries-Clichy Peterson. New York: Praeger, 1961.

———. Che Guevara Speaks: Selected Speeches and Writings. Ed. George Lavan. New York: Grove Press, 1968.

———. Che Guevara on Revolution: A Documentary Overview. Ed. Jay Mallin. Coral Gables, Fla.: University of Miami Press, 1969.

———. Che: Selected Works of Ernesto Guevara, Ed. Rolando E. Bonachea and Nelson P. Valdés. Cambridge, Mass.: MIT Press, 1969.

Hernández, Roberto E. "La atención médica en Cuba hasta 1958." Journal of Inter-American Studies, 11, no. 4 (October 1969), 533–57.

Horowitz, Irving Louis, ed. Cuban Communism. Chicago: Aldine, 1970. Articles from a special issue of Trans-Action (April 1969) by Richard R. Fagen, Arlie Hochschild, Carmelo Mesa-Lago, Joseph A. Kahl, Maurice Zeitlin, and Horowitz.

Huberman, Leo. "Revolution Revisited." Nation, August 2, 1965, pp. 51–54.

———, and Paul M. Sweezy. Cuba: Anatomy of a Revolution. New York: Monthly Review Press, 1960.

———. Socialism in Cuba. New York: Monthly Review Press, 1969.

International Bank for Reconstruction and Development, Economic and Technical Mission to Cuba in 1950. Report on Cuba. Baltimore: Johns Hopkins Press, 1951.

International Commission of Jurists. Cuba and the Rule of Law. Geneva, 1962.

Jenks, Leland H. Our Cuban Colony. New York: Vanguard, 1928.

John, Erwin Roy. "An American in Cuba." Nation, March 14, 21, 1966.

Karol, K. S. Guerrillas in Power: The Course of the Cuban Revolution. Trans. Arnold J. Pomerans. New York: Hill and Wang, 1970.

Lazo, Mario. Dagger in the Heart: American Policy Failures in Cuba. New York: Funk and Wagnalls, 1968.

Selected Bibliography

Leontief, Wassily. "Notes on a Visit to Cuba." *New York Review of Books,* August 21, 1969, pp. 15ff.
———. "The Trouble with Cuban Socialism." *New York Review of Books,* January 7, 1971, pp. 19ff.
Lockwood, Lee. *Castro's Cuba: Cuba's Fidel.* New York: Macmillan, 1967.
Macaulay, Neill. *A Rebel in Cuba: An American's Memoir.* Chicago: Quadrangle, 1970.
McClatchy, C. K. *Cuba 1965.* A reporter's observations as published in the *Sacramento Bee;* several articles bound together. Sacramento, Cal.: McClatchy Newspapers, 1965.
MacGaffey, Wyatt, and Clifford R. Barnett. *Cuba: Its People, Its Society, Its Culture.* New Haven, Conn.: HRAF Press, 1962.
Mallin, Jay. *Fortress Cuba: Russia's American Base.* Chicago: Henry Regnery, 1965.
Matthews, Herbert L. *The Cuban Story.* New York: Braziller, 1961.
———. *Fidel Castro.* New York: Simon and Schuster, 1969.
Mesa-Lago, Carmelo. *The Labor Sector and Socialist Distribution in Cuba.* New York: Praeger, for the Hoover Institution on War, Revolution, and Peace, 1968.
———. "The Economic Significance of Unpaid Labor in Socialist Cuba." *Industrial and Labor Relations Review,* 22, no. 3 (April 1969), 339–57.
———. "Availability and Reliability of Statistics in Communist Cuba." *Latin American Research Review,* 4, nos. 1, 2 (Spring, Summer, 1969).
———, ed. *Revolutionary Changes in Cuba.* Pittsburgh: University of Pittsburgh Press, 1971.
———, and Roberto E. Hernández. *Labor Conditions in Communist Cuba.* Cuban Economic Research Project. Coral Gables, Fla.: University of Miami Press, 1963.
Mezerik, Avrahm G., ed. *Cuba and the United States.* New York: International Review Service 140, 1960.
Mills, C. Wright, *Listen, Yankee: The Revolution in Cuba.* New York: McGraw-Hill, 1960.
Monahan, James, and Kenneth O. Gilmore. *The Great Deception.* New York: Farrar, Straus, 1963.
Nelson, Lowry. *Rural Cuba.* Minneapolis: University of Minnesota Press, 1950.
Nixon, Richard. *Six Crises.* Garden City, N.Y.: Doubleday, 1962.
Núñez Jiménez, Antonio. *Geografía de Cuba.* 3rd ed. Havana: Editorial Nacional de Cuba, 1965.
O'Connor, James. "On Cuban Political Economy." *Political Science Quarterly,* 69, no. 2 (June 1964), 233–47.
———. "Industrial Organization in the Old and New Cuba." *Science and Society,* 30, no. 2 (Spring 1966), 149–90.
———. *The Origins of Socialism in Cuba.* Ithaca, N.Y.: Cornell University Press, 1970.
Ortíz Fernández, Fernando. *Cuban Counterpoint: Tobacco and Sugar.* Trans. Harriet de Onis; prologue by Herminio Portell Vilá. New York: Knopf, 1947.
Pan American Union. *América en Cifras.* Statistical annual. Washington, D.C.: Pan American Union, various years.
Pflaum, Irving P. *Tragic Island: How Communism Came to Cuba.* Englewood Cliffs, N.J.: Prentice-Hall, 1961.
Phillips, R. Hart. *Cuba: Island of Paradox.* New York: McDowell, Obolensky, 1959.
———. *The Cuban Dilemma.* New York: Obolensky, 1962.
Plank, John, ed. *Cuba and the United States: Long Range Perspective.* Washington, D.C.: Brookings Institution, 1967.
Portell Vilá, Herminio. *Historia de Cuba, en sus relaciones con los Estados Unidos y España.* 4 vols. Havana, 1938–41.

231

Rauf, Mohammed A., Jr. *Cuban Journal: Castro's Cuba as It Really Is*. New York: Crowell, 1964.

Reston, James. "Cuban Diary: Bringing up Castro's 'New Man.' " *New York Times Magazine*, August 13, 1967.

Roberts, C. Paul, and Mukhtar Hamour. *Cuba 1968, Supplement to the Statistical Abstract of Latin America*. Los Angeles: University of California, 1970.

Ruiz, Ramón Eduardo. *Cuba: The Making of a Revolution*. Amherst: University of Massachusetts Press, 1968.

Schleifer, Marc. "Letter from Havana." *Nation*, April 17, 1964, pp. 442–44.

Schmid, Peter. "Letter from Havana." *Commentary*, September 1965, pp. 56–63.

Seers, Dudley, and Andrés Bianchi, Richard Jolly, and Max Nolff. *Cuba: The Economic and Social Revolution*. Chapel Hill: University of North Carolina Press, 1964.

Selzer, Gregorio. *Fidel Castro: La Revolución Cubana*. Buenos Aires: Editorial Palestra, 1960.

Smith, Robert Freeman. *Background to Revolution: The Development of Modern Cuba*. New York: Knopf, 1960.

———. *The United States and Cuba: Business and Diplomacy, 1917–1960*. New York: Bookman Associates, 1960.

———. *What Happened in Cuba? A Documentary History*. New York: Twayne, 1963.

Smith, T. Lynn, *Agrarian Reform in Latin America*. New York: Knopf, 1965. Contains English text of Cuban Agrarian Reform Law.

Suárez, Andrés. *Cuba: Castroism and Communism, 1959–1966*. Cambridge, Mass.: MIT Press, 1967.

Suchlicki, Jaime. *University Students and Revolution in Cuba, 1920–1968*. Coral Gables, Fla.: University of Miami Press, 1969.

———, ed. *Cuba, Castro, and Revolution*. Coral Gables, Fla.: University of Miami Press, forthcoming. Chapters by Suchlicki, Raymond Duncan, Lowry Nelson, Frank McDonald, Sergio Roca and Roberto Hernández, Gemma Del Ducca, Foy D. Kohler, Leon Gouré and Julian Weinkle, and Michael Kline.

Tetlow, Edwin. *Eye on Cuba*. New York: Harcourt, Brace, and World, 1966.

Thomas, Hugh. *Cuba: The Pursuit of Freedom*. New York: Harper and Rowe, 1971.

United Nations. Various statistical yearbooks of the UN and its specialized agencies, FAO, ILO, WHO, and UNESCO, are indispensable sources on Cuba, particularly for the early years of the revolution when direct information from Cuba was not available.

U.S., Congress, House, Subcommittee on Inter-American Affairs of the Committee on Foreign Affairs. *Cuba and the Caribbean*. 91st Congress, 2d Session, July–August 1970.

U.S., Department of Commerce, Bureau of Foreign Commerce. *Investment in Cuba*. Washington, D.C.: 1956.

———. *Economic Development in Cuba, 1958*. World Trade Information Service Economic Reports, April 1959. Washington, D.C.: 1959.

U.S., Department of State. *Cuba, Latin America, and Communism*. By Edwin M. Martin. Publication 7621. Washington, D.C., 1963.

———. *U.S. Policy Toward Cuba*. Publication 7690. Washington, D.C., 1964. Urrutia Lleó, Manuel. *Fidel Castro and Company, Inc.: Communist Tyranny in Cuba*. New York: Praeger, 1964.

Viator (pseud.). "Cuba Revisited after Ten Years of Castro." *Foreign Affairs*, 48 (January 1970), 312–21.

232

Selected Bibliography

Wilgus, A. Curtis. *The Caribbean.* Vols. 1–7. Gainesville: University of Florida Press, 1950–57.

Wilkerson, Loree. *Fidel Castro's Political Programs: From Reform to Marxism-Leninism.* Gainesville: University of Florida Press, 1965.

Wylie, Kathryn. *A Survey of Agriculture in Cuba.* Washington, D.C.: U.S. Department of Agriculture, Economic Research Service, 1969.

Yglesias, José. *In the Fist of the Revolution: Life in a Cuban Country Town.* New York: Pantheon, 1968.

————. "Cuban Report: Their Hippies and Their Squares." *New York Times Magazine,* January 12, 1969.

Zeitlin, Maurice. *Revolutionary Politics and the Cuban Working Class.* Princeton: Princeton University Press, 1967.

————, and Robert Scheer. *Cuba: Tragedy in Our Hemisphere.* New York: Grove Press, 1963.

Index

Index

237

238

Index

Index